The
Time-Crunched
Cyclist

Fit, Fast, and Powerful
in 6 Hours a Week

2ND EDITION

Chris Carmichael
& Jim Rutberg

VELO press

Boulder, Colorado

3002 Sterling Circle, Suite 100
Boulder, Colorado 80301-2338 USA
(303) 440-0601 · Fax (303) 444-6788
E-mail velopress@competitorgroup.com

Distributed in the United States and Canada by Ingram Publisher Services

Library of Congress Cataloging-in-Publication Data
Carmichael, Chris, 1960–
The time-crunched cyclist: fit, fast, and powerful in 6 hours a week /
Chris Carmichael and Jim Rutberg.—2nd ed
p. cm.
Includes bibliographical references and index.
ISBN 978-1-934030-83-7 (pbk.)
1. Triathlon—Training. 2. Physical fitness. I. Rutberg, Jim. II. Title.
GV1060.73.C37 2012
796.6—dc23
2012022856

For information on purchasing VeloPress books, please call (800) 811-4210, ext. 2138,
or visit www.velopress.com.

This paper meets the requirements of ANSI/NISO Z39.48-1992 (Permanence of Paper).

Cover and interior design by Anita Koury
Cover photo by John Segesta
Photographs in Chapter 11 by Don Karle

Text set in Minion Pro

12   13   14   /   10   9   8   7   6   5   4   3   2

Contents

Preface   vii

Acknowledgments   ix

1   Bringing Endurance Training into the 21st Century   1

2   The Science of the Time-Crunched Training Program   19

3   Measuring Intensity in the Information Age   59

4   Competitor and Century Workouts and Training Programs   91

5   The Commuter's Plan for Race-Ready Fitness   123

6   Cyclocross: A Perfect Application of the TCTP   139

7   Training for Endurance Mountain Bike Races   149

8   High-Speed Nutrition   161

9   Making the Most of Your Fitness   189

10   Supplementing Your Training: Endurance Blocks   207

11   Strength Training on Limited Time   219

References   245

Index   249

About the Authors   261

Preface

One of the first judgments I make about a book is based on how it feels in my hand. I want it to be substantial and have some weight, as if the heft of the book is an indication of the weight of its words. And therein lay the challenge of writing a book called *The Time-Crunched Cyclist*. This is a book for people who lead busy lives, people who wake up early and hit the ground running, juggle one or more jobs with raising one or more kids, all while trying to maintain healthy relationships with friends and maybe a spouse or significant other. Time is in short supply, and the whole point of this program is to get more from less, so it seemed absurd to make you sift through a 450-page volume to learn how to save time.

But I'm an old-school guy. Although I have embraced technology and the "short-attention-span theater" that dominates modern culture, given the chance I'll sit down with a thick, heavy book and disappear for a long while. And when I write, I write about subjects I'm passionate about and that make me want to keep explaining ideas and expanding concepts. My challenge with this book was to cut to the chase and respect the knowledge many of you already have about cycling and training, to be brief about the basics. After all, you most likely already have at least four books on your shelves that cover basic material and offer the same old conservative and mundane guidance.

For me, there was no point in adding more of the same to your collection of training books, so I'm going out on a limb with this one. The program described in this book breaks some of the "rules" of traditional endurance training. The workouts are hard, and the rewards are great, even if they are relatively brief. The program has limitations in the length of time that you'll be able to maintain top fitness, but it offers great opportunities for getting more out of limited training time. A marketing whiz would say I'm better off playing it safe and designing an easier program ("20 minutes a day and you don't even have to sweat!"), even if it produced smaller improvements in performance. I disagree.

This is a "go big or go home" kind of world, and you and I seek greater performance in everything we do. As a business owner or employee, you're not just punching in and punching out. And your idea of good parenting goes far beyond merely showing up. You're not afraid to put yourself out there and accept new challenges, so I'm going to step up and give you one. If you're open to new ideas and innovative ways of achieving superior performance, I have a new kind of program that will make you fit, fast, and powerful in the limited time you have available for training.

It's the promise of a new training paradigm that makes me believe this could be the most important book I've ever written. For years superior performance in cycling and other endurance sports has been out of reach for athletes who have limited time to train. The old model of endurance training is flawed, not because it doesn't work, but because it only works if you have more than 10 hours a week to spend on your bike. I don't have that kind of time anymore, and neither do a lot of the athletes who come to Carmichael Training Systems. But I have found a solution, a new way to train that leverages the largely untapped potential of high-intensity interval workouts to make high-performance cycling accessible to time-crunched athletes. It's backed up by science, it's been proven effective by real athletes, and it's your ticket to achieving the fitness necessary to obtain the results you desire. So although this book may be lighter in the hand than some, it is dense with new ideas.

The Time-Crunched Training Program will put you back at the front of the pack, where you belong. So let's get started.

Acknowledgments

CHRIS CARMICHAEL: To my wife, Paige; our life together is a wonderful and exciting journey and I am happy we are making it "hand-in-hand" together.

To my children, Anna, Connor, and little Vivian; you all are wonderful, sparkling balls of life for Paige and me.

I would like to thank all the people who make up Carmichael Training Systems for their dedication to making my vision a reality. You all are the best. And to the athletes who continue to prove the effectiveness of the program in this book, thank you for providing the feedback and results that convinced me this program could help an even wider population of athletes to achieve their goals.

Of course, my thanks to Lance Armstrong and all the athletes I have had the pleasure of coaching over many years. I cannot imagine a career more fulfilling than this one.

To my mother and father, who were my first and always my best coaches, you have my eternal gratitude. The same is true for my brother and sister, who have always been there for me.

Thank you to Ted Costantino and Renee Jardine at VeloPress for their support and encouragement on this project from beginning to end.

And finally, a very special thank you to Jim Rutberg, my close friend and colleague. It's hard to believe we've been at this for more than a decade.

JIM RUTBERG: My thanks go to the athletes I've had the pleasure of working with, especially Sterling Swaim, Taylor Carrington, and John Fallon, who trusted me with their training as well as with the telling of their stories.

This book would not have been possible without the help and support of Abby Ruby, Jim Lehman, Dean Golich, and Mike Durner. Thank you for your hard work making sure the training programs and research were perfect. Thanks as well to Jay T. Kearney for his insight and expertise, and to Brian Delong and the entire staff at Carmichael Training Systems for their support throughout the book-creation process.

Thank you to Ted Costantino, Renee Jardine, and Dave Trendler at Velo-Press for your support and guidance throughout. And thank you, Grant David, for contributing your expertise and invaluable viewpoint to this project.

Above all, my greatest thanks go to my wife, Leslie. Thank you for your support during the long days and late nights that always accompany big projects. And to Oliver and Elliot; in case you were wondering, this book is the reason you and Mom went to visit Ama and Gramps for a month.

CHAPTER

1

Bringing Endurance Training into the 21st Century

I'm a cyclist at my core, but these days my life doesn't revolve around my bike the way it did when I was 20. I'm a cyclist, but I'm also a father, husband, and business owner. I don't have endless hours to spend building up the massive endurance base that characterizes so many classic training programs. I don't have time to be the cyclist I was 30 years ago, and to be honest, I don't have any desire to be that guy again. My life is fuller—and more fulfilling—than it has ever been, and although I'm glad cycling is an important part of my life, I'm equally glad that it ranks behind my family and business in priority.

My current relationship with cycling is not unique; there are tens of thousands of cyclists in the United States who still love to ride but used to ride a lot more than they do now. Almost every cyclist I talk to over the age of 30 has some version of the same story. They all used to go out on epic 4-hour-plus rides on weekends and put in 15 to 20 hours of training on a weekly basis. Many raced, and some even claim to have kicked butt. Then they got a real job, fell in love, bought a house, had kids, and so on. Cycling is still their passion and still takes up significant space in the garage, but now the car is worth more than the bike on the roof (instead of the other way around), and the kids' soccer games and recitals take precedence over a long training ride or driving 3 hours each way to race a 1-hour criterium.

Our relationship with our sport may have changed, but our desire to be fit, fast, and powerful hasn't diminished. I hate being slow, especially because I know what it feels like to be fast. I hate getting dropped, because I know what it feels like to drive the pace and make others suffer. And I hate to see riders soft-pedaling ahead of me at the tops of rolling hills, because I used to be the one politely slowing down so my friends could keep up.

I love the feeling of being on top of the gear, spinning along effortlessly in a fast-moving pack. I love knowing I have the power to accelerate up a small hill, jump out of a corner, bridge a gap, or take a good pull through a strong headwind. I love how it feels to look around and know I have more left in the tank than some of the other riders, and that they're closer to their limits than I am to mine. I like being fit, fast, and powerful on the bike, and after talking to thousands of cyclists on my travels around the world, I know you do, too.

For the majority of working cyclists, your training program is the only thing *stopping* you from enjoying cycling the way you used to. Why? Because predominant theories in training are still stuck in the 1980s. Yes, we have dramatically improved the precision of training with power meters, heart rate monitors, and global positioning system (GPS) units, but the fundamental infrastructure of training hasn't changed in a long time. As athletes, our lifestyles have changed dramatically, but our approach to training has remained essentially the same.

The Time-Crunched Training Program (TCTP) is a new approach to training that takes a different path to endurance fitness. It works around busy schedules by systematically applying greater intensities to achieve bigger gains with fewer and shorter rides. But that doesn't mean it's a shortcut to fitness; there's no such thing. The workouts are strenuous and the workload is high. Because of that the benefits match and sometimes exceed those achieved through programs that call for twice the weekly training hours. If your ambition is to race at a high level, either again or for the first time, the TCTP will make you competitive in local and regional races. If you just want to improve your strength and stamina on the bike, it will give you the fitness you need to push the pace at the local group ride and enjoy challenging rides. If you want to achieve high-performance fitness in the limited time you have available for training, it's time to embrace a new approach to endurance training.

Case Study:
The Decline of Sterling Swaim

The limitations of the classic endurance training model, and the benefits of the time-crunched model my coaching staff and I have developed, are clearly illustrated through the experiences of three CTS athletes, who coincidentally all work in the financial industry. Sterling Swaim, Taylor Carrington, and John Fallon are cyclists who could show up at any group ride across the country and fit right in. They're not pros or former pros, they're not freakishly gifted in terms of VO₂max (maximum aerobic capacity), and they probably wouldn't be the strongest or the weakest riders in your local ride. In other words, they're good, and a very good representation of the modern American cyclist. We'll start with Sterling.

Sterling has lived in Winston-Salem, North Carolina, pretty much all his life, and he's been racing since he was 13 years old. As a young man he raced the junior version of Paris–Roubaix and rode the United States Cycling Federation (USCF) National Road and Criterium Championships as a junior and senior rider. Throughout his 20s, he raced as a Category (Cat.) III in criteriums and road races up and down the eastern seaboard and as far west as the Mississippi River. For years his brother (a Cat. I) and other racing buddies urged him to devote more time to training and move up to the Cat. II or Cat. I level, but Sterling had other priorities. He built a lucrative car-detailing business in his driveway to raise tuition money so he could attend the University of North Carolina–Greensboro at night and earned a degree in business administration. All the while, he continued training about 14 to 16 hours a week and went racing on weekends.

After graduation Sterling gave his car-detailing business to his brother, Ben, and went to work as an investment broker. Though the work was less backbreaking, the hours were longer, and he cut his training back to about 10 to 12 hours a week. Falling in love, getting married, buying a house, and having a daughter all followed in short order, and soon after Sterling was struggling to find 10 hours a week for training.

With his years of experience, Sterling had become accustomed to placing in the top 10 on a consistent basis in Cat. III criteriums and road races in the Southeast. But as his training time fell below 10 hours, racing became more difficult. He found himself in the middle of the pack, then the back. Where he used to push the pace on group rides, he now followed wheels. He started opting out of most of the long loops he used to enjoy with his brother and friends because he didn't want to deal with struggling to keep up or being the "slow guy." Cycling rapidly lost its appeal, his fitness declined, his weight went up, and his bikes started collecting more dust than miles.

The Promise of a New Paradigm

Sterling's case is remarkably common. Here's a guy who loves cycling, is pretty good at it, has been doing it for years, and would genuinely like to continue doing it for years to come. But being slow and out of shape isn't much fun, and cycling is too difficult a sport to bother with when it's not fun. I can't change the reality of Sterling's life to magically create more time for him to use for training. I can't—or at least I never would—ask him to give up time reading to and playing with his daughter so he can put in more time on the bike and race for $50 primes and $200 purses at regional criteriums. The value proposition (trade-off) there doesn't make any sense (rightfully so, I might add). Yet cycling will not regain its appeal for Sterling, or for thousands of cyclists facing similar value propositions, unless he's able to perform at a level that's worth the effort of training.

The classic endurance training model won't work for Sterling because he doesn't have enough time to go through the slow and gradual buildup of deep aerobic fitness. He has 6 hours a week, up to 8 if he's lucky, and that's it. Under the old training paradigm, there is no way for him to be competitive in Cat. III criteriums.

The reason this section refers to a new paradigm and not just a new training program is that the changes I'm going to ask you to make go way beyond adding a new interval workout to your routine. For this to work—and it will—you have to be willing to rethink your overall approach to endurance training. When CTS coach Jim Rutberg suggested the TCTP to his longtime friend and former teammate, Sterling thought he was nuts. For someone who had been a bike racer for more than 15 years, the time-crunched program Rutberg wanted to put Sterling on didn't look like anything he'd done before. Though he was an investment broker, he had read numerous cycling training books and had subscriptions to *Bicycling*, *VeloNews*, and even *Winning* magazine back in the day, and Rutberg was suggesting he train in ways those trusted publications told him not to! Then again, Sterling missed being a strong cyclist and wasn't very happy being mediocre, so what did he have to lose?

Cyclists in the Carolinas are fortunate to have two significant blocks of criterium racing each year, one from May to June and the other from September to October. In the spring the traveling circus that is professional cycling swings through the Southeast for races such as the Hanes Park Classic, the Dilworth Criterium, and the Athens Twilight Criterium. Then in the fall there are a bunch of local criteriums, leading up to the Carolina Classic in Greensboro, North Carolina, and the Greenville Cycling Classic near George Hincapie's adopted hometown of Greenville, South Carolina. There is some racing at other times in the year, but not as much, and nothing that attracts such large and strong fields of pros and amateurs.

Rutberg put Sterling on the TCTP six weeks before the start of the spring races in the Carolinas. He rode four times a week, never more than 7 hours total, raced four times in 8 weeks, and finished fourth, eighth, first, and third. In the only race he had entered the previous fall, he hadn't even finished.

Purists will tell you the TCTP won't work, and some will even tell you it's dangerous. Well, I'm telling you it does work, I'll show you exactly how and why it works, and it's no more dangerous than being a cyclist in the first place. What's more, it's based on sound science, has been proven effective by real athletes, and offers the opportunity of high-speed, high-power, full-throttle fun for cyclists who can't get there using antiquated training methods.

A Brief History of Training

Even though we can trace some theories of athletic training, such as periodization, back to the ancient Greeks, the level of sophistication in training was very low until the middle of the 20th century. That's not to diminish the abilities or accomplishments of athletes such as Major Taylor, Jesse Owens,

Babe Ruth, and Jim Thorpe. They were great athletes in their time and would be great champions today as well. But early Olympians and professional athletes rose above their competitors based largely on natural talent and their ability to endure great punishment. Some trained for their sports, a few trained maniacally, and the best athletes were those who managed to survive and adapt to brutal training regimens that destroyed everyone else. With relatively little scientific knowledge of how and why the training worked, training methods came and went as athletes observed and copied the workouts used by each new champion. Coaches saw this and theorized that improvement was based on the load an athlete could handle (recovery was largely ignored), and subsequently they based the process of athlete recruitment on pushing relative beginners harder and harder, until only a handful were left standing.

On a side note, if you want to have an interesting (although ultimately pointless) discussion, ask a sports scientist or coach how much better the greatest athletes of the early 20th century could have been if they had been trained using present-day methods. In other words, how would Jesse Owens perform against Usain Bolt in a 200-meter race if Owens could take advantage of the technologies and training methods used today? How would Major Taylor perform against Chris Hoy on the velodrome? We'll never know for sure, but it's a good cocktail party question to get a sports scientist riled up.

Structured interval training started appearing in the 1930s, when German scientist Woldemar Gerschler refined the less formal but highly effective practices already used by the Swedes and Finns (inventors of "Fartlek" running, which used natural terrain to interject periods of intensity and recovery into long runs). Gerschler made intervals more intense, kept the recovery periods short, and even used heart rate to govern the intensity of efforts. If you're interested in reading more about training during this period, I recommend *The Perfect Mile*, by Neal Bascomb, which describes the training methods used by elite runners as they sought to become the first to run a mile in less than 4 minutes.

The science of training took significant steps forward after World War II, largely because of the cold war. Even though the basic idea of periodization—systematically changing the focus and workload of training to maximize the positive impact of overload and recovery on training adaptations—had been around in various forms for thousands of years, it gained more widespread acceptance after Tudor Bompa and other Eastern Bloc coaches started creating detailed systems for improving athletic performance and winning medals by the truckload. With the world's greatest armies in a perpetual standoff, the Olympics became both a real and a symbolic battleground between East and West. Right along with the arms race and the race for space was an ongoing battle to see who could win more Olympic medals. From 1945 to 1989 the space and arms races pushed technology ahead faster than at any previous period in human history, and the cold war fight for athletic supremacy also led to giant advances in sports science. As a result, by 1990 our understanding of the athlete's response to exercise, altitude, hydration, nutrition, and recovery had never been greater. There was still plenty left to learn, and there still is, but we know more about how the body adapts to training than ever before.

Unfortunately, with great advances came horrible abuses. Doping existed before World War II, but it was largely unscientific and often pretty bizarre (cigarettes and brandy before major mountain climbs?). Applying modern science to training led to great advances in our understanding of how the body performed and how performance could be enhanced. That knowledge was used for both good and bad. On the positive side, structure was applied to training schedules to take advantage of the body's ability to adapt to alternating periods of stress and recovery. On the negative side, scientists also learned to create and use drugs to manipulate the body's adaptations to training. To make matters worse, it's almost impossible to completely separate the honest science from the science of the cheaters, because a lot of the same research was used to advance both legitimate and illegal methods for enhancing performance. For example, the same research that helped us understand the mechanism and benefits of altitude training also helped the cheaters devise new methods for blood doping. As long as there are athletes willing to cheat, there will be scientists and coaches working to pervert good science, and there will always be honest athletes, coaches, and agencies fighting against them. Doping is an ugly and unfortunate part of the history of sports science and training, so as much as I hate to waste ink on the subject, I'd be remiss to ignore it here. Now let's move on.

When I started training seriously in the 1970s, we had a basic understanding of interval training, but all we did was break down the different aspects of bike racing and train them individually. Monday was a rest day, Tuesday was sprinting, Wednesday was endurance, Thursday was climbing or a training race, Friday was a short spin, and then you raced on the weekend. If a race was particularly important, you rested a little more than usual during the preceding week. In the winter you used smaller gears and focused more on endurance, and maybe did some cyclocross racing. As amateurs, we did exactly what the pros did, but we rode fewer hours and did fewer intervals.

In the 1980s we started doing more lab testing. We were poked and prodded and informed of our VO$_2$max and lactate threshold values, but those numbers were largely useless outside the lab. By the mid-1980s you could use a heart rate monitor during your rides (although they were huge and not very accurate). Dr. Edmund Burke, a physiologist with the U.S. Cycling Team who later became a great mentor and friend of mine, was one of the first scientists to realize that endurance athletes could use heart rate ranges to target specific training adaptations. It was a big step forward because it allowed athletes to establish personal training intensities instead of relying on pace and perceived effort.

In the early 1990s, as heart rate monitors became widely available and heart rate training gained widespread acceptance, a new technology was being developed that would greatly increase the effectiveness and precision of cycling training. I think I first saw an SRM power meter in 1990 at the world championships in Japan, on the Germans' team time trial bikes. In 1993, I was the U.S. National Team coach and brought Lance Armstrong to Colorado Springs for testing immediately following his victory at the world championships. Working with a team that included U.S. Olympic Committee biomechanist Jeff Broker and sports scientists Ed Burke and Jay T. Kearney, we mounted a prototype wheel-based power meter from Look on Lance's bike and evaluated the aerodynamic advantages of different time trial positions. The next year, Dean Golich, who worked for me at USA Cycling and is now a CTS Premier coach, mounted SRMs on the bikes of U.S. National Team riders to study the power output of individual cyclists during the Tour DuPont.

Power meters finally provided the ability to use the power numbers derived from VO$_2$max and lactate threshold tests in everyday training out on the road. We developed individual power ranges to target specific training adaptations, then developed field tests to monitor and evaluate athletes' progress without having to go back into the lab. The science and technology were later pushed even further by Hunter Allen and Andrew Coggan when they developed Trainingpeaks software, which dramatically improved the ability to analyze the data from power files.

Despite the distance that training and technology have come since the end of World War II, however, the training programs used by most modern cyclists still don't meet their needs. That is because there's a fundamental problem with the classic training model for endurance cycling (including criteriums, cyclocross, mountain biking, and road racing).

The Classic Endurance Training Model

The classic endurance training model has always taken a top-down approach, meaning we have taken principles proven at the elite level and modified them to the needs and constraints of average and novice athletes. This is where the idea of long-term base training, or foundation training, came from. For decades pro athletes have spent a significant portion of the fall and winter engaged in high-volume, low- to moderate-intensity training. This was followed by a gradual increase in intensity and the inclusion of some longer intervals at intensities around lactate threshold. Hard intervals and training races were then thrown into the mix in the four to eight weeks prior to racing. Once the racing season started, training volume and intensity varied according to the athlete's racing schedule, but racing itself provided a significant amount of the overall training stimulus. During the season, athletes cycled through a series of race-and-recover periods in which there was very little actual training on the days between competitions. Because alternating between high-intensity racing and easy recovery days can only sustain competitive fitness for about six to eight weeks, athletes would shift to a lighter racing schedule—or a series of second-tier events they were doing for training rather than results—while devoting more attention to endurance and lactate threshold training. Then it was back to the race-and-recover cycle for several weeks in an effort to get results, earn some prize money, and keep their jobs.

And so it went from March to October. After the final race of the season, we were all so tired that we tossed the bike into the garage and slept for a month. Then the process started all over again and we were ready to race by March. It was like that in the 1970s, and it's like that today for many young men and women trying to make a living as bike racers.

Lance Armstrong's Impact on the Classic Endurance Training Model

My views on training had changed very little between the time when I was racing as an amateur in Europe in the 1970s and the day Lance Armstrong was diagnosed with testicular cancer in October 1996. Technology had improved, and so had my understanding of physiology, coaching, and training methods, but none of that had changed my fundamental approach to preparing athletes for competition. In terms of workouts I was as old-school as they come; I pushed my athletes to their limits, and those who could adapt and grow stronger were the ones who stayed on the team, went to Europe, became Olympians, and then pros. Basically, I coached the way I had been coached, but with the benefit of hindsight it's clear there were major flaws in that method.

The problems really became apparent after Lance completed his cancer treatment and set his sights on returning to professional cycling. I set up a training program that was pretty light, compared to his precancer programs, but followed the same basic structure. It crushed him physically, and he didn't have the motivation to push through the efforts. The solution was to reduce the intensity of his interval training and focus on efforts that were slightly below his lactate threshold power output. A rider's lactate threshold marks his or her maximum sustainable effort level. You can complete efforts above this power output, but only for a limited time before you're forced to slow down.

Earlier in Lance's career, we had relied more heavily on very difficult intervals at intensities well above lactate threshold. At the time we believed it worked because those intense efforts generated a lot of lactate in his muscles and forced his body to improve its ability to buffer and process that lactate. As I'll explain later, the actual mechanism may have been a bit different. Either way, the result of the training was that his lab-measured power at lactate threshold increased. And he was winning some of the biggest races in the world, which was the ultimate confirmation that the training was effective.

What we learned during Lance's comeback was that the maximal efforts weren't as necessary as we thought. Longer, submaximal efforts at power outputs just below his lactate threshold elicited similar increases in lactate threshold power, and because the training intensity was lower, Lance could do more of this targeted training in a given week or month than he could using the older, harder method. Going a little bit easier actually made him stronger and faster. This training, coupled with the loss of significant muscle mass during his cancer treatment, enabled him to return to the top of professional cycling in the fall of 1998 with fourth-place finishes at the three-week Tour of Spain and both the road race and time trial events at the world championships. The following July, he won the first of seven consecutive Tour de France titles.

Lance's focus on subthreshold interval work and higher cadence ranges on all terrains became the most enduring training innovations from his comeback period. The concepts were explained in detail in *The Lance Armstrong Performance Program* (Rodale, 2000) and later in *The Ultimate Ride* (Penguin, 2003), and are widely used by novice, amateur, and professional athletes and their coaches to this day. Now, lest you think I'm arrogant enough to believe I'm the only one to figure out the value of this approach, many of the same concepts—especially the importance of submaximal efforts in improving sustainable power at lactate threshold—were discussed in books such as *The Cyclist's Training Bible* by Joe Friel, *Serious Training for Endurance Athletes* by Rob Sleamaker and Ray Browning, *Serious Cycling* by Ed Burke, *High Performance Cycling* by Asker Jeukendrup, and later *Training and Racing with a Power Meter* by Hunter Allen and Andrew Coggan.

But perhaps Lance's greater impact on training was his level of specificity. In my opinion, Eddy Merckx will forever be regarded as the greatest cyclist who ever raced a bike. He won just about every race there was, more than once in many cases, and he won races from the earliest part of the spring to the latest events in the fall. His commitment to racing and winning throughout the season was shared by all professional cyclists of the time, and indeed by most riders well into the 1990s. Riders focused a bit more on particular races they wanted to win, but for the most part they raced full bore from

Milan–San Remo in March through the Giro di Lombardia in October. Lance changed that when he decided to focus his entire season on winning the Tour de France.

Instead of racing week in and week out through the spring, Lance's program focused on training first and using select races for training. There's no way to completely replicate the physical and psychological demands of racing in training, so difficult races such as Paris–Nice and the Dauphiné Libéré were typically included in his Tour de France preparation. However, relative to other yellow jersey contenders, he often had fewer days of racing in his legs before starting the Tour in July. And most years from 1999 to 2005, Lance's season was essentially over once he left the Champs-Élysées. He focused on being his best at the Tour de France and winning the race every time he said he would. It was an enormously successful strategy, and now we see groups of pro riders specializing in different portions of the season—the spring classics, the grand tours, the fall classics and world championships, and so on.

Adapting Pro-Level Training for Amateurs

As I mentioned previously, I launched CTS to deliver world-class coaching to athletes of all abilities. I was frustrated by the gap between the level of expertise available to elite athletes and the relatively archaic training methods that were being used by novice cyclists and amateur racers. Over the next 10 years I coached, taught other coaches new training methods, hosted camps and clinics, wrote books and countless articles, and built a multimillion-dollar coaching business. Along the way, CTS raised awareness about the benefits of coaching and helped give rise to an industry. In 2000 there were fewer than 200 licensed USA Cycling coaches. As demand grew from the cycling community, so did the number of coaches, and by 2008 there were more than 1,400.

There are dozens of reasons why the coaching industry thrived and grew, and I believe the subtle shift to submaximal training intensities was an important factor. It made training easier and therefore more pleasant, yet still prepared athletes for great personal performances. Initially it was pretty simple for my coaches and me to adapt the principles I'd been using with pros to athletes who were training for one-third to one-half of the pros' weekly training hours. If pros were riding 24 hours a week and completing four 30-minute climbing efforts, then it was absolutely reasonable to prescribe three 15-minute climbing efforts to a Cat. III rider who was training 12 hours a week. The relative intensities were the same, expressed as an identical percentage of each rider's lactate threshold power output (if the rider had access to a lab) or average power from the CTS Field Test (the performance test used for the workouts and training programs in this book; see Chapter 3). Although heart rate intensities are less accurate than power measurements, we also derived them for athletes who did not have access to power meters.

Effective training comes down to applying a workload to an athlete that is both specific to his or her activity and goal appropriate for that person's current levels of fitness and fatigue. The load has to be enough to stimulate a training response from the body, but not so great that it creates more fatigue than the body can cope with. And you have to give the body enough recovery time to replenish energy stores and adapt to the applied stress. Physically, the principal differences between training an elite athlete and an amateur are the workloads necessary to cause positive adaptations, the workloads the athletes can handle, and the time the athletes have available to train.

From 2000 to 2008, CTS coaches worked with thousands of cyclists, and more than 95 percent of them were novices, recreational riders, and amateur competitors. In the early years, through about 2004, the average CTS athlete was training about 10 to 12 hours a week. The riders who raced Cat. II or Cat. III or fast masters categories were closer to 12 to 16 hours a week, and some of the recreational riders and century riders were at about 8 to 10 hours a week. They were all being coached using the same method I was using with pro athletes, essentially an updated version of the classic endurance training model. It worked beautifully, and amateur athletes experienced incredible gains in their sustainable power outputs and race performances. They were finishing centuries faster than ever before, winning criteriums and road races left and right, leaving their riding buddies behind on climbs, and having more fun on their bikes than they had in years.

The biggest complaint we heard in those days was that the training was too easy. We had to have the same conversation with almost every athlete who signed up for coaching. My coaches would build the first few weeks of the athlete's schedule, then the athlete would log onto our Web site to see it and immediately call to let the coach know he or she could handle more. The intensity was too low, the intervals weren't long enough, the rides weren't long enough, and there were far too many rest days in the week. Yes, we'd say, we know it looks different than what you've done for the past 5 years (which was based on 30-year-old science), but try this for 6 weeks and then tell us if you want to go back to the way you trained before.

With rare exceptions, the coaching program adapted straight from what I was doing with pros worked for novices, recreational riders, and amateur racers, and athletes were ecstatic about the results. As time went on, however, I started hearing about athletes for whom the program wasn't working. At first they were few and far between, and it was tempting to dismiss them as "uncoachable" (a term I despise, and a circumstance I don't believe in) or just within that small percentage of people you can never satisfy. But if that were true, I reasoned, the number—or at least percentage—of those athletes should remain somewhat constant. If my coaching methodology worked 95 percent of the time, it should always work 95 percent of the time.

But toward the end of 2004, I started to see an increase in the percentage of athletes who were achieving results that were below my expectations. Many of the athletes were perfectly happy with their results, but their coaches expressed concern about what they saw as diminishing returns. The athletes were still making progress, but not as much, and the gains were more difficult to come by.

It took some digging to find the common link among these athletes, but as it turned out, it was remarkably simple. The problem was time.

Endurance Training at the Crossroads

The common factor shared by athletes who were experiencing subpar results from their coaching programs was a lack of training time. In almost every case I examined, the athletes in question were training fewer than 8 hours a week, some as few as 5. Many had training schedules that called for 10 to 12 hours and weren't able to complete all the training sessions because of their hectic work and family schedules. Others had worked with their coaches to build 6- or 8-hour schedules and were following their programs to the letter but were still not seeing results.

Time and intensity add up to workload, and all other things being equal, too little training time means there's an insufficient training stimulus. That's when it hit me. We had found the point at which the classic endurance training model breaks down. Once you get below 8 hours of training a week, the old tried-and-true methods derived from pro-level athletes no longer work. With the kind of workouts and interval intensities typically used in classically based programs, there's simply not enough time to generate the workload necessary to overload the body's systems and force them to adapt and grow stronger. Athletes stop improving and stagnate instead. And after a few months of training at a level that's insufficient to move them forward, they get frustrated, lose their motivation, complete halfhearted workouts, and subsequently experience a decline in fitness and performance.

We were seeing an increase in the percentage of people struggling to make progress, because in those years the popularity of cycling and coaching was increasing, and a growing number of the athletes signing up for coaching were leading extremely busy lives. At the same time, athletes who had been working with CTS coaches for two or three years were experiencing changes in their lifestyles: marriage, kids, promotions, mortgages, and so on.

As I saw it, there were two choices: Write off a highly motivated population of athletes because they weren't able to commit enough time to fit into the classic endurance training model, or change the model. Since the only time I ever encouraged athletes to stop exercising was when their physicians said their sport or activity level might kill them, I chose to change the model.

Overview of the Time-Crunched Training Program

By the time Jim Rutberg started preparing Sterling Swaim for his comeback, my coaches and I had taken the loose concept of "time-crunched" training and refined it into a structured program that could be effectively used by a wide variety of athletes. Before stepping through the details and the science of how it works, I want to give you a broad overview of the program.

The TCTP consists of a maximum of 4 workouts per week. There's some latitude in terms of scheduling, but generally it comes down to a combination of the following:

- Two to three weekday workouts, each lasting 60 to 90 minutes
- One to two weekend rides, each lasting 1 to 3 hours

Three-hour rides are rare in the program, and there's nothing longer than that. Weekly training volume will be 6 hours, with the option to increase workout duration and accumulate up to 8 hours. The exceptions to these rules will be in the Ultraendurance and Commuting chapters. The ultraendurance training program features more volume on the weekends while maintaining shorter interval workouts during the workweek, and there are a few weeks of that schedule that feature a fifth workout day. The commuter training plans assume that you're commuting to and from work 4 to 5 days a week, although the actual weekday workouts stick with the 60- to 90-minute range.

In the absence of time, intensity is the key to performance. Remember, workload is a product of time and intensity, so if you want to keep the workload constant as time decreases, then intensity must increase. For a training program to work on fewer than 8 hours a week, you pretty much have to focus entirely on intensity. Make no mistake: The workouts in this program are hard. Very hard. You will be performing some efforts just below your lactate threshold power output and some right at it, but many efforts will be much more difficult, at maximum intensity.

The TCTP is a high-intensity, low-volume training program that produces the fitness and power necessary to push the pace in local group rides and to be competitive in local and regional criteriums, cross-country and short-track mountain bike races, and cyclocross races. If you're not a competitive cyclist but want to be stronger than you are right now, this program will give you the fitness to fully enjoy weekend rides, bike tours, and cycling camps.

However, there are limits to what you're going to be able to accomplish on fewer than 8 hours of training per week. For instance, with this program you can prepare to have a good day on a century ride, but it's not likely to be the fastest 100 miles you've ever ridden. And although the program lets Sterling race for the win, there's a reason he's focusing on the spring and fall series instead of trying to win races throughout the entire season. The TCTP will not be the perfect solution for every cyclist, and I have included an important section in Chapter 2 called "Terms and Conditions" to help you decide whether this program is for you.

Placing your family and career ahead of your cycling goals is a wise choice for pretty much anyone who has either a real career or a family, and pretty much the only choice if you have both. But focusing on your career and your family doesn't change the fact that you're a cyclist, nor does it invalidate your desire to be fit, fast, and powerful. Simply put, a reduction in training time doesn't automatically doom you to back-of-the-pack finishes or another season of fruitless suffering. If you're willing to work hard with the limited time you have, and if you're ready to let go of antiquated training methods and try something new, then it's time to get off your butt and retake your rightful place at the front of the pack.

CHAPTER

2

The Science of the Time-Crunched Training Program

Whether you have unlimited time to train or only a few hours a week, your performance depends on developing the same physical systems. The human body has three primary energy systems, which power all activities: immediate (adenosine triphosphate [ATP] and creatine phosphate [CP]), aerobic, and glycolytic (anaerobic). The end product of all three is ATP, which releases energy when one of its three phosphate bonds is broken. The resulting adenosine diphosphate is then resynthesized to ATP so it can be broken again, and again, and again. The best way to think of these three energy pathways is from the viewpoint of demand.

The Immediate Energy System: Do or Die

The ATP/CP system supports high-power efforts that last fewer than about 10 seconds. You use it when you have to jump out of the way of a speeding bus, and from an athletic standpoint it's most important in power sports such as football. As a cyclist, you mostly use this system for a powerful standing start or when you almost rip the cranks off trying to avoid getting run over by a car. During those few seconds, you demand energy faster than either the glycolytic or aerobic energy system can deliver it. The ATP/CP system is immediate because the ATP part is the energy-yielding molecule produced by the other systems. The very limited supply that is stored in your muscles can provide energy without the more than 20 steps required to produce ATP through the aerobic system. However, because endurance cycling doesn't rely heavily on this energy system, cyclists have little reason to focus on it during training.

The Aerobic Engine

The aerobic system is the body's primary source of energy, and it's an utterly amazing machine. It can burn carbohydrate, fat, and protein simultaneously and can regulate the mixture it burns based on fuel availability and energy demand. It's a flex-fuel engine that's remarkably clean and efficient; when the aerobic system is done with a molecule of sugar, the only waste products are water and carbon dioxide. In comparison, the glycolytic system (discussed in more detail below) produces energy faster, but it can only use carbohydrate, produces less ATP from every molecule of sugar it processes, and produces lactate as a by-product (more on that later, too).

The rock stars of the aerobic system are little things called mitochondria. These organelles are a muscle cell's power plants: Fuel and oxygen go in, and energy comes out. For an endurance athlete, the primary goal of training is to increase the amount of oxygen your body can absorb, deliver, and process. One of the biggest keys to building this oxygen-processing capacity is increasing mitochondrial density, or the size and number of mitochondria in muscle cells. As you ride, having more and bigger power plants running at full capacity gives you the ability to produce more energy aerobically every minute.

When training increases the power you can produce aerobically, you can go harder before reaching the point where you're demanding energy faster than the aerobic engine can deliver it, otherwise known as *lactate threshold*. But increasing your power at lactate threshold is only part of the equation. With specific training at intensities near your lactate threshold power output, you can also increase the amount of time you will be able to ride at and slightly above threshold.

The Glycolytic Energy System

There's been a lot of confusion about the glycolytic system, mainly because of semantics. This is the system people often refer to as "anaerobic," which literally means "without oxygen." The terminology causes confusion because it implies that the body has stopped using oxygen to produce energy, which is not the case. As exercise intensity increases, you reach a point at which your demand for energy matches your aerobic engine's ability to produce it in working muscles. Then you decide to push the pace, you hit a hill or a headwind, or your buddy attacks and you have to respond. Your energy demand increases, and in order for your mitochondria to continue producing enough energy, your body uses a metabolic shortcut called anaerobic glycolysis. Although the actual process involves many chemical reactions, glycolysis—to put it in its simplest terms—rapidly delivers the ATP necessary to meet your increased energy demand by converting glucose (sugar) into lactate in order to keep other energy-producing reactions moving.

Lactate is a partially used carbohydrate that leads to trouble when it builds up in your muscles. The molecule is created as a normal step of aerobic metabolism, and lactate is constantly being broken down to usable energy. The problem isn't that more lactate is being produced; instead, as exercise intensity increases, you reach a point where lactate removal or processing can no longer keep up with production. A disproportionate amount of lactate builds up in the muscle and blood, and this accumulation is what we look for when we're determining an athlete's lactate threshold.

The conversion of glucose to lactate in order to keep energy production going is a lot like using a credit card. You're getting the currency you need as you need it, but you don't have unlimited credit, and pretty soon you're going to have to pay back every cent you borrowed. What's more, you have to cut back on spending while you're paying it back, which means you have to slow down. One of the key adaptations you're seeking as an endurance athlete is an improvement in your ability to get that lactate integrated back into the normal process of aerobic energy production so it can be oxidized completely. The faster you can process lactate, the more work you can perform before lactate levels in your muscles and blood start to rise. To continue the financial analogy, a stronger aerobic system puts more cash (aerobic metabolism) in your pocket so you're not so quick to use credit.

VO₂max

Lactate threshold is the point at which your demand for energy outstrips the aerobic system's ability to deliver it, but lactate threshold doesn't define the maximum amount of oxygen your body can use. When your exercise intensity reaches its absolute peak, and your body is pulling in, absorbing, and burning as much oxygen as it possibly can, you're at VO_2max. This is your maximum aerobic capacity, and it is one of the most important indicators of your potential as an endurance athlete.

An exceedingly high VO_2max doesn't automatically guarantee you'll become a cycling champion; it just means you have a big engine. To make a comparison to car engines, some people are born with eight cylinders, whereas others have four (and extremely gifted athletes are born with twelve). A finely tuned four-cylinder Acura can go faster than a poorly maintained V8 Corvette, and twelve-cylinder supercars can beat everything, but they can be finicky and difficult to control. You have to have a big engine to be a pro, but no matter what size engine you start with, you can optimize your performance with effective training.

It takes a great effort to reach intensities near your VO_2max, and during VO_2max-specific workouts you generate an enormous amount of lactate and burn calories tremendously fast. But the reward is worth the effort, because increasing your power at VO_2max gives you the tools to launch and respond to attacks. We all know cyclists who can ride at a hard and steady pace all day but can't accelerate to save their lives. They're the guys you love to have around in a breakaway, because they'll pull all day long, and then you can ditch them with one or two strong accelerations in the final mile. Their training gives them tremendous power at lactate threshold but fails to develop the ability to handle repeated maximal efforts.

Not only does increasing your power at VO_2max, and the amount of time you can sustain that power, give you the ability to accelerate hard during an attack, but the training further improves your ability to process lactate. This means you'll be able to better handle the inevitable surges and pace changes that push you over your lactate threshold power during everything from criteriums to training races, centuries, and local group rides.

The Endurance String Theory

Delineating the various ways your body can produce energy is both a blessing and a curse. On the positive side, knowing how each system works gives us the information necessary to design training that makes each system produce energy more quickly and sustainably. On the downside, the same information has inadvertently led people to believe that these systems operate independently of each other. Sports scientists and coaches, myself included, have told you that training at 86 to 90 percent of your maximum sustainable power output will target your glycolytic energy system and increase your power at lactate threshold. And although that is true, the glycolytic system isn't the only one doing the work at that intensity, nor is it the only one that will reap a training benefit.

You are always producing energy through all possible pathways, but your demand for energy determines the relative contribution from each. At low to moderate intensities, the vast majority of your energy comes from the aerobic engine (mitochondria breaking down primarily fat and carbohydrate). As your intensity level rises above about 60 percent of VO_2max, the contribution from the glycolytic system starts to increase, and then it really ramps up quickly once you reach lactate threshold. Because glycolysis only burns carbohydrate, the overall percentage of energy coming from carbohydrate increases dramatically as your intensity increases from lactate threshold to VO_2max. You're still burning a lot of fat, however, because your mitochondria are also still chugging along as fast as they can.

Rather than seeing your various energy pathways as separate and distinct, it's better to think of them as segments of one continuous string, arranged based on the amount of work you perform with each. At one end is the immediate energy system, which can only power your muscles for 5 to 8 seconds. Next comes a large segment representing the aerobic system, because it could theoretically power your muscles at a moderate intensity level forever if there were sufficient oxygen and fuel available. After that is the glycolytic system, which can do a lot of work but can only run at full tilt for a limited period of time before lactate accumulation causes you to reduce your exercise intensity. And finally, we have the segment for VO_2max, which is the maximum amount of work you can do, an intensity that is only sustainable for a few minutes. Training to improve your performance at VO_2max is like pulling up on the VO_2 end of the string—all the other segments rise with it. Focusing your training entirely on improving aerobic performance is like picking up the string in the middle: Power at lactate threshold will dip a bit, and power at VO_2max will only move a little. All of these systems are interconnected, and how you focus your training affects the amount of work you can do, not only with the system you're focusing on but with all the others as well.

The Science of High-Intensity Training

When you view the energy systems as interconnected parts of the same string, it starts to make sense that when training pulls up on the VO_2max end of the string, you'll see a subsequent increase in performance from the aerobic and glycolytic systems. To use an old phrase, a rising tide lifts all boats. High-intensity training has been extensively studied, and the basic premise of a training program that utilizes intervals at and near an athlete's VO_2max is that efforts at this intensity level lead to many of the same physiological adaptations that result from more traditional endurance training models. In fact, Burgomaster et al. (2005) found that high-intensity interval training doubled an athlete's time to exhaustion on a ride performed at 80 percent of peak VO_2. This is appealing to the time-crunched athlete because the efforts required are up to five times shorter than the traditional intervals used to target power at lactate threshold. I know a lot of athletes are genuinely interested in the science of performance, so let's take a closer look at the science that supports a high-intensity, low-volume training program.

What Constitutes Improvement?

At the end of the day, improvement can be measured by whether you can produce more power at the same relative effort level as before and/or whether you can sustain that power output longer than you could before. After training, if you can go faster from point A to point B (in similar conditions), then you have made progress. But many factors are involved in getting from A to B more quickly, including a learning curve that helps athletes become faster over familiar territory even when they have made no improvement in fitness. So how do you know whether an athlete's improved performance is due to physiological changes or the fact he or she has learned how to perform better when tested? You look inside the muscles.

Having more mitochondria in muscle cells allows you to oxidize more fat and carbohydrate through aerobic metabolism. For a long time we thought the most effective way to increase mitochondrial density was to perform long rides at moderate intensities. And although there's still debate about the exact mechanism at work, evidence suggests that the depletion of ATP in muscle cells, which happens when intense exercise leads you to consume ATP faster than it can be produced, may kick-start a cascade of biochemical processes that ends with increased production of mitochondria (Willett, 2006). Studies examining the effectiveness of short high-intensity intervals for improving aerobic performance have shown an increase in muscles' oxidative capacity (the maximum amount of oxygen a muscle can utilize) and in levels of key enzymes used in the process of aerobic metabolism. In 1982, Dudley et al. reported that intensities of 95 percent and above throughout a 20-minute maximum power output are required to create the largest concentration of mitochondrial enzymes. Conversely, they also reported that there is no increase in muscle enzyme density after 60 minutes of continuous work. Although the original research was completed using rat muscle fiber, the study has been frequently cited in later research performed on athletes. It has been suggested that the lack of increased muscle enzyme activity after 60 minutes of continuous work (such as during a long, moderate-intensity endurance ride) may occur because the increased exercise duration lowers the athlete's power output below what is needed to stimulate up-regulation of enzymes.

You can also measure an athlete's VO$_2$max to determine whether a training program has improved his or her capacity to utilize oxygen. In 1986

Dempsey found a 19 percent increase in VO_2max (from 50 to 61) using a 12-week program of four workouts a week, featuring 3-minute intervals at VO_2max and 2-minute recovery periods between efforts. Rodas et al. (2000) were able to take the research a step further because of advances in power meter technology; they reported a 30-watt increase in maximal load and an increase in VO_2max from 57.3 to 63.8 in their high-intensity interval training research. Barnett et al. (2004) found a 7.1 percent increase in mean power output and an 8 percent increase in peak VO_2. Their research also showed a 17 percent increase in resting intramuscular glycogen content; an increase in the amount of carbohydrate fuel a muscle can store is another indicator of improved aerobic conditioning.

I'd be the first to tell you that riders who look great in the lab are sometimes the first to be shot out the back in real races. A few studies have included actual cycling time trials in their protocols, and Laursen, Shing et al. (2002) found that it took only four high-intensity training sessions to bring about a 4.4 to 5.8 percent improvement in 40K time trial performance. Hawley et al. (1997) found that after only four to six interval sessions performed over two to three weeks, peak power output was increased by 15 to 20 watts, which can translate to riding 1.5 to 2 km/hr. faster in a 40K time trial, or a 90- to 120-second improvement. These findings support the notion that after training with high-intensity intervals, athletes are able to sustain work at a higher percentage of their peak VO_2 (90 percent versus 86 percent in Hawley's study). Hawley stated that this improvement is likely due to an increased efficiency in fatty acid metabolism and a "decreased reliance on carbohydrate as a fuel source" due to an increased density of mitochondria in muscle cells.

Similarly, Brooks and Mercier (1994) reported a reduction in carbohydrate oxidation and lactate accumulation following high-intensity interval training when subjects were asked to perform at the same absolute work rate as they had at the beginning of the study. This is crucial for understanding how high-intensity training ends up increasing endurance performance. After the high-intensity training, when athletes ride at higher power outputs, they will be less reliant on the glycolytic system and derive a higher percentage of energy from the aerobic system. As a result, they will use more fat for energy and produce less lactate. Harmer et al. (2000) also found a reduction in glycogen utilization and lactate accumulation following a high-intensity training protocol.

Does It Matter How Strong You Are Now?

Research has shown that if an athlete has a VO_2max over 60 ml/kg/min., endurance performance will not improve without high-intensity interval training (Londeree, 1997). Londeree also found that even with a VO_2max lower than 60 ml/kg/min., after three weeks of training there will be very few positive training adaptations unless there is an increase in training stimulus. As a matter of perspective, a moderately trained cyclist will have a VO_2max of about 50 to 55, a well-trained cyclist (Cat. III to IV or good in fast group rides) will likely be between 55 and 65, and a high-level amateur or domestic pro is likely to have a VO_2max above 70 ml/kg/min. Laursen and Jenkins (2002a), who defined "moderately trained" athletes as having a VO_2max less than 60 ml/kg/min., provided a very useful summary of relevant research. They defined high-intensity training as an interval of 30 seconds to 5 minutes at intensities above lactate threshold, and they looked at a wide range of markers to identify improvement in aerobic metabolism, including changes in muscle fibers and the small blood vessels (capillaries) that deliver oxygenated blood to muscle tissue:

> *High-intensity training in sedentary and recreationally active individuals improves endurance performance to a greater extent than does continuous submaximal training alone. This improvement appears due, in part, to an up-regulated contribution of both aerobic and anaerobic metabolism to the energy demand, which enhances the availability of ATP and improves the energy status in working muscle. An improved capacity for aerobic metabolism, as evidenced by an increased expression of Type I fibers [otherwise known as slow-twitch muscle fibers and in contrast to Type II, or fast-twitch muscle fibers], capillarization and oxidative enzyme activity is the most common response to high intensity training in untrained or moderately active individuals. (Laursen and Jenkins, 2002b)*

Although far less research has been conducted on professional-level cy-clists (it's difficult to get them to participate in a study that requires them to try something different), Laursen and Jenkins put together a table that sum-marizes the results of research into the effectiveness of high-intensity train-ing for highly trained endurance athletes (see Table 2.1).

How High Is High Intensity?

Now we're getting to the really important part of this discussion of the sci-ence behind the Time-Crunched Training Program (TCTP). Sports scientists have shown that high-intensity intervals improve an athlete's ability to per-form at workloads below and above lactate threshold, but their research has also included efforts that range from 15 seconds to more than 5 minutes, and intensities ranging from 95 percent of 20-minute maximum power to well above 120 percent of VO_2max power. For instance, Burgomaster et al. (2005)

TABLE 2.1 | **Summary of Findings in High-Intensity Interval-Training (HIT) Studies in Highly Trained Cyclists**[a]

REFERENCE	N	HIT SESSIONS	REPS	INTENSITY (% P_{PEAK})
Lindsay et al.	8	6	6-8	80
Weston et al.	6	6	6-8	80
Westgarth-Taylor et al.	8	12	6-9	80
Stepto et al.	4	6	4	80
Stepto et al.	4	6	8	85
Stepto et al.	4	6	12	90
Laursen et al.	7	4	20	100
Stepto et al.	3	6	12	100
Stepto et al.	4	6	12	175

[a] Changes indicated based on statistical significance at the $p < 0.05$ level.
3-HCoA = 3-hydroxyacyl coenzyme A dehydrogenase activity;
CHO$_{ox}$ = carbohydrate oxidation rates; **CS** = citrate synthase activity;
HK = hexokinase activity; **n** = number of participants;
PFK = phosphofructokinase activity; **P$_{peak}$** = peak aerobic power output;

found that six sessions of 30-second all-out sprint intervals over 2 weeks doubled athletes' time to exhaustion (from 26 to 51 minutes) at a sustained intensity of 80 percent of peak VO_2. Their results prompted Dr. Ed Coyle, a prominent researcher from the University of Texas, to submit an invited editorial to the *Journal of Applied Physiology* in which he wrote, "Indeed, it is likely that if an experienced runner or bicyclist had only two weeks and very limited time to prepare for a race of about 30 minutes' duration, that sprint interval training would become a mainstay of their preparation."

Now, even though you may not have a ton of time available for training, 6 to 8 hours a week is a lot more time than the subjects in many of the extremely short-interval (15 to 30 seconds) studies. You also have more than two weeks to prepare for your next cycling goal, and most likely achieving that goal is going to take longer than 30 minutes. That's why I prefer to limit the most difficult intervals in the TCTP to about 1 to 4 minutes, at intensities that generally will be "as hard as you can sustain for the whole interval." I discuss

WORK DURATION	REST DURATION	HIT DURATION (WK)	RESULTS
5 min	60 sec	4	$\uparrow P_{peak}$, $\uparrow TF_{150}$, $\uparrow TT_{40}$
5 min	60 sec	4	$\uparrow P_{peak}$, $\uparrow TF_{150}$, $\uparrow TT_{40}$ $\uparrow ß$, $\leftrightarrow HK$, $\leftrightarrow PFK$, $\leftrightarrow CS$, $\leftrightarrow$3-HCoA
5 min	60 sec	6	$\uparrow P_{peak}$, $\uparrow TT_{40}$, $\downarrow CHOox$
8 min	1 min	3	$\leftrightarrow$
4 min	1.5 min	3	$\uparrow P_{peak}$, $\uparrow TT_{40}$
2 min	3 min	3	$\leftrightarrow$
1 min	2 min	2	$\uparrow P_{peak}$, $\uparrow T_{vent}$, $\uparrow TF_{100}$,
1 min	4 min	3	$\leftrightarrow$
30 sec	4.5 min	3	$\uparrow P_{peak}$, $\uparrow TT_{40}$

Reps = repetitions; **TF_{100}** = time to fatigue at 100%;
TF_{150} = time to fatigue at 150% of P_{peak}; **TT_{40}** = 40km time-trial performance;
T_{vent} = ventilatory threshold.
ß = buffering capacity; $\downarrow$ = decrease; $\uparrow$ =increase; $\leftrightarrow$ = no change.

this more in Chapter 3, but for now suffice it to say that you'll be working at intensities between lactate threshold and VO$_2$max, and sometimes at VO$_2$max. You will also be performing longer intervals (6 to 10 minutes) at slightly lower intensities, closer to your lactate threshold power output.

In high-intensity training programs, the recovery times between intervals are just as important as what's referred to as the "work time." If you're doing a set of intervals in which each effort is 2 minutes of work time, there's a big difference between taking 1, 2, and 5 minutes of easy spinning recovery between efforts. Though you will get some additional recovery time in the early portions of the TCTP, once you're into the heart of it, many of the interval workouts will use recovery ratios (work time:recovery time) of 1:1 and 1:0.5. In other words, you'll see interval sets of 2 minutes "on" and 2 minutes "off," or even 2 minutes "on" and 1 minute "off." You won't be completely recovered from one effort before it's time to begin the next, and that's the point. The efforts will generate a lot of lactate, and your body will be working to process it, but starting your next high-power effort while your lactate levels are still elevated helps drive the necessary adaptations that will make you a faster, stronger cyclist.

Things You Can't Cut Out

Even though the scientific literature and our experiences with real-world athletes show that you can perform well as an endurance athlete even when you cut out a great deal of the volume typically found in endurance training programs, there are some essential principles and components of training that cannot be eliminated.

PRINCIPLES OF TRAINING

In 2003 I wrote a book called *The Ultimate Ride*, which described the five principles of training and the five major components of a productive workout. The training philosophies in that book illustrated the modifications I had made to the classic endurance training model in the process of coaching Lance Armstrong through his comeback from cancer. Those training philosophies are all still valid, and my coaches and I use them every day with athletes who have more than 8 hours a week to commit to training. Yet even though I needed to make dramatic changes to the classic endurance training model to optimize performance for time-crunched athletes, this new paradigm is still governed by the same principles and workout components as that model. Rather than reinvent the wheel here, I have revisited some of the material from *The Ultimate Ride* and updated it to reflect the unique demands of the TCTP.

When you distill the world's most successful training programs, across all sports, you arrive at five distinct principles of training:

1. Overload and recovery
2. Individuality
3. Specificity
4. Progression
5. Systematic approach

OVERLOAD AND RECOVERY PRINCIPLE

The human body is designed to respond to overload, and as long as you overload a system in the body properly and allow it time to adapt, that system will grow stronger and be ready for the same stress in the future. All forms of physical training are based on the body's ability to adapt to stress (or overload). To achieve positive training effects, this principle must be applied to individual training sessions as well as entire periods of your training. For instance, a lactate threshold interval workout must be difficult enough and long enough to stress your glycolytic energy system, but lactate threshold workouts must also be scheduled into a block of training so that the training loads from individual workouts accumulate and lead to more significant adaptations.

Organizing training into blocks of similar workouts was one of the changes we made to the U.S. National Team programs in the early 1990s. When I was racing, the common training program was structured to hit all aspects of cycling every week: Monday was a rest day, Tuesday was sprinting, Wednesday was a long day, Thursday was for hills, and Friday was a short ride to rest up for racing or group rides on the weekends. The limitation of that program was that there was never enough load on any one energy system to lead to significant growth. A full week was too long to wait between climbing repeats for one workout to build on the benefits from the previous one. When we started restructuring training weeks to tilt the balance to specific energy systems, the athletes made significant gains very quickly.

To benefit from overloading an energy system, you have to give that system time to rest. When you are out on the road and you've got the hammer down in the middle of a PowerInterval (a maximum-intensity interval workout), you are not improving your fitness; you are applying stress. Later, when you are home reading bedtime stories to your kids, then you are improving your fitness. Gains are made when you allow enough time for your body to recover and adapt to the stresses you have applied. This is why I don't separate recovery from training. Recovery is part of your training, and thinking of it that way helps you remain as committed to recovering as you are to working out.

Table 2.2 shows general guidelines for recovery following specific amounts of time at given intensities. Remember that these are only guidelines. Recovery from training varies among individuals.

Adapting the Overload and Recovery Principle for Time-Crunched Cyclists

Athletes who train 10, 12, or more hours a week tend to have no problem achieving the overload portion of the equation. If anything, they have more trouble setting aside as much time as they need for optimal recovery. For

TABLE 2.2 | Guidelines for Recovery

VOLUME OF INTENSITY	SUGGESTED TIME NEEDED FOR RECOVERY
0–6 hours at aerobic endurance intensity	8 hours
30–60 minutes at tempo intensity	8–10 hours
75–120 minutes at tempo intensity	24–36 hours
15–45 minutes at lactate threshold	24 hours
60–90 minutes at lactate threshold	24–36 hours
10–30 minutes above lactate threshold	24–36 hours
45 minutes or more above lactate threshold	36–48 hours

time-crunched cyclists, the opposite is true. With only 6 to 8 hours available for training, recovery is less of a problem because your relative lack of training time means there's plenty of downtime built into your week. The challenge is to accumulate the workload necessary to cause an overload. Fortunately, the relationship between volume and intensity is not linear. Training workload is the product of volume and intensity, but compared with the effect of increasing volume, increasing intensity results in an exponential increase in workload. As a result, high-intensity training programs can generate great workloads despite very low training volumes.

Some athletes and coaches initially fear that the TCTP will lead to overtraining—which is perhaps more accurately termed "under-recovery"—because it includes so much intensity. Their fear is based on the fact that classic endurance training programs typically only include very high-intensity intervals in the final weeks leading up to big competitions. In those training programs, you couldn't add harder intervals any earlier because the training volume was so high. There's a limit to the total workload an athlete can handle in a week, and in classic programs the volume takes up such a large percentage of that workload that you can't add more high-intensity intervals to it without compromising the athlete's ability to recover and adapt. The workouts and training programs in this book start out with hard intervals and progress to really difficult ones within only a few weeks. This works because your low training volume gives you the opportunity to use high-intensity intervals in ways high-volume trainers cannot.

INDIVIDUALITY PRINCIPLE

I have always been surprised by how many athletes ignore the individuality principle. The training program that works for you, right down to the individual workouts and interval intensities, has to be based on your physiological and personal needs. Training is not a one-size-fits-all product. All parts of your program—the total mileage, the number and type of intervals, and even the terrain and cadence—must be personalized. That doesn't mean that you can't train with your friends or training partners; it just means that while you're with them you have to stay true to your own training program.

Individuality is rarely a problem for time-crunched athletes, because your busy schedule already means training at different times and with different workouts than do your friends who have more free time on their hands. Once you start on the TCTP, your training is going to be extremely different from what they're doing, so much so that they may question the wisdom of your choices. But don't give in to peer pressure telling you to revert back to a training model that's no longer relevant for you. Let them tell you this is crazy; the best way to convince them that the TCTP works is to do the program and then ride them off your wheel in a group ride or race.

"About three weeks into the program, I was out on the road doing maximum-intensity PowerIntervals when some of my cycling buddies came rolling by," Sterling Swaim remembers. "They asked what I was doing and nodded politely as I told them, but I could tell they thought I was insane. That night I got a call from a guy I'd been riding with and racing against for 10 years, because he was 'concerned' I was going to ruin my season. A few months later, after I'd killed him in the spring race series, he approached me at a barbeque and asked if I'd let him see my 'radical' new training program."

It may seem paradoxical to talk about the individuality principle and then include 12-week training programs in this book. Ideally, every cyclist would work with a coach and get a training program built from scratch, but I understand that personal coaching is not an option for everyone. The workouts and training programs in this book are rooted in the principles my coaches and I use to create custom schedules for our athletes, and you'll be able to apply the individuality principle to them when you establish your personal intensity ranges and fit the workouts into your busy work and family schedules.

SPECIFICITY PRINCIPLE

Your training must resemble the activity you want to perform. In a broad sense, this means that if you want to be a road cyclist, you should spend the vast majority of your training time on two wheels. In a narrower sense, it means you have to determine the exact demands of the activity you wish to perform and tailor your training to address them. Conversely, it also means that your training is going to prepare you optimally for specific events and activities.

The specificity principle is especially important for the time-crunched cyclist. Traditionally we talk about narrowing the focus of a broad endurance training program to enhance the specific skills and power outputs that will lead to success in goal events. But you don't have the time to build broad endurance fitness in the first place, so you need to look at specificity from the opposite direction. With very limited time available for training, the fitness you're going to develop with the TCTP will be best applied to a specific set of events and goals. You will have many opportunities for success (probably more than you have right now), but as I explain in more detail in the section "Terms and Conditions" later in this chapter, there are some inescapable consequences to having fewer than 8 hours a week to train for an endurance sport.

PROGRESSION PRINCIPLE

Training must progressively move forward. To enjoy continued gains in performance, you have to increase training loads as you adapt. Time and intensity are the two most significant variables you can use to adjust your workload. For instance, you can increase the number of hours you devote to training, increase the overall intensity of your rides, include more intervals, make the intervals more intense, make the intervals longer, or shorten the recovery periods between the intervals. You can use these two variables to manipulate training a hundred different ways, but the end result must be that you're generating a training stimulus great enough to make your muscles and aerobic engine adapt. Just as important, once you adapt and grow stronger, you have to manipulate the time and intensity variables again so you further increase the workload to generate another training stimulus.

Interestingly, some of the most compelling evidence supporting the effectiveness of high-intensity interval training relates to the principle of progression. Neither training time nor intensity is limitless, even for professional cyclists. There are only 24 hours in the day, and the human body can only be pushed so hard. Professional racing cyclists are pretty much maxed out in terms of the annual hours and mileage they can accumulate while still performing at a high level. Indeed, studies have shown that for highly trained athletes, even if they could add more training volume, it wouldn't lead to additional improvements in VO_2max, power at lactate threshold, or mitochondrial density (Laursen and Jenkins, 2002a). With volume effectively maxed out and therefore not a limiting factor for improvement, you can observe the impact of increasing an athlete's workload with high-intensity intervals. Professional cycling has advanced so far that no amount of moderate-intensity training volume will be enough to generate the speed and power necessary to keep up, let alone win. To make the additional progress that's required for success at the highest levels of the sport, pros have to incorporate high-intensity intervals—on top of the intensity they get in races—into their training programs.

Time-crunched athletes aren't maxed out in terms of training volume, but you are maxed out in terms of the amount of time you can devote to training. Even though there are advantages to training more than 6 hours a week, the other commitments in your life mean you have to do what you can in that time. To achieve progression without adding hours, the TCTP manipulates the type and number of intervals, their length, and the recovery periods between them. Progression is fast in this program, and by the end of 11 weeks the workouts you thought were challenging at the beginning will look like child's play. But around the same time you'll also notice that you're pushing the pace at the front of the group ride or sprinting for the win in a criterium instead of suffering like a dog at the back.

SYSTEMATIC APPROACH

For novices, even a haphazard training schedule produces results. Just the act of getting on the bike, or throwing in a few intervals here and there, is enough to develop fitness. Pretty soon, however, that progress plateaus. Just as an architect follows a step-by-step blueprint when designing a house, training must take a systematic approach. A successful training program must be well thought out and organized so your body advances through a planned series of training and recovery periods. If you wake up each day and simply flip a coin to determine your daily workout, you will soon find you are making little progress in your training. This is especially true for athletes who have limited training time.

Athletes using high-volume training programs have the luxury of being able to waste some percentage of their training time without experiencing much of a penalty. For one thing, they have time to make up for a poor ride by adjusting a workout later in the week. High-volume training programs are also more forgiving, in that they generate such deep aerobic fitness that small transgressions aren't enough to knock an athlete off course. The less time you have available for training, the greater the penalties for wasted efforts.

Some people seem to be able to remain super-fit regardless of what they do or how much they do. Some stay thin regardless of what they eat. These people are the fortunate anomalies. Most athletes, even those of you who like to think of yourselves as rebels, thrive with structure. As you embark on the TCTP, remember that with limited training time, every hour and every interval counts.

THE FIVE WORKOUT COMPONENTS

When you throw your leg over your saddle and head out on the road, you can use the following five variables to address the five principles of training discussed in the previous section:

1. Intensity
2. Volume
3. Frequency or repetition
4. Terrain
5. Cadence

You can completely change the goal of a workout by changing one of its components. For instance, climbing intervals that are 10 minutes long can target two completely different energy systems if you simply change the cadence. Climbing at a cadence of 70 revolutions per minute (rpm) will tend to push an athlete to his or her climbing lactate threshold, which is slightly higher than the flat-ground lactate threshold due to an increase in muscle recruitment. I prescribe such workouts to develop an athlete's ability to sustain prolonged climbing efforts in races. But if the same climbing workout is done at a cadence of 50 rpm, the tension applied to the leg muscles increases greatly, and the stress on the cardiovascular system decreases. I use slow-cadence climbing efforts to increase leg strength and muscular power development. In this case, varying the cadence of an effort transforms a lactate threshold workout into an on-the-bike resistance-training workout.

Intensity

Intensity is a measure of how hard you are working, and it should be clear by now that you will be working quite hard in this training program. Because you don't have the time to ride moderately hard for 2 hours, you'll have to achieve the necessary training stimulus in 1 hour. The impact of a workout is directly related to the intensity at which you are working, and over the years we have become increasingly precise in the methods we use to measure intensity.

Precision is important for success with the TCTP, so I strongly encourage you to use a power meter, or at the very least a heart rate monitor that records average heart rates for individual intervals. Training with power and heart rate is covered in more detail in Chapter 3.

Volume

Volume is the total amount of exercise you're doing in a single workout, a week of training, a month, a year, or a career. By definition, *time-crunched* means low volume, at least in terms of the hours you spend training. But there's another concept here that makes up for some of that reduction in volume, called volume-at-intensity. Classic endurance training programs contain a lot of hours riding at moderate intensity, but relatively little time training at higher intensity. The TCTP strips out most of the moderate-intensity volume of those programs but retains—and may even increase—the volume-at-intensity, especially volume-at-high-intensity. In a given week in this program, you're most likely going to spend more time riding at and above your lactate threshold power output than you have during any portion of your previous training programs.

Frequency or Repetition

Frequency is the number of times a workout is performed in a given period of training, whereas repetition is the number of times an exercise is repeated in a single session. Riding 3 PowerInterval workouts in a week is frequency; riding 12 PowerIntervals in a single workout is repetition. Frequency and repetition are used to ensure the quality of your training sessions. In the TCTP your goal is to accumulate time at high workloads, because that's the driving force behind the adaptations you're seeking. PowerIntervals are maximum-intensity intervals, and their effectiveness is based on sustaining your highest possible power output for a given period of time.

Let's say you have a lactate threshold power of 250 watts, and that you can sustain that output for 20 minutes. You might be able to average 300 watts for 3 minutes during a PowerInterval. There's no point in trying to complete a 20-minute PowerInterval, because your output will fall so dramatically after the first 3 to 5 minutes that the rest of the effort will no longer be useful as a PowerInterval. It would feel ridiculously hard, and your heart rate would stay elevated, but once your power output drops, that effort is no longer addressing the goal of a PowerInterval. On the other hand, if you do seven 3-minute PowerIntervals at 300 watts each, separated by recovery periods, you'll accumulate 21 minutes at 300 watts. That's why interval training is so effective for improving performance (and burning calories) compared to exercising at a steady pace or level of effort.

Frequency gives you another way to accumulate workload, by repeating individual interval sessions during a given week, month, or even year. For instance, a week with two PowerInterval workouts like the one above means 42 minutes at 300 watts. The harder the intervals, the more recovery you need before you'll be ready to complete another high-quality training session. Fortunately, this works in favor of the time-crunched cyclist, because your relative lack of training time leaves plenty of time for recovery during the week. This program has four workouts per week, and ideally you'll be able to complete them on the days and in the order they are prescribed. However, because the workouts are so short and the overall volume is so low, you have a lot of latitude to move the workouts around without much risk of diminishing the quality of your training. In other words, if you have to pile 3 hard days of intervals back-to-back in 1 week, that's not ideal, but it's probably better than skipping them because you couldn't do them on the days they were originally planned.

Terrain

As I discuss more in the section about training with power, workload is most accurately expressed as the number of kilojoules—the amount of mechanical work—you produce during a training session. (How rapidly you produce those kilojoules determines your power output.) You can use terrain to manipulate your workload, and this is especially useful for time-crunched athletes, who need to get as much as possible done in 60 to 90 minutes. Riding uphill and performing efforts on hills can significantly increase the overall workload for your intervals, even though it can sometimes decrease the overall workload for the session (depending on the difference between the time spent at higher power outputs going uphill and the time spent going downhill at much lower power outputs).

Intervals on hills can also be useful for overcoming lagging motivation. Sometimes it can be difficult to push yourself through maximum-intensity intervals on flat ground, but a hill adds resistance and a visible challenge, and sometimes that's the little something extra you need to make your workout more effective.

Of course, training on hills is important from a specificity standpoint. If you want to go faster on climbs, it helps to train on them. But if you live in Kansas or some other pancake-flat location, increasing your sustainable power at lactate threshold is the number one thing you can do to help you go faster uphill (when you finally encounter one). Riding into the wind can be a useful strategy for flatlanders who are training for hills; your power output and effort level will be high as you push against a significant resistance, which will likely bring your cadence down to similar levels you would use on a climb (80 to 85 rpm instead of 90 to 100).

Cadence

I have been a proponent of high-cadence cycling for a long time because it improves your ability to maintain high-power efforts longer by pedaling faster in a lighter gear. You can produce 250 watts at 80 rpm or 100 rpm, but your leg muscles will fatigue faster riding a bigger gear at 80 rpm than a lower gear at 100 rpm, even though the power output (wattage) is the same. Power is a measure of how rapidly you can do work. Think in terms of moving a pile of 250 bricks in a minute. When you divide the work into smaller portions but get it done in the same amount of time, each load is lighter and you can move faster. If you double the number of bricks you carry in each load, you'll move the pile in half as many loads, but you'll have to work harder to move each load, and each trip will take longer. As an endurance athlete, your training optimizes your muscles' ability to work continuously and contract frequently. High-cadence cycling takes advantage of the adaptations already provided by aerobic training, not only muscular adaptations but also cardiovascular ones. Your heart and lungs don't fatigue the same way skeletal muscles do, and maintaining higher cadences helps shift stress from easily fatigued skeletal muscles to the fatigue-resistant cardiovascular system.

Learning to produce a lot of power while pedaling fast is also helpful when it's time to accelerate. The workouts in the TCTP are high-intensity, high-power efforts, and I encourage you to keep your cadence above 90 rpm for maximal efforts like PowerIntervals. You'll improve in aerobic power, power at lactate threshold, and power at VO_2max from the intensity of the efforts. But maintaining a higher cadence during the efforts will also give you the snap necessary to accelerate hard when it's time to attack, cover an attack, bridge a gap, or just lift out of the saddle to get over a small climb with the group. Keep in mind, however, that there's no magical cadence everyone should shoot for. Rather than aim for a specific number, I recommend athletes try to increase their normal cruising cadence and climbing cadence by 10 percent in a year (with the understanding that very few cyclists can ride effectively at sustained cadences above 120 to 125 rpm on flat ground).

Terms and Conditions

If you have only 6 hours available for training each week, the TCTP is your best option for developing the fitness and power necessary to ride at the front of the group, push the pace, and sprint for the win. It's your best option for building the fitness you need for an enjoyable century or cycling tour, or for feeling strong at your local Tuesday Night World Championship.

The TCTP is designed to maximize the effectiveness of the training you can complete in the limited time you have available. When you complete this program, you'll be more fit, more powerful, and faster than you would otherwise have been on so few training hours. On the flip side, I can't tell you that you'll be able to do everything that riders who train 16 to 20 hours a week can do. The TCTP would not prepare European or American pros for the rigors of their long seasons. The classic endurance training model works great for pros and athletes who have more than 10 to 12 hours to devote to training, and my coaches and I still use the classically based concepts from *The Ultimate Ride* with elite athletes and many of our amateur racers and cycling enthusiasts. In fact, if you have the time to commit more than 10 hours to training each week, a more traditional endurance training program may serve you better than the one in this book, because you have the time to reap the benefits that additional training volume provides. But if you have fewer than 10 hours, you're at the low end of what I consider to be enough time to make the classic endurance training model work. If your performance is neither stellar nor terrible right now, I encourage you to give the TCTP a try. Based on my coaches' experiences with CTS athletes in similar circumstances, you're far more likely to see significant improvements than appreciable drops in your performance.

The information in this section is vital to your success. There are some inescapable consequences to having only 6 hours a week to train for an endurance sport, and there are limitations on the types and lengths of events you'll be optimally prepared for. It is also true that the TCTP may not work for everyone. I can't sugarcoat the realities that time-crunched cyclists face: There are terms and conditions you need to accept if you want to reap the rewards of this training program.

THE 3-HOUR LIMIT

The reason training volume is so beneficial is that it enables you to build the aerobic endurance to ride all day. More than that, high-volume training that incorporates high-intensity intervals prepares athletes to ride aggressively all day. As you can imagine, this is crucial for success in pro events, which range from 100K criteriums to epic mountain stages in the grand tours and 250K classics such as the Tour of Flanders. Pros have to be able to attack, chase, and sustain tremendous power outputs at the end of long races, sometimes after 5, 6, or even more hours in the saddle. With only 6 hours available to train each week, you can still ride all day when you get the chance, but your best performances will come in rides and events that are 3 hours or shorter.

Before you scoff indignantly at the notion that your best performances may be limited to events that are shorter than 3 hours, take a good look at the events you actually participate in. An informal survey of CTS athletes and coaches, coupled with common sense, suggests that the vast majority of 30- to 50-year-old cyclists regularly compete in or participate in events that last between 45 and 90 minutes. If you want to ride the local criterium series, a bunch of cyclocross races in the fall, or even a regional cross-country mountain bike series, you need the fitness to be fast and powerful for less than 2 hours. Yes, this means you might struggle in 100-mile road races, but how many of those do you enter in a year? For amateurs, most road races even races that are 60 to 70 miles long—typically take less than 3 hours to complete.

There's a persistent myth in cycling that to be a "real" cyclist you have to be equally adept at the longest epic ride and the shortest criterium or cyclocross race. Like the idea that all training should be modeled on what the pros do, that myth comes from observing what pros are able to do. Professional cyclists are the best of the breed; they're the top dogs, the guys and gals who are head and shoulders above average athletes. They can race—and win—criteriums, cyclocross races, major stage races, and epic one-day classics because they started out with genetic gifts and devote all their time and attention to maximizing their performance. It's understandable that amateur racers and enthusiasts admire and even try to emulate them, but it's equally important to realize that there's no shame in being a cyclist with a more limited range.

Here's the bottom line: Do you want to be mediocre at every distance, or is it OK to be strong enough to be really good at a smaller selection of the distances and disciplines in cycling? A 3-hour limit covers a large percentage of the events most amateur cyclists participate in, and I'm betting that you don't like being mediocre at anything. That's why I regard the 3-hour limit in a positive light: By accepting that you may not be optimally prepared for every event on two wheels, the TCTP gives you the opportunity to excel in the events you most frequently participate in anyway.

But haven't I been saying this program could be used to prepare for a century? Riding 100 miles takes more than 3 hours, so how does it fit into the 3-hour limit? Well, as you'll see later when we get to the workouts and training programs, there are separate programs for century riders and competitors. The differences are in the interval intensities. The competition program focuses more on developing power for repeatable efforts at VO_2max, and the century program focuses more on developing sustainable power at lactate threshold. But regardless of which program you use, you're still going to see a change in your performance at about the 3-hour mark of your long rides.

The 3-hour limit was derived purely from anecdotal evidence. My coaches and I noticed that athletes on the TCTP experienced a significant change in their performance about 3 hours into long rides. They got noticeably tired, stopped talking, started skipping pulls, and struggled on climbs. A high-intensity, low-volume training program delivers many of the same physio-logical adaptations we see in higher-volume training programs, but it stands to reason that there are some adaptations that actually require more time in the saddle.

Epic rides are a defining benchmark for every cyclist. Even if you only get one or two chances a year to get out there for 5, 6, or 7 hours with a couple of buddies or for a long day of wondrous solitude, those rides are part of the very essence of being a cyclist. For beginners, your first ride longer than 5 hours is a rite of passage, and I suspect that many cyclists cling to their an-tiquated training programs because they fear losing the ability to complete those long days. They view that as an unacceptable step backward. But being undertrained because you're a low-volume rider on a high-volume training program means you'll suffer from start to finish the next time you get the chance to escape the clutches of normal life and go out for an all-day ride. The 3-hour limit doesn't mean you aren't allowed to go out for epic rides; it just means your best performances will be in rides and events shorter than 3 hours. You can still take advantage of that weekend when your spouse takes the kids and goes to Grandma's house; in fact, I encourage you to. Using the TCTP, you'll feel better for the first half of the ride, and if you use your fit-ness wisely you can stretch your range and have a good ride all the way to the finish. In Chapter 9 I cover the details of adjusting your habits, from the way you ride to the way you eat and the role you play in the group, so you can ef-fectively extend your range.

TIME-CRUNCHED TRAINING LEADS TO
TIME-CRUNCHED FITNESS

The TCTP is a limited-time offer. You will gain fitness and power rapidly, and you will be able to have a lot of fun with it while it lasts, but 10 to 12 weeks after you start the program, you'll have to back off and recover. This program can be used two or three times in a 12-month period, but you should not run through the 11 weeks and then immediately start over at week 1.

To understand why it's necessary to restrict the TCTP to 12 to 16 weeks (the training programs are 11 weeks, but some athletes will be able to stretch the fitness for up to an additional month), we have to refer back to the classic endurance training model. In that model, we built a huge foundation of aerobic fitness with months of long, moderate-intensity training. That aerobic fitness supported the more intense intervals that followed, allowing athletes to handle the workload of repeated interval workouts at or near lactate threshold. By the time these athletes reached the point where they were using high-intensity intervals near VO_2max, their efforts were being supported by a huge aerobic engine and thoroughly built glycolytic system.

Having deeper aerobic fitness means that the aerobic engine is capable of handling a relatively large percentage of the workload even when you're working above lactate threshold. That's important, because the glycolytic system burns through your carbohydrate stores very rapidly, whereas a highly trained aerobic system can burn more fat than carbohydrate (a moderately trained athlete burns about a 50–50 mixture of fat and carbohydrate riding at subthreshold intensities). With a stronger aerobic system, you can sustain higher power outputs before you reach the intensity at which you start eating into your limited carbohydrate reserves.

The high-intensity intervals in the TCTP build high-end fitness. Your power at VO_2max will increase, and so will your power at lactate threshold. Your glycolytic system will get stronger because of intervals performed at or near lactate threshold, and your body will learn to process and tolerate lactate better as well. At the same time, however, these high-intensity intervals will also lead to greater mitochondrial density and improve your ability to produce power with your aerobic system. Just like athletes on traditional high-volume training plans, athletes who perform lactate threshold tests after training on the TCTP have lower blood lactate levels during the early stages of the test, compared to their early-stage blood lactate levels from previous lactate threshold tests. Once the body has produced more and bigger mitochondria, you can process more fat and carbohydrate aerobically, which means you can produce less energy from glycolysis and hence produce less lactate.

The more you rely on glycolysis, the faster you'll fatigue. This not only applies to individual efforts and training sessions but also means that your body has to work harder to perform and recover as the weeks of high-intensity training build up. Deeper aerobic fitness derived from high-volume training helps those athletes recover more quickly (and they often have less acute fatigue to recover from after individual workouts), which means they can go longer (like the entire summer) before having to take an extended recovery period. Without that massive endurance base, you're on a much shorter timeline.

I'm not kidding about the timeline, either. Your relative lack of training time allows you to take advantage of a high-intensity training program, but the workouts in this program generate a lot of fatigue. You don't have the aerobic system to support that fatigue forever; your fitness is essentially top-heavy and will collapse under its own weight if you stretch the program too far. How can you tell when it's time to back off? If you're using a power meter, you'll notice that your average power output for maximum-intensity intervals starts to drop, and that you have trouble completing interval workouts without a dramatic decline in your power outputs during the final set. Quite simply, you'll know because you're really tired, and your performance on the bike is going to decline rapidly and noticeably.

The impact of overextending the TCTP is more dramatic than when you overextend a peak as a high-volume trainer. For high-volume cyclists, the decline in performance is relatively slow when they try to perform past peak fitness, again because of the depth of their aerobic foundation. With far less of a foundation supporting your fitness, performance falls fast when you overdo it. If anything, this reduces the chances you'll end up overtrained, under-recovered, or injured, because the TCTP is more self-limiting than a high-volume training program. Your body will tell you, much more clearly than if you were riding 12 to 16 hours a week, that you're done and it's time to rest.

Initially I had a lot of trouble with the relatively short-term nature of the fitness gained using this program. Coming from the old-school mindset of endurance training, I struggled with the idea of a top-heavy training program that built high-end power without the deep aerobic fitness necessary to support it long-term. But for athletes with limited time to train, the alternative is sticking with old programs that can't possibly generate the fitness necessary to be a successful cyclist. Again and again I kept going back to the value proposition: Would you want to be really good for about 2 months at a time, even if it meant having to back off for 4 to 6 weeks before starting again? Or put another way: Do you want to be really good a couple of times a year, or mediocre all year long?

What really won me over about the TCTP was the realization that this program closely matches the realistic performance demands of most cyclists who are balancing their athletic ambitions with a family and a full-time career. Every region of the country has some seasonal concentration of events. It might be a formal spring series of criteriums or a summer mountain bike series, and cyclocross races are almost always packed into an 8- to 10-week season in the fall or winter. Sometimes the concentration of events is informal but not coincidental. Event promoters know they'll attract more riders to their events if cyclists are already active in the area or already motivated to participate because the weather is just right and there are other events nearby. This is the way we ride and race, so why do we have to train like we're going to start racing in February and go nonstop until October?

Another reason I was won over by this program was that because the high-intensity intervals build aerobic fitness as well as power at lactate threshold and VO₂max, many athletes who use the TCTP two or three times in a 12-month period get incrementally stronger each time. In other words, an athlete who starts the program in the spring may average 250 watts during the CTS Field Test (used to establish training intensities for workouts; see Chapter 3). If he or she reduces the training workload to an endurance or maintenance level for 4 to 6 weeks after finishing the program, and then decides to use it again to prepare for a series of late-summer races, he or she will perform another CTS Field Test, and this time the average power output is likely to be higher than 250 watts. So although the TCTP is a relatively short-term, high-intensity, low-volume training program, it produces lasting performance gains and gives athletes the opportunity to continue growing stronger season after season.

Case Study:
The Resurgence of Taylor Carrington

Taylor Carrington is another of CTS coach Jim Rutberg's longtime friends. The two met as students at Wake Forest University, where Rutberg was majoring in sports science and was president of the school's two-man collegiate cycling team. Carrington was a former soccer player who had discovered mountain biking in the summer between high school and college. Being the only two competitive cyclists on campus (after the team's third rider graduated), they trained and traveled to races together, and even worked together as mechanics at the same off-campus bike shop.

After college, Rutberg and Carrington packed their belongings into their cars and split up to travel the country and race their bikes full-time for a few years. They were moderately successful. Rutberg upgraded his way to Cat. I on the road, and Carrington raced as a semipro mountain biker, but by their own admission they were fighting for top-10 finishes in regional events and just hoping to finish in the money at national events. After a few years it was time to put those Wake Forest degrees to work, and both settled into careers out West, Rutberg as my editorial director at CTS, and Carrington as a financial adviser in Denver, Colorado.

A few years later, after both had married, bought and sold their first homes, and had their first children (it's kind of scary how parallel their lives have been since college), Carrington decided he wanted one more shot at elite-level racing before he put it behind him. He and Rutberg talked about it during a mountain bike ride in Crested Butte, Colorado. Taylor wanted to race U.S. Cyclocross National Championships in December 2006. More than that, he wanted to do well, which meant traveling to races throughout the fall to earn UCI points (points earned by good finishes in races sanctioned by cycling's top governing body, the Union Cycliste International) so he could get a decent starting position for nationals.

As he had with their mutual friend, Sterling Swaim, Rutberg described the TCTP, including its terms and conditions. Taylor, who hadn't trained in a structured program for nearly 4 years and had only entered a few races a year for the fun of it, was a perfect candidate for the program. He was married, working a high-stress job more than 50 hours a week, and paying a hefty mortgage to own a modest home in downtown Denver, and he and his wife were doing their best to share the work of caring for their daughter, Sally. His wife, Megan (an accomplished endurance athlete in her own right), supported his goal, especially because most of the travel required coincided with trips he had to take for work anyway. The only caveat was that because some portion of the time he was going to spend training, traveling, and racing was time she would have to cover for him around the house, she figured she had some ownership of how he spent "her" time. In other words, she told him, "If you're going to do this, do it right and kick some butt."

I think a lot of cyclists face similar expectations. Even in a low-volume training program, we spend a considerable amount of our "free" time on our bikes. Our spouses, significant others, and kids don't necessarily suffer, but there's no denying that time spent training is time you're not spending fixing the windows or cooking Saturday-morning breakfast for the family. For the most part, families figure out the balance that works for them, but I think it's a lot easier for your family to understand and accept your time commitment when spending that time away from them makes you really happy. I don't know too many athletes who enjoy back-of-the-pack finishes or riding home alone after being dropped from the group ride, and I've found that coming home frustrated by your performance makes it more difficult for your family to understand your desire to go in the first place.

Cyclocross is a great place to apply the TCTP, because it's extremely difficult and both the races and the season are very short. Elite races are only an hour long (sometimes shorter). Other categories can be as short as 20 minutes, and the season generally runs from October to December. Taylor did what he could to stay in reasonable shape throughout the summer and then started the TCTP in October. Before daylight saving time ended, he did the workouts outdoors because he was out of work by about 4:00 p.m. (Like many in the financial industry, his hours are based on Wall Street's, which means he starts work at 5:30 a.m. in Denver.) As the days got shorter, he moved his training indoors. Fortunately the workouts in the TCTP are well suited to indoor trainers, and the relatively short high-intensity efforts make the time pass quickly.

Because he had to start racing soon after he started the program, Taylor struggled in his first few events. He and Rutberg knew that would be the case, and they focused those races on honing Taylor's handling skills and equipment choices. Within a few weeks, though, Taylor's power came up to the point where he was competitive in Colorado cyclocross races, even hanging with and finishing with guys who regularly finish in the top 20 at nationals. He traveled and earned his UCI points and even won a minor race in St. Louis before traveling to Providence, Rhode Island, for the U.S. National Championships.

His UCI points earned Taylor a spot in the third row of the starting grid, and after about 62 minutes of battling the pros, he finished 17th out of 90 finishers. Rutberg and Carrington had talked about a top-30 finish as a realistic goal, but within the top 20 was beyond their expectations. Fellow CTS athlete Ryan Trebon won the U.S. National Championship that year, and race fans who look up the results will recognize most of the names between Trebon and Carrington. He was beaten by the best in the United States, but he finished in the top 20 at Elite Cyclocross National Championships on only 6 hours of training per week. Six hours a week!

The unexpectedly good result from a relatively small investment of time convinced Taylor that he could do it again the following year. Fortunately his wife was still supportive as well. In 2007, having barely ridden his bike during the spring and summer, and using roughly the same program he had used in the fall of 2006, Carrington drove to Kansas City for much muddier U.S. National Cyclocross Championships. Proving that his 2006 result wasn't a fluke, he finished 20th out of 99 starters in 2007, and unlike nearly everyone in front of him, he did so without a pit crew to hand him a clean bike every few laps.

Taylor didn't win at the national championships, but his performances in 2006 and 2007 were comparable to 1999's, when he was training and racing full-time. More than simply achieving his personal goals, Taylor's results showed him that he didn't have to turn his back completely on high-performance goals. Many athletes look back longingly at the days when they felt fit, fast, and powerful. Taylor successfully recaptured that fitness after 7 years of focusing on other important aspects of his life, and he did it without sacrificing the career or family he'd spent so much time and effort building. The TCTP isn't about reclaiming your youth so much as it is about reclaiming your identity. Being a cyclist is an important part of who you are, and it's a lot easier to proudly identify yourself as a cyclist when you're good at it.

The Time-Crunched Periodization Plan

Taylor's and Sterling's experiences with the TCTP demonstrate not only that the program works, but also that it calls for a shift in the way endurance training is typically organized. As I mentioned in Chapter 1, periodization

SHORT, INTENSE WORKOUTS = LONG-TERM BENEFITS

As the first edition of *The Time-Crunched Cyclist* was being written in the winter of 2009, researchers were demonstrating that the same high-intensity workouts prescribed in this book produced many of the same physical benefits found in a cyclist following a traditional high-volume endurance-training plan. Even more remarkable, the research discovered how dramatically little training (in volume) is necessary to spark the body's ability to process more fuel aerobically before switching to anaerobic systems.

A study with cyclists in Canada (Burgomaster et al. 2008) compared the effects of training 3 days a week for 6 weeks doing four to six 30-second all-out sprints to the effects of training 5 days a week for 40 to 60 minutes at a comfortable aerobic pace. At the end of 6 weeks, the scientists found no difference in the improved metabolic adaptations between the test groups. In other words, the group who trained for 90 minutes a week saw the same energy processing benefits as the group who spun through 5 hours of aerobic training.

If you've been training for any appreciable time, you're not likely to be surprised by those study results—not because you think the intervals are too short, but because they were being compared to riding at a comfortable aerobic pace. But isn't accumulating time at a comfortable aerobic pace exactly what cyclists have been doing when they ride "base miles" for several weeks or months?

Time-crunched cyclists don't have time to build a giant aerobic base, and what the research is showing is that the sprinting/interval group did a grand total of 10 minutes of hard, all-out effort per week. That's it. The other 80 minutes were devoted to spinning easily through a warm-up, a recovery from each sprint, and a cool-down. And in return they accomplished the same metabolic adaptations as the other group.

Along the same lines of these 2008 findings, a 2010 study in the *Journal of Physiology* (Little et al.) tested the effects of lactate threshold intervals (which are somewhat easier than all-out max efforts) on cyclists and found the same biological adaptations as those found in cyclists who

CONTINUED

CONTINUED

follow large-volume endurance training plans. The length and number of these intervals were doubled compared to the 2008 study, but that still only totaled roughly 40 minutes of high-intensity work per week spread over 2.5 hours of riding. As you'll see in the TCTP, the harder the efforts, the shorter the intervals and the lower the total amount of "work time" during an interval session. During a VO_2max session you might do 16 minutes of total work at VO_2max intensities, whereas you might spend 24 to 36 minutes at lactate threshold intensities during LT workouts.

Originally, the TCTP was designed to deliver race-winning fitness relatively quickly, with the understanding that this peak fitness would be short lived—sort of a "make hay while the sun shines" program. Then we noticed that athletes grew incrementally stronger each time they utilized the program—provided they took 4 to 6 weeks to recover and focus on endurance-paced rides. Their program-starting field test results were higher the second, third, and fourth time around. And so were their peak power numbers for PowerIntervals. Race results provided the final confirmation of these incremental gains. Now that the program and the book have been around for a few more years, we've had the opportunity to see its impact on long-term fitness and performance.

Take Taylor Carrington as an example (see page 47 for his case study). His training, lifestyle, and race results in 2006 and 2007 made him the poster child for the TCTP. But in the summer of 2009, Taylor called Jim Rutberg to let him know he was embarking on an ambitious project at work. If he succeeded, it would be one of those career-making, life-altering, dragon-slaying kind of accomplishments. But the cost would be 18 to 24 months of nose-to-the-grindstone work. It would completely disrupt the balance of his life, but he had weighed the costs and benefits and realized this was the relatively short-term cost to take a giant leap forward in his career and prosperity. And with that he hung up his race wheels for two years.

Fast forward to the summer of 2011, and Taylor's time in purgatory had reached its end. It took two years but he closed a monster of a deal. And then he called Rutberg to ask about Masters Cyclocross

World Championships. It was late August, and he wanted to race those championships in Louisville, Kentucky, in January. The biggest unknown was how much detraining had occurred during his time away from structured training and competition.

They reviewed Taylor's activity level over the preceding two years. During the busiest parts of putting the deal together, Taylor rode 1 to 2 times a week. When times were a bit easier, he managed to squeeze in 3 rides a week. And perhaps due to his earlier experiences with the TCTP, or because hard intervals are great stress-relievers, his rides were endurance miles, big climbs, or PowerIntervals. Lots of 1- and 2-minute PowerIntervals.

Remember the string analogy I used earlier? By consistently challenging the top end of your capacity (VO$_2$max), even for just 10 to 20 minutes a week, you pull up the right (VO$_2$max) side of the string; in turn, that pulls up on your power at lactate threshold and at more moderate effort levels.

Instead of making incremental gains from cycling through the TCTP 2 to 3 times in a 12-month period, Taylor and other athletes have used the concepts from the TCTP to minimize detraining during prolonged periods away from competition. Contrast this with most people's usual idea of time off from a structured, multimonth training plan, which is to get out on the bike when they can and take it easy because they can't believe their bodies can handle a tough workout.

The science of high-intensity training shows that by sticking with the concepts of the TCTP—or the program itself—when you're severely time-crunched or need to buckle down and focus on something in your career or personal life, you can maintain a large portion of the fitness you've already earned. If you don't have time for the long stuff, make sure to stick with the hard stuff. And when your schedule frees up and you can recommit to some racing goals, you'll find that you haven't lost all that much power.

In Taylor's case, his field test power outputs were only about 10 watts lower than they had been two years earlier. But while his ability

CONTINUED

CONTINUED

to produce power was good, the efforts took more out of him, and it took him longer to recover from intervals and from hard workouts. Rutberg used a modified version of the TCTP with Taylor to ramp him up for Masters Worlds from September into January. Though Taylor's fitness and power responded quickly, his somewhat rusty racing skills yielded a mixture of race results. Nevertheless, he came good in time for his big race and finished 9th in the Men's 35–39 race, behind winner and fellow CTS athlete Scott Frederick. It's not an earth-shattering result, but it's testament to the power of short high-intensity workouts to keep you in the game—or within shouting distance of the game—during prolonged periods away from competition.

has been around, at varying levels of sophistication, since the days of the ancient Greeks. The general concept of periodization is now so widespread that pretty much anyone who has prepared for an event or goal with a training plan designed by a coach or found in a book or magazine published since 1980 has trained using periodization. The general concept is to break up the training year into progressively smaller segments to focus the training stressors. Perhaps most important, the technique organizes the scheduling of rest days and weeks to ensure athletes get the right amount of time to adapt to their training.

The periodization plan most often used by athletes in a classic endurance training program starts with a base building period in the winter and follows with a preparation period that focuses on improving sustainable power at lactate threshold. These workouts prepare the athlete for the high-intensity workouts in the specialization—or competition—period, which leads an athlete to a planned peak of conditioning and competitive readiness. Depending on the length of the athlete's season, there may be a second period of preparation training, followed by another specialization period and peak, before moving on to a transitional period of lighter, less-structured training. This final period is meant to help the athlete recuperate from the cumulative mental and physical fatigue of a long season.

Just about any cycling training book will include a year-long periodization plan that looks something like what I have just described. It's what most people use, because it works very well for athletes who plan on being strong or competitive from April through October. Time-crunched cyclists should definitely do their best to ride and train year-round, but the TCTP follows a very different periodization plan because of the nature of the workouts you'll be doing and the kind of fitness you'll be developing.

The principal reason that a year-long periodization plan is necessary for high-volume trainers is that the volume's contribution to overall workload is so high that it takes a long time to gradually add small increments of intensity. If you try to accelerate the process by quickly ramping up the intensity on a high-volume trainer, you'll soon reach the point where you can't recover and adapt quickly enough to continue making progress. Low-volume training plans can progress faster because the intensity contributes a greater percentage of the total workload, and there's plenty of built-in recovery time. At the same time, the intensity of the program leads to a lot of fatigue, which limits the length of time an athlete can successfully maintain top fitness before needing to back off and recover.

If you think of the classic endurance periodization plan as a dimmer switch (workload and fitness move up and down slowly and gradually), the TCTP is more like an "on/off" switch. When you're "on," it's full on, and you go straight through until you flip the switch to "off." The classic endurance periodization plan has four major periods: foundation (base aerobic training), preparation (aerobic and lactate threshold work), specialization (high-power work

TESTIMONIAL

Dear Chris,
I just wanted to take this opportunity to say that I think The Time-Crunched Cyclist *is the new standard. I'm 40 years old and coming back to the sport after a 15-year absence. After 8 months back on the bike and following your training plans, I joined my first fast club ride. I felt and rode like I never missed a beat. I felt good drafting, jumping, and riding at high speeds in a pack of riders at 40–45 kmh [25–28 mph]. Now I know what I have to do to improve my conditioning and make my way to the front again.*

—Simon Jagassar

and event-specific training), and transition (recuperation and active recovery). The TCTP essentially cuts this down to two hybrid periods: preparation/specialization ("on") and foundation/preparation ("off").

PREPARATION/SPECIALIZATION
(GO TIME)

This period is pretty much defined by the 11 weeks that constitute the TCTP included in this book (see Chapters 4, 5, 6, and 7). You'll notice that the plans start off with a few moderate-intensity interval workouts and then rapidly progress to incorporate more maximum-intensity PowerIntervals. In 3 to 4 weeks you should start seeing dramatic improvements in your power output and performance in group rides or races, and you'll reach your peak performance about 8 weeks into the program. Some athletes, especially less experienced riders, may start to see performance declining about 10 weeks into the program, whereas riders with more than 5 years of experience can typically maintain peak performance through the 11th week. It's important to incorporate that information into your planning. If you're going to compete in a local criterium series that lasts 8 weeks, start the program 3 to 4 weeks before the first race. You won't be in optimal condition for the first event, but the racing will enhance your training, and your performance will improve all the way through the rest of the series. If you're preparing for a series of events over a 3- to 5-week period, you should start the TCTP 4 to 5 weeks before the first event so you will have made more training progress before you start racing.

Normally, programs from CTS follow a pattern that features a recovery week after 3 weeks of training. There are some recovery or regeneration weeks built into the TCTP program as well, but because of the already low training volume, we're really only talking about backing off the intensity of 1 or 2 workouts, 4 weeks into the program.

I mentioned previously that some athletes may be able to stretch their fitness for up to an additional month. Cyclists who have raced for many years will have greater success extending the period of time they can maintain their high-performance fitness. For instance, Sterling and Taylor have 10 to 15 years of miles in their legs and have been able to stay competitive for 14 to 16 weeks after starting the program, but their best performances were still in the 8- to 12-week period.

FOUNDATION/PREPARATION (MAINTENANCE)

For high-volume trainers, the scientifically proven recipe to prevent detraining is to decrease the volume and retain—or even increase—the intensity. This is the technique most often used to taper athletes before big events and hold on to hard-earned fitness through an end-of-season break or transition period (Mujika et al. 2003). In reality, the technique leverages the same science this program is based on, just for a slightly different purpose. During the TCTP, you're using intensity to *increase* your workload above what you'd normally be able to achieve, to generate enough stimulus to improve your power at VO_2max and lactate threshold. In contrast, high-volume trainers use a short period of high-intensity, low-volume training to reduce their overall workload while retaining just enough stimulus to keep power at VO_2max and lactate threshold from declining.

Recovery and maintenance are the goals of the periods between the times when you're using the TCTP, but unlike high-volume trainers, aerobic endurance should be your highest priority. When you're done and you flip the switch to "off," you have to back off the intensity. But you can and should maintain your volume. In other words, if you're riding 6 to 8 hours when you're on the program, you should continue riding for 6 to 8 hours a week during the time between build periods. The intensity is what you have to recover from, not the volume. If anything, you should stick to your riding schedule so the time doesn't get siphoned away to other priorities.

Your rides during this period should be less structured but focused on maintaining steady intensities at about 65 to 85 percent of your maximum sustainable power output. This means maintaining a good tempo that's more challenging than an easy cruising pace. You will see a significant decline in your high-end fitness (power at VO_2max and your ability to handle repeated maximal efforts), but that's normal, and those performance markers respond quickly when you return to high-intensity training. By riding at a more challenging tempo, you'll still be getting a reasonable amount of energy from the glycolytic energy system, which will help prevent significant detraining of your aerobic system and power at lactate threshold. Including some intense efforts once a week will further aid in preventing significant detraining, which means that I encourage you to continue going to the local group ride or pushing yourself on the local climb.

Four weeks is the minimum amount of time you must allow between the end of any use of the TCTP and the start of another. Six weeks is better, or you can make the maintenance period as long as you like. At CTS we have had the most success cycling athletes through the program twice in a year. Depending on an athlete's goals and location, it is sometimes possible to add a third cycle. The TCTP is perfect for having a great spring season and another surge in performance in the late summer or early fall (late fall or early winter for cyclocross racers). To fit in three cycles, you have to start early (February) to be prepared for an early spring season, then prepare again for a midsummer peak, and then prepare again for one in the fall. Although this can work for anyone, it is most often an option for athletes in warm climates because their season can start earlier and end later than the cycling season in northern states.

For specific week-by-week recommendations on the "off" period, see the Q&A section at the end of Chapter 4. While I don't think you need much structure during this period, I've included a 4-week program that you can follow or modify to suit your own needs and training schedule.

CHAPTER

3

Measuring Intensity in the Information Age

Advanced training technology may be the most important factor working in your favor as a cyclist with a busy schedule. Looking back at my years as a professional cyclist, it saddens me to think about all the energy I wasted. I trained religiously and was advised by many of the sport's top coaches and sports scientists, but training technology hadn't advanced to the point where I could accurately determine how hard I was working. My extreme training volume masked its inefficiency; somewhere in all those hours I managed to ride at the intensities necessary to improve performance, but I also wasted a ton of time at ineffective power outputs or riding when I should have been resting.

Journalists have asked me innumerable times to explain how and why today's pros are so much faster than they were 20 or 30 years ago. There are many factors, including improved road surfaces, lighter and stiffer bikes, slipperier aerodynamics (for riders as well as their equipment), and far superior wheels and bearings. But beyond the mechanical and aerodynamic advancements, today's cyclists have the ability to train with greater precision than any previous generation.

Precision comes from having detailed, real-time performance data you can use to monitor, evaluate, and adjust your training. And by far the best piece of equipment for providing that information is a power meter, which measures the true amount of work you produce as you ride.

Cyclists are fortunate because we have access to more accurate data than any other endurance sport. The most accurate power meters use strain gauges located in the crank or rear wheel to directly measure the mechanical work you're producing (kilojoules) and how rapidly you're producing that work (watts). This information is not available to runners or swimmers, or to athletes in any sport played on a field, court, or rink.

Even if you don't own a power meter, as a cyclist you have benefited, and will continue to benefit, from the fact that others do. The work coaches have done with power-equipped athletes has broadened our understanding of how the body responds to training and fatigue, and that knowledge has led to positive changes in how workouts are arranged and prescribed. So although I highly recommend investing in a power meter and using it to advance your training, I also know—from experience—that the TCTP works whether you're training with power or heart rate.

Gathering Data

Your power meter provides a detailed record of every ride, with heart rate, power output, speed, and cadence information for every effort you put forth. As you'll see in the following sections, that information is crucial during your ride, but it's also very important afterward. One of the most important things you can do with a power meter is download the data from every ride, race, or event to your computer and into software products that can log and analyze the information. Currently the best power-analysis software out there is WKO+ from Peaksware (www.trainingpeaks.com). My coaches and I use it to analyze power files from our athletes, and if you're training with power, I highly recommend that you use it as well.

To make sure the data you gather are accurate, it's also crucial that you calibrate your power meter before every ride. This simple procedure only takes a few seconds (see the manufacturer's instruction manual for directions), but it means the difference between getting valuable information and recording junk. And more than just ensuring accuracy for individual work-outs, accurate calibration is especially important when you're adding data to cumulative training logs. The accuracy of the analysis performed by software programs such as WKO+ depends on the accuracy of the data you input.

Keeping It Simple

Dr. Edmund Burke was a good friend of mine throughout my cycling career and was one of my primary mentors as I made the transition from athlete to coach. Ed was a pioneering sports scientist, one of the first to apply individual heart rate ranges to endurance training to target efforts to specific energy systems. In addition to working for the U.S. Olympic Committee and USA Cycling, he was a professor at the University of Colorado at Colorado Springs, where he taught exercise physiology to undergrads and graduate students. He was one of the smartest men I've ever known, but even more impressive than the depth and breadth of his knowledge was his ability to make complex physiological concepts accessible to athletes whose last experience with physiology was in high school biology class. When you asked him a question, you knew there was a 30-minute answer in his head, complete with graphs, diagrams, and references, but he knew how to distill that information into a 5-minute answer that an athlete could understand completely and begin using immediately.

As a coach, an educator of coaches, a public speaker, and an author, I have tried to emulate Ed in the way I explain training and nutrition. Nowhere is that more important than during discussions about training with power. There are a thousand ways to slice and dice the massive amount of data athletes generate, and some very serious minds have spent, and continue to spend, enormous amounts of time doing just that. I have a few of these people on my staff, including Dean Golich, who has been one of the leading experts on training with power for more than 15 years. There are athletes who love numbers, too, and many spend their free time analyzing and reanalyzing data from power files. If you're one of them, I recommend the book *Training and Racing with a Power Meter*, by Hunter Allen and Andrew Coggan. It is the most complete resource I have seen for anyone who wants to delve into the nitty-gritty details of training with power.

Now, if you were to give me a Ferrari, I would want to know how to get the most out of it. I'd probably know how to drive it better if I understood some key principles about how the engine and suspension work, but I wouldn't necessarily need to know how to build it from scratch. Similarly, my philosophy about physiology is that an athlete doesn't need to be able to diagram the individual chemical reactions within the Krebs Cycle to understand that aerobic metabolism breaks fat and carbohydrate down into usable energy. And being able to diagram the Krebs Cycle doesn't make one athlete faster than another. Likewise, a power meter is a tremendous tool that can dramatically enhance the quality and effectiveness of your training, and my point is that it can do so whether you have a basic or an advanced understanding of how it works and the data it produces.

Training with Power

If you're training with power, especially using the TCTP, you need to focus on three main pieces of information: power, kilojoules, and fatigue.

POWER

Power, expressed in watts, is derived from the following equation:

$$\text{Power in Watts} = \text{Torque} \times \text{Angular Velocity}$$

To generate more power, you can push harder on the pedals to generate more torque or pedal faster to create greater angular velocity, or you can do both. Power is a direct measure of the work you are doing right now, and it is unaffected by many of the factors that can distort heart rate data, including dehydration, heat, humidity, anxiety, excitement, and stimulants such as caffeine. These factors can influence your motivation or ability to produce power on the bike, but they don't alter the validity of the numbers you see on the power meter readout.

The two primary uses of power are to determine the demands of the rides, events, and races you want to participate in, and to establish training intensity ranges that you can use to develop the fitness necessary to meet those demands. That is why it is very helpful to race with a power meter and examine

POWER-TO-WEIGHT RATIO

Along with providing athletes with an accurate way of measuring work-load, a power meter gives us a good method for comparing the relative climbing strengths of two athletes. Your ability to go uphill quickly depends on the amount of power you can produce and the amount of weight you need to move against gravity. With a power meter we can quantify this by determining your Power-to-Weight Ratio (PWR).

The PWR can be used to compare your abilities as a climber before and after a period of training, or to compare your abilities as a climber against those of a rider who is a different size. For instance, right now you may be able to sustain 250 watts on a local climb, and if you weigh 70 kilograms (154 pounds), your PWR would be 250/70 or 3.57 watts per kilogram. After completing the TCTP, your sustainable power may increase to 275 watts and your weight may decrease to 68 kilograms, bringing your PWR to 275/68 or 4.04 watts per kilogram. Even without climbing-specific workouts, you should reach the summit of the local climb faster with a PWR of 4.04 watts per kilogram than with a PWR of 3.57.

When comparing riders of relatively equal fitness, a taller and heavier rider will tend to have more muscle mass and longer levers, with which to generate greater power, than a smaller rider. However, the bigger rider also has more mass to carry uphill, so you need more than just the two riders' sustainable power outputs to determine which one has an advantage on a climb. This is where PWR ratio comes into play. Let's say Big Boy weighs 85 kilograms and has a sustainable power output of 320 watts, and Little Guy weighs 65 kilograms and has a sustainable power output of 250 watts. Despite having the strength to sustain 320 watts, Big Boy would reach the summit of the climb behind Little Guy, because his PWR is 3.76 watts per kilogram and Little Guy's is 3.85.

A higher PWR also gives a cyclist a tactical advantage, because it gives you a greater ability to accelerate on a steep pitch. You're able to use more power to lift each kilogram of your body weight against gravity, which means that during a hard acceleration on a steep pitch, you'll go faster than a rider with a lower PWR. Racers and group riders of all

CONTINUED

CONTINUED

sizes can use this information to their advantage. If you know you have a lower PWR than other riders in the group, your best option is to keep the pace high on the flat roads before the climb and any moderate grades on the climb itself in an effort to make the smaller riders work harder. If your tactic works, you'll effectively reduce the other riders' PWRs by tiring them out and reducing the power outputs they're able to sustain on the steep sections. If you're the little climber with a high PWR, you want to conserve energy before the climb and hit the big guys hard as soon as you come to a really steep pitch. You'll force them to make a choice: dig deep to stay with you or let you go and hope you'll tire so they can gradually catch you.

It's important to realize that PWR is entirely dependent on time. You can't just say a rider has a PWR of 4.0 watts per kilogram. That value has to have a time associated with it, like 4.0 watts per kilogram for 20 minutes. The shorter the climb, the higher your PWR will be. For instance, I've often said that I consider 6.8 watts per kilogram for 30 minutes to be a performance marker that a rider needs to accomplish to be considered a contender for overall victory at the Tour de France. That doesn't mean that a Tour contender can ride a 45-minute climb during the Tour at 6.8 watts per kilogram. Beyond the fact that the climb is longer than the 30-minute test, climbs in the Tour are contested after many days of racing and sometimes more than 4 hours of hard riding earlier in the stage. That's why top riders average PWRs in the 4 to 5 watts per kilogram range at the Tour, even though they can hit the 6.8 watts per kilogram threshold during a pre-Tour test.

An athlete's weight and stature can make a big difference in time trials and the cycling portion of a triathlon, not only because these characteristics impact PWR but because they also affect the relationship between aerodynamics and power production. No matter how aerodynamic you make a bicycle, the human on top of it is the biggest impediment to going faster. But as athletes get bigger, the hole they have to punch in the air doesn't grow proportionally with their height and weight. As a result, tall athletes tend to have an advantage over shorter ones when riding in an aerodynamic position; they generate more power because of longer levers and more muscle mass, but the hole they have to punch in the air isn't that much larger than that of a much shorter rider. (One instance where a shorter rider has an advantage, however, is illustrated by American cyclist Levi Leipheimer. He has tremendous power, and he is small enough that he can tuck his head behind his hands, essentially filling the gap between his upper arms in order to smooth the airflow around his body. Taller riders can't take advantage of this position as well because of the more significant distance between the top of the saddle and the top of the handlebars.)

On courses with significant climbs, smaller athletes can level the playing field by using their superior PWR to gain time on the hills. Instead of utilizing a steady effort level (which is often the preferred plan on low rolling hills or flat courses), you may benefit from surging up and over the top of climbs, and then use your best aerodynamic position to maximize speed and minimize power output during the descents and flat portions of the course. On descents and flat ground, bigger riders can use their power advantage to go faster, but that extra speed costs them a lot of energy. When you go faster uphill, you can take significant amounts of time away from them, and the energy cost of gaining that time is lower than trying to out-ride them on flat ground. Over a 40 kilometer course of rolling hills, the rider with a higher PWR ratio will eventually ride away from a bigger rider who has more power and more weight to drag along with it.

power files from centuries, group rides, and other events. For instance, let's say there's a particular climb on the local group ride where you frequently get dropped. Looking at your power file, you may see that you're able to stay with the group when your power output for the 5-minute effort is 250 watts, but you get dropped when you have to ride at 265 watts on the same climb. To avoid getting dropped there, your training program has to be designed to increase the wattage you're able to maintain for 5 minutes from 250 to 265.

Many athletes have less specific goals for improving their power output; they just want to be able to go faster and ride longer. For these athletes, and even for athletes who are trying to meet specific demands, increasing sustainable power at lactate threshold and increasing power at VO₂max are the best ways to improve cycling performance. In addition, it's important not only to focus on achieving higher wattages at these levels but also to work on increasing the amount of time you can sustain those intensities.

In order to increase the power you can produce for efforts ranging from a few seconds to several hours, you need to establish training ranges that challenge your body and lead to the adaptations you seek. I cover this subject in more detail later in this chapter.

KILOJOULES

I don't have to tell you that pedaling a bicycle is work, but the number of kilojoules you produce during a ride provides an accurate accounting of exactly *how much* work you do during each ride. A kilojoule is a unit of mechanical energy, or work produced, and 4.184 kilojoules is equal to 1 kilocalorie. You expend kilocalories to produce kilojoules, but the human body is not a perfectly efficient machine, so only a portion of the kilocalories you expend do the mechanical work of turning your pedals. In fact, a cyclist's efficiency is about 20 to 25 percent, meaning that about 75 to 80 percent of the energy you expend is lost, mostly as heat, which is why strenuous exercise is such a sweaty affair. If every calorie you expended was used for producing kilojoules, you would have to multiply your kilojoule count by 4 to come up with the number of kilocalories you burned during your workout (X kilojoules × 4.184 = Y kilocalories). However, because of the 25 percent efficiency of the system, it takes about 4 kilocalories to produce 1 kilojoule of mechanical work. That brings the ratio of energy expended to work produced back to about 1:1. In other words, when you return from a ride or race, you can generally consider the number of kilojoules displayed on your power meter to be equal to the number of kilocalories you burned during your time on the bike. There is actually some error in this number, in that your efficiency may have been between 20 and 25 percent, but the error is typically so small that it's not worth worrying about.

Kilojoules can be a more accurate way of prescribing the desired workload for a ride than either time or mileage. Basing workout duration on distance is convenient but notoriously bad in terms of determining the actual work done during the ride. From downtown Colorado Springs, for instance, I can complete 30-mile rides that are either entirely flat or extremely hilly. When I return home I've completed 30 miles, but the workload and training effect of the flat ride would be completely different than those of the hilly ride. Similarly, basing workouts on time has some of the same problems. A 2-hour ride on a hilly route and a windy day could be far more challenging than a 2-hour ride on flat terrain on a windless day. Based on time, you'd cover more distance on the 2-hour flat ride (let's say 40 miles), but the workload could still be lower than covering 30 miles on the hilly ride on a windy day. And if I rode really hard on the flat ride but easy on the hilly ride, the flat ride could actually end up being harder than the hilly one. With so many variables and so little objective data (even heart rate is relatively easily influenced by outside factors), it can be difficult to accurately determine the true workload of your rides.

With a power meter, however, you can make an apples-to-apples comparison of one ride with another. A 1,500-kilojoule ride is a 1,500-kilojoule ride, whether it took you 90 minutes or 2 hours to complete, and whether it was uphill into a headwind or ripping along on flat roads with a tailwind. It's important to note, however, that kilojoules provide information about the endurance component of your training, but this must be considered in conjunction with time and intensity (*how* you produced those kilojoules) to evaluate the ride's impact on your fitness, performance, and fatigue.

Races and events are among the most useful places to gather kilojoule data. If you're doing 45-minute criteriums and you race with a power meter, you can see how many kilojoules of energy you produced during your event. Let's say you return from a local race and your power meter says you produced 800 kilojoules. That's the total energy demand of your event, which means you can use that information to guide your training. For instance, to develop the endurance for your events, you may want some of your rides to be at least 800-kilojoule sessions. But your training rides aren't as intense as your races, so it may take you 60 to 75 minutes to reach 800 kilojoules in training, compared to 45 minutes during a race.

For century riders and athletes preparing for cycling tours, it's difficult to match the energy expenditure of your goal event in training. During a 6-hour century, you might produce 3,000 to 4,000 kilojoules, and during even the hardest training sessions it's difficult for any athlete to achieve more than 1,200 kilojoules in an hour. As a matter of perspective, a 170-pound cyclist is likely to produce 800 to 1,000 kilojoules during the 75- to 90-minute interval sessions featured in the TCTP. Ideally, you would complete a few challenging 3- to 4-hour rides that pushed your energy production to about 3,000 kilojoules, but you can be adequately prepared for your long days without these rides if necessary.

There's an inverse relationship between power output and exercise duration, meaning that your average power output—and hence the kilojoules produced per hour—will decline as the length of rides increases. Most cyclists realize this without ever being told; it's called pacing. When you leave your house for a 90-minute ride, you innately know you can afford to ride more aggressively than when you roll out for a 5-hour ride. If you didn't know this and attempted to ride aggressively right from the start of a century, you'd ride at a high power output and energy expenditure for the first 2 hours and end up crawling home at a very low output in the last hour. Almost every novice cyclist makes this mistake at least once. It's like a rite of passage that helps us learn how to pace ourselves.

The inverse relationship between power output and exercise duration also means that relatively short training sessions can prepare you for longer events. As you build a bigger aerobic engine, you're gaining the fitness necessary to produce more kilojoules per hour through primarily aerobic metabolism. Let's say that right now 600 kilojoules an hour is an endurance pace you can comfortably sustain for 3 hours. As I discussed in Chapter 2, riding at 600 kilojoules an hour for an additional hour isn't going to do you much good in terms of increasing your mitochondrial density, a key marker of increased oxidative capacity in skeletal muscle. However, because shorter, higher-intensity interval workouts can increase mitochondrial density and give you the tools to burn more fat and carbohydrate through aerobic channels, these workouts can increase the number of kilojoules you can produce aerobically each hour. This increased fitness can be used two ways: You can use it to ride at a higher power output that may get you up to 700 kilojoules an hour, or you can ride at 600 kilojoules an hour for more hours because you're relying more on fat and carbohydrate through aerobic metabolism and deriving less energy from the glycolytic system.

FATIGUE

Fatigue gets a bad rap, but it is not always a bad thing; it's actually one of the most important components of an effective training program. It is always created in the process of overloading a physical system, which makes it an integral part of the stimulus your body is responding to as you adapt and grow stronger. And like any other part of training, fatigue has to be managed properly so it can enhance your performance rather than destroy it. A power meter can be a very effective tool for helping you manage fatigue, not only during individual workouts but also within entire periods of training.

Power is a direct measure of the work you're doing right now, so it provides a very accurate way to tell if you're too tired to continue with effective intervals. As you fatigue, you'll see a decline in the power output you're able to sustain for interval efforts as well as endurance-pace riding. But there's a difference between knowing that you're getting tired and making the right decisions about what to do about it. This is covered in more detail in the section "Knowing When to Say When" in Chapter 4; for now it's important to realize that there are times when you will want to push through the fatigue and complete your intervals but also times when skipping those intervals will be the better choice.

One of the most important things cycling coaches learned once we started training athletes with power was that there were times when athletes were less fatigued than we originally believed. Before power meters were widely used, we used heart rate and perceived exertion to judge an athlete's level of fatigue and then adjusted training accordingly. The day after a lactate threshold or VO$_2$max interval session, we noticed that an athlete's exercise heart rate was often suppressed (lower heart rate values at similar paces) and ratings of perceived exertion were often elevated (efforts at similar paces felt harder). This suggested that the athlete was fatigued and needed more recovery before performing another effective interval workout.

In fact, heart rate and perceived exertion were lying. Once riders started using power meters, we saw that despite the suppressed heart rates and elevated ratings of perceived exertion, athletes were often able to complete interval workouts on back-to-back days at matching—and sometimes even higher—power outputs. Yes, there was fatigue present, as illustrated by heart rate and perceived exertion, but the power meter provides context for that fatigue. In the days before power meters, we knew fatigue was present but couldn't tell how much. When a power meter reveals that an athlete can sustain efforts at outputs equal to those of the day before, despite a suppressed exercise heart rate and an elevated rating of perceived exertion, that means there's fatigue, but not enough to warrant a full recovery day. If, on the other hand, during the second consecutive day of intervals an athlete's power output is more than 10 to 15 percent lower than on the previous day, exercise heart rate is suppressed more than 10 percent, and perceived exertion is elevated, that is an indication that the athlete's level of fatigue is high enough that a rest day is a better option than another training session.

Power meters have led to an increase in the use of 2-day training blocks, and they are featured prominently in the training programs in this book. The benefit of block training is that you generate a strong training stimulus by completing the second day of interval training in a somewhat fatigued state. Put simply, you're reinforcing the training stimulus from the first day and giving your body a more urgent request for adaptation.

Training with Heart Rate

After the preceding discussions of the benefits of training with power, it should come as little surprise when I tell you that heart rate training is not as effective as using a power meter. However, power meters are still quite expensive ($900 to $5,000), and it's unrealistic to expect all cyclists to invest in them. The truth is, in terms of effectiveness, the difference between training with power and with heart rate is a matter of degree. The fact that training with power is more effective doesn't mean that training with heart rate is not effective at all. My coaches and I have been working with heart rate for more than 20 years, and our athletes have won and continue to win races and achieve personal goals using heart rate alone.

Research published in 2010 backs me up. Scientists (Robinson et al. 2010) at the University of Florida broke 20 men and women into two groups, one assigned to train with power meters, and one with heart rate monitors. At the end of 5 weeks of 90-minute sessions of once-a-week, high-intensity lactate threshold intervals, both groups saw roughly the same improvement in power. So if all you can afford is a heart rate monitor, don't sweat it. You're still using a powerful tool, and you won't be short-changing your training.

In fact, the nature of the TCTP actually makes it better suited to heart rate training than many other programs. There are two main types of workouts in the program: lactate threshold intervals and VO_2max intervals. As you'll see in the description of the CTS Field Test below, it's relatively easy to establish accurate heart rate and power training intensities for intervals that improve your sustainable power at threshold. In terms of VO_2max intervals, heart rate has never been a good way to evaluate these efforts anyway. They're very short (2 to 3 minutes), and because your heart rate is an observation of your body's response to effort, it lags too far behind these efforts to provide useful information. Most likely your heart rate will steadily increase throughout the interval even though your power output may stay relatively constant. Whether you're using a power meter or a heart rate monitor, VO_2max intervals are governed by a relatively unscientific prescription: You go as hard as you can. Power meters provide more accurate information about exactly how hard you went, but at the end of the day, these intervals can be just as effective whether you have that detailed information or not.

One of the greatest disadvantages of using heart rate alone to gauge training intensity is "cardiac drift." Because up to 75 percent of the energy produced in muscles is lost as heat, your body has to work to dissipate that heat to keep your core temperature from rising out of control. As you exercise—and especially as you ride at higher intensities—your body uses your skin as your car uses its radiator. Heart rate increases, not only to deliver oxygen to working muscles but also to direct blood to the skin so it can donate fluid for sweat. The sweat is released onto the skin so it can evaporate, which carries much of this excess heat away from the body. Much of the fluid that appears as sweat on your skin was most recently part of your bloodstream. As you lose blood plasma volume to produce sweat, your heart has to pump even faster to continue delivering the same amount of oxygen to working muscles. As a result, your heart rate will increase slightly as exercise duration increases, even if you maintain the same level of effort. The impact of cardiac drift will be lower if you're better at staying hydrated; you're replacing the fluid lost by sweating and helping to maintain a higher overall blood volume. However, no matter how diligent you are about consuming fluids, some level of cardiac drift is unavoidable during intense endurance exercise.

You can see the impact of cardiac drift in Figure 3.1. In this power file from a lactate threshold interval workout, the athlete performs three intervals at roughly the same power output, but his or her heart rate gets progressively higher for each effort. When athletes train with heart rate alone, they are instructed to maintain the same heart rate range for each interval. Ideally this would result in efforts of equal intensity, but as a result of cardiac drift, this often means that the first interval is actually completed at a higher power output than the subsequent ones. To the athletes, heart rate and perceived exertion seem right on target, but they don't realize that power output is actually falling, and as a result, the workout loses some of its potential effectiveness.

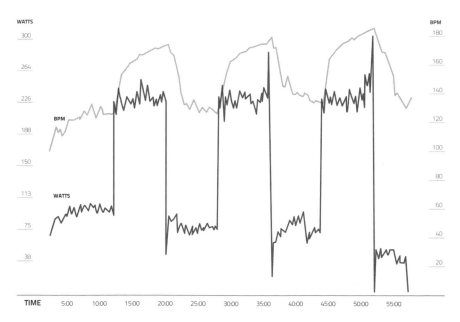

FIGURE 3.1: CARDIAC DRIFT
You can see how the rider's heart rate (BPM) increases from the first hard effort to the third. This is a clear example of cardiac drift, where workload remains relatively stable but heart rate increases by an average of 10 beats from first to final interval. (Note: cadence and speed traces removed from all power files for clarity.)

The next logical assumption is that athletes training with heart rate should adjust their heart rate ranges during interval workouts to compensate for cardiac drift. In other words, some athletes ask if they should ride their first interval at 160 to 165 beats per minute, the second one at 163 to 166, and the last one at 166 to 169. The problem with this idea is that without a power meter you can't accurately determine the extent to which an athlete's performance is being affected by cardiac drift. Raising your heart rate ranges during a series of intervals could either under- or overcompensate for cardiac drift, so the best option for heart rate trainers is to focus on staying hydrated and controlling core temperature (to minimize cardiac drift) and stick to the prescribed heart rate ranges for all intervals in a given workout.

Again, the fact that the workouts in the TCTP are short works to the advantage of athletes training with heart rate. Cardiac drift is more pronounced during workouts longer than 2 hours, so the relatively short nature of the workouts in this program helps to minimize its detrimental impact on actual interval intensities.

Establishing Effective Training Intensity Ranges: The CTS Field Test

Performance testing is a crucial part of training, because an accurate test provides a snapshot of your current level of fitness and allows athletes and coaches to determine whether progress has been made. As you grow stronger, testing provides a means for adjusting training intensities so you can continue to challenge yourself.

There are two primary categories of performance testing, lab and field. In the lab we put you on an ergometer and run you through a series of steps at ever-increasing power outputs. At the same time, you're breathing into a tube so we can analyze the composition of your inspired and expired air, and we're pricking your finger to measure the amount of lactate present in your blood. At the end of a combined Lactate Threshold/VO_2max Test, the information is analyzed, and we can provide you with an accurate determination of your power output at lactate threshold, power at VO_2max, and blood lactate levels at both points.

In the field, we can determine the power output and/or heart rate you can sustain for an effort of a given duration. And although that probably sounds like a paltry amount of information compared to a lab test, the fact is that there's a strong correlation between the accuracy of lab and field tests. Having tested thousands of athletes using both methods, I generally prefer field testing, because it is easier to fit into an athlete's schedule, it's cheaper and more accessible to more athletes, and it provides data that are just as useful for achieving all the aforementioned goals for performance testing. In addition, because the field test is often completed in real-world conditions out on the road, it provides athletes with greater context for their performance. They experience all the sensations (speed, wind, road feel, etc.) of riding an all-out effort, which can help them better judge their efforts during rides and races when they may not be able to see information from a power meter or heart rate monitor.

There are numerous methods for field testing involving efforts of varying durations. The CTS Field Test consists of two 8-minute, all-out time trials separated by 10 minutes of easy spinning recovery. If you have read my previous books, you'll notice this is different from the original recommendation of two 3-mile time trials. The difference is mostly one of semantics: Instead of gauging improvement by completing 3 miles faster, I have changed the test so you can gauge improvement by covering more distance in 8 minutes. This updated recommendation also translates better to indoor trainers, where distance isn't typically measured at all. It also reflects the increased use of power meters, because training with power relies heavily on information about your sustainable output for a given period of time rather than on distance.

In a study published in the *Journal of Strength and Conditioning Research* (Klika et al. 2007), the CTS Field Test was shown to be an effective method for establishing training intensities. Fifty-six participants performed both a lactate threshold test in a lab and the CTS Field Test on an indoor trainer before a CTS-designed, 8-week, power-based indoor training program. At the end of 8 weeks, participants performed both tests again and, on average, experienced a 12.9 percent increase in power at lactate threshold. There was a statistically significant correlation between their improvement in the lab and their improvement as measured by the CTS Field Test. The study concluded that the CTS Field Test is "a valid measure of fitness and changes in fitness, and provided data for the establishment of training ranges." Figures 3.2, 3.3, and 3.4 show examples of results from the CTS Field Test.

WHY 8 MINUTES?

Some athletes and coaches ask me about the rationale behind the two 8-minute efforts that make up the CTS Field Test. My field test is unique in its brevity; it's not a 60-minute or even a 20-minute time trial because I've found that I don't need to put athletes through such an effort to gather the necessary data. It's not that a 60- or 20-minute time trial effort won't work; in fact, those tests work quite well. However, my coaches and I work with a very broad spectrum of athletes, and a field test of two 8-minute efforts can be performed well by novices as well as by experienced masters competitors and even pros.

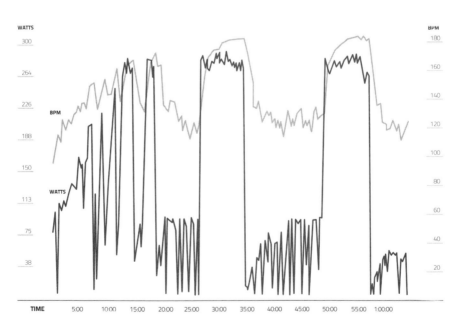

FIGURE 3.2: GOOD FIELD TEST
The test depicted shows a proper warm-up with some high-intensity efforts
before two steady field test efforts. Power is consistent in the first 8 minutes. The second
8 minutes also show a relatively even effort until the final drop in power, indicating that
the athlete has reached fatigue. This is a good indicator that the field test was run
properly and that the athlete gave a full effort.

I prefer two 8-minute efforts over one longer effort because I believe there's valuable information to be gained from observing your ability to recover from and repeat a hard effort. With a 10-minute recovery period between efforts, an athlete with a well-developed aerobic engine will be able to complete the second effort with an average power output within 5 percent of the first effort. If your average power from your second effort is more than 10 percent lower than your first effort, that doesn't change your training prescription, but it gives you one more marker by which you can evaluate progress the next time you complete the test. For example, as the average power outputs for your two field test efforts become more equal, that is a sign that your training has improved your ability to buffer lactic acid and process lactate. The first effort took less out of you, and you were able to recover from the effort more quickly, leading to the ability to perform a second effort at an equal power output after just 10 minutes of easy spinning recovery.

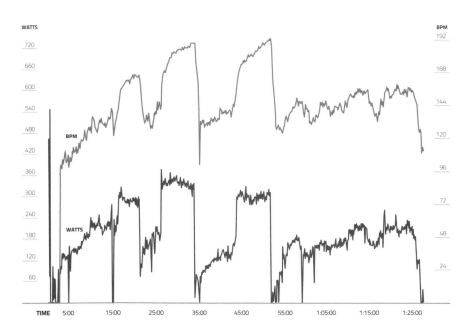

FIGURE 3.3: INEXPERIENCED FIELD TEST
In contrast to the steady effort in Figure 3.2, this graph shows a strong first field test followed by a significant drop in power (watts) for the second test. This indicates that the rider, while strong, lacks endurance and the ability to hold high power for repeatable efforts. This is not a "bad" field test; in fact, it reveals a tremendous amount about the athlete's specific need to develop the aerobic energy system.

Sometimes an athlete has a higher average power on the second effort of the CTS Field Test, and this can often be attributed to one of two factors: You were cautious on the first effort and held back, or you didn't warm up well enough before the field test (the first effort, then, was in essence the end of your warm-up). In either case, your training ranges are established from the higher of your two average power outputs or heart rates, so the fact that the CTS Field Test consists of two efforts allows you to establish accurate training ranges despite performing poorly on one part of the test. In a test that consists of one longer effort, either the learning curve of the test or a poor warm-up is more likely to result in training intensities that are lower than they should be. In the long run, this isn't all that harmful to an athlete's training, because training intensities will most likely be corrected by subsequent tests, and most athletes make performance gains even if their training intensities are a little lower than they could be. Nevertheless, through testing

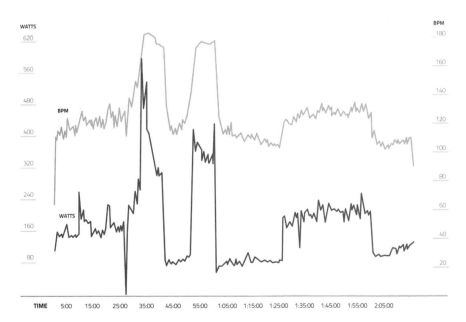

FIGURE 3.4: BAD FIELD TEST
You can see from the sharp spike in power at the start of the field test and the rapid decline that this athlete did not pace himself well for the entire 8-minute effort. He went out too hard, had to slow down, and then pushed again at the end of the effort (indicated by the sharp upward slope of the wattage data). To achieve a better field test result, you want to use the first 45–60 seconds of each effort to gradually get up to speed.

thousands of athletes with the CTS Field Test, I have found that it provides greater accuracy the first time around as well as in subsequent tests.

THE CTS FIELD TEST VERSUS OTHER PERFORMANCE TESTS

The other major question my coaches and I are asked about field testing is whether the power or heart rate we use to establish training ranges is equal to an athlete's power or heart rate at lactate threshold. The answer is no, but the results from the CTS Field Test correlate predictably with results from laboratory testing, so a conversion factor can be applied to your numbers to establish accurate training ranges.

One of the reasons some coaches prefer longer field test efforts is that longer tests result in average power numbers that are closer to actual lab-tested lactate threshold power outputs. The reason for this is that you can maintain an effort well above your lactate threshold for a short period of time, but because lactate threshold pretty much defines the upper limit of your sustainable power output, if you ride long enough you'll settle into a pace that's very close to—and most likely below—your lactate threshold power output. But this is another situation in which sports science doesn't necessarily work to an athlete's benefit. Yes, a 60-minute time trial could provide a relatively accurate estimation of your lactate threshold power output, but only if you can stay motivated to ride all-out for a full hour. If you can't—and there's no shame in that; most novices and amateur racers struggle with such a long, intense effort—your numbers are going to be low, and you'll establish training intensities that are lower than they should be. And even if you could stay motivated enough to complete a great 60-minute time trial, it would be difficult to integrate that into your training program on a regular basis because it's such a demanding workout in and of itself.

After thousands of tests, my coaches and I have found that the CTS Field Test generates average power outputs that are about 10 percent above an athlete's lab-tested lactate threshold power output. In the calculations that I present for establishing your own training intensity ranges, this 10 percent is already factored into the equations in the tables. In other words, you'll take your actual power output or heart rate from the field test and plug it directly into the equation. We have been using the CTS Field Test and the corresponding training intensity calculations for many years, and the accuracy of this method was proven in the Klika et al. study (2007), which was conducted in Aspen, Colorado. The study found that participants' maximum sustainable power outputs, as measured by the CTS Field Test on an indoor trainer, were 7.5 percent higher than their lab-tested power at lactate threshold. However, it is important to remember that the study was conducted at an elevation of 9,000 feet, where not only is power at lactate threshold lower than at sea level, but the ability to sustain efforts above threshold is even more limited. Therefore, I have continued to use the 10 percent conversion factor for calculating training intensity ranges from CTS Field Test data.

One popular field test, published in *Training and Racing with a Power Meter* by Hunter Allen and Andrew Coggan, is a 20-minute time trial. This test is a good one; it's short enough that many athletes can complete a high-quality effort. Allen and Coggan also use a conversion factor to account for the difference between an athlete's field test power and his or her predicted lactate threshold power. In their system, athletes record their average power output from a 20-minute time trial, multiply this number by 0.95, and then apply a series of percentages to the resulting power output to establish power training intensities. They multiply by 0.95 initially because an athlete's 20-minute power output will be about 5 percent higher than that same athlete's power output in a 60-minute effort—which is also about equal to an athlete's lab-tested lactate threshold power output. Essentially, if you consider a 60-minute test to be roughly equal to power at lactate threshold, then a 20-minute test will give you a power output 5 percent higher than that, and the CTS Field Test will give you a power output another 5 percent above that.

Before describing exactly how to perform the CTS Field Test, I want to point out that it is important not to get too caught up in performance testing. It's a valuable component of training, but some athletes train for the tests the same way some schools teach to standardized exams. Your performance as a cyclist goes beyond your ability to produce more wattage in a performance test, and regardless of improvements in your power at threshold, you'll still get dropped from the local group ride or finish at the back of the pack in a criterium if you fail to learn how to apply your strength in real-world cycling situations. Races are not won in the lab or on the indoor trainer, and I've yet to meet a cyclist who describes his or her best day on the bike by talking about a performance test. Do the testing, use the results to enhance your training, but always remember that your identity as a cyclist is much more than a collection of testing data.

COMPLETING THE CTS FIELD TEST

The CTS Field Test should be completed before you begin the TCTP the first time. If you decide to use the program more than once in a season, you should complete the field test again before starting the program each time. When you view the workouts and training programs (see Chapter 4), you'll notice that the CTS Field Test is not included as a workout at the very beginning of the schedule. I want you to complete it a few days before you begin one of the training programs. Make sure you're well rested before completing the test. Don't perform the test the day after a major race or hard century ride because you won't be able to determine how fatigue affects your results.

The field test itself consists of two 8-minute efforts, but it's important to be properly fueled and warmed up before beginning the first time trial. Refer to the pre-workout nutrition tips in Chapter 4 for more information on optimal pre-workout meals and snacks. When you get on the bike, you'll need time to complete the warm-up, the field test, and a good cool-down, so budget a total of an hour for the entire field test workout. Start with 10 minutes of easy- to moderate-intensity riding and then complete the following warm-up routine:

Pre–Field Test Warm-up

1 minute FastPedal (in a light gear, bring your cadence up as high as you can without bouncing in the saddle)

1 minute easy spinning recovery

2 minutes FastPedal

1 minute easy spinning recovery

1 minute PowerInterval (maximum-intensity interval at 90 to 95 rpm; bring the intensity up gradually over the first 30 seconds and hold that effort level through the end of the interval)

2 minutes easy spinning recovery

1 minute PowerInterval

4 minutes easy spinning recovery

Begin CTS Field Test

VO₂MAX TESTING

An athlete's VO₂max is defined as the maximum amount of oxygen the body can take in and use per minute, and it's often expressed relative to body weight. During their professional careers, some elite cyclists have recorded VO₂max values of more than 80 milliliters per kilogram per minute (ml/kg/min.). The average sedentary human has a VO₂max of about 40, and a well-trained cyclist will often have values from 55 to 65 ml/kg/min. Genetics play a pivotal role in determining your VO₂max, but it also responds to training. You can increase your absolute VO₂max, the power you can produce at VO₂max, and how long you can sustain efforts at this maximal intensity. However, on a percentage basis, lactate threshold responds to training better than VO₂max does. An untrained athlete could conceivably double his or her power at lactate threshold but would not be able to raise a starting VO₂max of 40 ml/kg/min. all the way to 80 unless he or she was born with the genetics to have a VO₂max of 80 ml/kg/min. In other words, you can improve your power at threshold to a greater extent than you can your power at VO₂max. On the other hand, a relatively small improvement in power at VO₂max—and the amount of time you can sustain that power—can have a significant impact on performance at lower intensities.

A scenario we often aim for in training is to improve both power at VO₂max and power at lactate threshold, with the overall goal of getting an athlete's lactate threshold power to be a higher percentage of his or her VO₂max power. For example, when CTS Premier coach Nick White was coaching triathlete Craig Alexander in preparation for the 2008 Ironman World Championships, he found that Craig's LT power was only 77 percent of his power at VO₂max. Through training, Craig's power at VO₂max increased, but perhaps more important, his power at threshold increased to about 85 percent of his VO₂max power. That meant he was able to use a greater percentage of his aerobic capacity for sustained efforts. In Kona he stayed near the leaders in the swim, rode conservatively on the bike to save energy, and came from minutes behind during the marathon to win his first Ironman World Championship.

CONTINUED

CONTINUED

Because VO$_2$max intervals are a major part of the TCTP (CTS Power-Intervals are VO$_2$max intervals), many athletes want to know whether they should have a VO$_2$max test done. There's certainly no harm in getting a VO$_2$max test, especially because it can often be tacked onto the end of a lactate threshold (LT) test. However, some performance labs only have the equipment to perform the LT test, which requires small blood samples to be tested for lactate. The VO$_2$max test requires analysis of inspired and expired gases, and that equipment is much more expensive. Labs that have the equipment to perform VO$_2$max tests, such as the CTS lab in Colorado Springs, can analyze inspired and expired gases during the LT portion of the test as well, which is useful for determining an athlete's VO$_2$ at LT as well as VO$_2$max.

If you can't get your VO$_2$max tested, don't worry about it. The reason that LT testing or field testing is so important is that we need to establish an accurate training range for efforts that are somewhere between moderately challenging and very strenuous. Accuracy counts because riding too easy won't provide the necessary stimulus, and riding too hard means you'll fatigue before you accumulate enough interval time. With VO$_2$max intervals, the intensity is as hard as you can go, which simplifies matters greatly because it means the intervals can be just as effective whether you've had a VO$_2$max test or not.

CTS FIELD TEST INSTRUCTIONS

When performing the CTS Field Test, collect the following data:

- Average heart rate for each effort
- Max heart rate for each effort
- Average power for each effort
- Average cadence for each effort
- Weather conditions (warm vs. cold, windy vs. calm, etc.)
- Course conditions (indoors vs. outdoors, flat vs. hilly, point-to-point vs. out-and-back, etc.)

- Rating of Perceived Exertion (RPE) for each effort (how hard you felt you were working)

Step 1: Find a Suitable Course

The CTS Field Test can be completed on an indoor trainer, which offers the ultimate in controlling conditions, but I have found that many athletes achieve higher power outputs in outdoor tests. I don't believe this is due to any inherent problem with indoor trainers, but rather that the sensations of speed and wind outdoors help motivate some athletes to perform better tests outside. The difference tends to be minor, however, so there is no need for a conversion factor between a field test completed indoors and one completed

RATING OF PERCEIVED EXERTION (RPE)

Even as technology has delivered remarkably accurate data about an athlete's true workload, a seemingly archaic measure of intensity refuses to disappear. Rating of Perceived Exertion, or RPE, is the ultimate in simplicity, nothing more than a scale of how hard you feel you are exercising. Not one single piece of data is collected, and you don't need any special equipment. All you need is the scale.

In the physiology lab my coaches and I use the Borg Scale, which ranges from 6 to 20 (6 being no exertion at all and 20 being a maximum effort). Why 6 to 20? Well, Borg's research has shown that there's a high correlation between the number an athlete chooses during exercise, multiplied by 10, and his or her actual heart rate at that time. In other words, if you're on an ergometer during an LT test and tell me that you feel like you're at 16, there is a pretty good chance your heart rate is around 160 beats per minute. This isn't absolutely true of all athletes, but you'd be surprised how accurate the 6 to 20 scale tends to be.

Outside the lab, however, I haven't found the Borg Scale to be as helpful for athletes. Most athletes find it easier to relate to a simpler 1 to 10 scale (1 being no exertion at all and 10 being a maximum effort). Using this scale, an endurance or "cruising" pace would be 4 to 5, a challeng-

CONTINUED

CONTINUED

ing aerobic tempo would be 6, LT work occurs at about 7 to 8, climbing and time trial efforts are a solid 8 (sometimes 9), and VO_2 intervals and all-out sprints are the only efforts that reach 10. Just as the Borg Scale multiplies the perceived exertion number by 10 to correlate with heart rate, the number chosen on the 1 to 10 scale, multiplied by 10, seems to correlate closely to the percentage of VO_2max that an athlete is currently maintaining.

With power meters providing an accurate and direct measure of workload, some athletes are tempted to relegate RPE to the trash bin of sports science history, but power meters have actually made RPE more important than ever. Although it's true that 200 watts today is the same workload as 200 watts tomorrow, RPE provides valuable context for your power files. When you're fresh, 200 watts may feel like a moderate spin, but when you're fatigued you may feel like you're working harder than normal (sluggish, heavy legs, pedaling through peanut butter, and similar terms may come to mind) for those same 200 watts. RPE is a great early warning device for revealing fatigue; your body is telling you it can still do the job, but that even though the work being done is the same, the effort to complete it is greater.

RPE can also indicate progress, even without a change in your power outputs. For example, at the beginning of the season, a 20-minute climb at 250 watts average power may feel strenuous enough to rate a 7 or even an 8. Later in the season, when your fitness has improved, riding at 250 watts up the same climb may take less out of you and feel more like a 6. An RPE of 7 to 8 on the climb may end up being 275 watts at the height of the season.

I have included RPE values with each workout in this book, and I encourage you to record your RPE during each effort in the CTS Field Test. Not only is perceived exertion important for providing context for power and heart rate files, but it also helps you learn to accurately evaluate your intensity level in the absence of all other technologies. Part of becoming a skilled cyclist is learning to use technology effectively while also reducing your dependence on it.

outdoors. If you're completing the test outside on the road, try to find a relatively flat course or one that is a consistent climb of no more than about a 5 to 6 percent grade. A course that contains rolling hills or a significant descent is not going to produce a good test. Likewise, a test performed on a steep climb is problematic because you end up in a situation where you're just doing whatever you need to in order to keep the pedals turning over; the terrain ends up dictating your effort more than you do. Above all, find a course that's safe and allows you to complete the 8-minute efforts without having to stop for stop signs, traffic lights, etc. For the sake of being able to compare one effort with the other, and one test with another, complete the test in weather conditions that are reasonably common for your area (not on a particularly hot or cold or windy day). You should also use the recovery time between efforts to return to your original starting point so you can complete the second effort over the same section of road.

Step 2: Begin Effort No. 1

Ideally, begin the effort from a standing start. Slow to almost a complete stop and rotate your cranks around so your dominant leg's crankarm is at the two o'clock position so you can take advantage of your body weight on the first power stroke. Your gear selection should allow a fast, stable start, not so small that you spin the gear out before you are able to sit down, and not so large you can barely get it moving. As you gain speed, but before you spin out your starting gear, shift up one gear and accelerate until you have reached a cadence of 90 to 100 rpm. Shift again and bring your cadence back up to 90 to 100, then sit and select the gear you're going to use to maintain a high power output at 90 to 100 rpm. Resist the urge to start too fast; you should reach your top speed about 45 to 60 seconds after you start, not before.

Step 3: Find Your Pace and Gear

Keep accelerating and shifting until you reach a speed you feel you can barely maintain for the length of the effort. I don't want you to hold back or think about the second effort that is still to come. Focus entirely on completing this effort at the highest power output you possibly can. Avoid the temptation to mash big gears. Pushing a bigger gear at a lower cadence may feel more powerful for a little while, but your leg muscles will fatigue quickly, and your power output will drop precipitously before the end of the effort. Try to maintain a cadence above 90 rpm on flat ground or an indoor trainer, and above 85 rpm if you're completing the test on a climb. The effort will be challenging from this point on, but do your best to keep breathing deeply. If you're hyperventilating (panting uncontrollably) during the first half of the effort, you started too fast.

Step 4: Stay on It

Every pedal stroke counts, so it's important to force the pace all the way through the end of the effort. Again, don't think about the second effort; just live for the one you're doing now. When you get to the final minute of the time trial, really open the throttle. As I repeatedly remind athletes during the indoor trainer classes at Carmichael Training Systems, you can do anything for 1 minute. Don't let up at 7:30 or even 7:55. Push all the way through to 8:00.

Step 5: Recover and Prepare for Effort No. 2

When you reach the end of Effort No. 1, you should be drained. But don't stop pedaling. Shift into an easy gear and keep turning the pedals over. Active recovery spinning helps your body circulate oxygenated blood to your tired muscles and flush away waste products. In the first minute of this recovery period, you may feel there's no way you can possibly repeat the effort you just completed, but you can if you spend these 10 minutes wisely. Take a drink of water, sit up with your hands on the tops of the bars, and relax as you spin. If you're completing the test outdoors, return to the same starting point you used for the first effort. If it takes you a little more than 10 minutes to get back there, that's OK. It's more important for the efforts to be completed over the same stretch of road than for the recovery time to be exactly 10 minutes.

Step 6: Complete Effort No. 2

Just as you did at the beginning of Effort No. 1, slow until you're nearly standing still and use your gears and cadence to accelerate to your top speed over the first 45 to 60 seconds of the effort. If you're using a power meter, avoid the temptation to pace your effort based on the average power output from your first effort. There's a good chance your second effort will result in a higher power output, but the only way you'll know that is if you give it everything you have.

Step 7: Cool Down; Record Your Data

Once you finish Effort No. 2, you're done with the CTS Field Test. All that's left is to cool down with some easy spinning for 15 to 30 minutes (or however long it takes to get home). When you get off the bike, make sure to consume carbohydrates and fluids per the post-workout recommendations in Chapter 8, and record your CTS Field Test data in a training log or software program. You can also use Table 3.3 (page 89) to record your data.

Calculating Training Intensities
for CTS Workouts

In the spirit of keeping things simple, I use a relatively small number of training intensity ranges (see Table 3.1). The whole idea of intensity ranges is to focus your efforts on specific regions of the energy system continuum. As I mentioned in Chapter 2, you're always using all your energy systems, but the percentage of energy coming from each system changes as you move from lower to higher intensities. One of the key principles of interval training is

TABLE 3.1 | **Establishing Training Intensities**

WORKOUT NAME	PRIMARY TRAINING GOAL	% OF CTS FIELD TEST POWER	% OF CTS FIELD TEST HEART RATE
Endurance Miles	Basic aerobic development	45–73	50–91
Tempo	Improved aerobic endurance	80–85	88–90
Steady State	Increased power at lactate threshold	86–90	92–94
Climbing Repeat	Increased power at lactate threshold	95–100	95–97
Power Interval	Increased power at VO₂max	Max effort (101 at absolute minimum)	100–max

that by spending focused time at specific points along this curve, you can stimulate greater training adaptations than by riding at self-selected speeds.

To calculate your individual training intensities for the CTS workouts (see Chapter 4), you need to know either the highest of the two average power outputs or the highest of the two average heart rates from your CTS Field Test. If you have both pieces of information, you should calculate both power and heart rate training intensities, but use the power ranges to gauge your interval efforts whenever possible.

INSTRUCTIONS FOR CALCULATING CTS
TRAINING INTENSITIES

1. Find the higher of the two average power outputs and/or the higher of the two average heart rates from your CTS Field Test.

2. Multiply the power output and/or heart rate by the percentages listed in Table 3.1 to establish the upper and lower limits of your training ranges.

TABLE 3.2 | **Intensity Ranges for Joe Athlete**

WORKOUT NAME	PRIMARY TRAINING GOAL	% OF CTS FIELD TEST POWER	CTS POWER INTENSITY RANGE (WATTS)	% OF CTS FIELD TEST HEART RATE	CTS HEART RATE INTENSITY RANGE (BPM)
Endurance Miles	Basic aerobic development	45–73	135–219	50–91	88–159
Tempo	Improved aerobic endurance	80–85	240–255	88–90	154–158
Steady State	Increased power at lactate threshold	86–90	258–270	92–94	161–165
Climbing Repeat	Increased power at lactate threshold	95–100	285–300	95–97	166–170
Power Interval	Increased power at VO$_2$max	Max effort (101 at absolute minimum)	300+	100–max	175–max

TRAINING INTENSITIES FOR JOE ATHLETE

Let's say Joe Athlete completed the CTS Field Test and recorded average power outputs of 300 watts and 296 watts. During the same efforts, his average heart rates were 172 and 175, respectively. He would use the 300 watts and the 175 heart rate for calculating his training intensities, even though they came from different efforts during the CTS Field Test.

The lower limit of Joe Athlete's SteadyState intensity ranges would come out to $300 \times 0.86 = 258$ watts. The upper limit of his SteadyState intensity range would come out to $300 \times 0.90 = 270$ watts. So Joe Athlete should complete SteadyState intervals at a power output between 258 and 270 watts. Table 3.2 shows Joe Athlete's intensity ranges.

YOUR CTS TRAINING INTENSITIES

After completing the CTS Field Test, use Table 3.3 to record your intensity outputs and calculate your CTS training intensities. You should also record your data in a training log or software program, whichever you use.

TABLE 3.3 | Recording Your CTS Intensities   DATE OF FIELD TEST:

WORKOUT NAME	PRIMARY TRAINING GOAL	% OF CTS FIELD TEST POWER	CTS POWER INTENSITY RANGE (WATTS)	% OF CTS FIELD TEST HEART RATE	CTS HEART RATE INTENSITY RANGE (BPM)
Endurance Miles	Basic aerobic development	45–73		50–91	
Tempo	Improved aerobic endurance	80–85		88–90	
Steady State	Increased power at lactate threshold	86–90		92–94	
Climbing Repeat	Increased power at lactate threshold	95–100		95–97	
Power Interval	Increased power at VO₂max	Max effort (101 at absolute minimum)		100–max	

CHAPTER

4

Competitor and Century Workouts and Training Programs

CTS Workouts

Over the years I have developed an extensive list of workouts for improving cycling performance. The selected workouts included here are featured in the training programs that appear later in this chapter. Power and heart rate training intensities are included for every workout and are based on your CTS Field Test (see Chapter 3, page 73). Rating of Perceived Exertion (RPE) is also included for each workout, using the 1 to 10 scale described in Chapter 3 (page 83).

FastPedal (FP) This workout should be performed on a relatively flat section of road. The gearing should be light, with low pedal resistance. Begin slowly working up your pedal speed, starting out with around 15 to 16 pedal revolutions per 10-second count. This equates to a cadence of 90 to 96 rpm. While staying in the saddle, increase your pedal speed, keeping your hips smooth, with no

Training Intensities for FastPedal
RPE: 7
HR: NA
Power: NA

rocking. Concentrate on pulling through the bottom of the pedal stroke and pushing over the top. After 1 minute of FP, you should be maintaining 18 to 20 pedal revolutions per 10-second count, or a cadence of 108 to 120 rpm for the entire time prescribed for the workout. Your heart rate (HR) will climb while doing this workout, but don't use it to judge your training intensity. It is important that you try to ride the entire length of the FP workout with as few interruptions as possible, because it should consist of consecutive riding at the prescribed training intensity.

EnduranceMiles (EM) This is your moderate-paced endurance intensity. The point is to stay at an intensity below lactate threshold for the vast majority of any time you're riding at EM pace. The heart rate and power ranges for this intensity are very wide to allow for widely varying conditions. It is OK for your power to dip on descents or in tailwinds, just as it is expected that your power will increase when you climb small hills. One mistake some riders make is to stay at the high end of their EM range for their entire ride. As you'll see from the intensity ranges for Tempo workouts, the upper end of EM overlaps with Tempo. If you constantly ride in your Tempo range instead of using that as a distinct interval intensity, you may not have the power to complete high-quality intervals when the time comes. You're better off keeping your power and/or heart rate in the middle portion of your EM range and allowing it to fluctuate up and down from there as the terrain and wind dictate. Use your gearing as you hit the hills to remain in the saddle as you climb. Expect to keep your pedal speed up into the 85 to 95 rpm range.

Training Intensities for EnduranceMiles
RPE: 5
HR: 50–91% of highest CTS Field Test average
Power: 45–73% of highest CTS Field Test average

NOTE ON COMBINATIONS

When a combination workout calls for "60 min. EM with 3 × 8 min. SS," that 60 minutes is your total ride time; your warm-up, SteadyState Intervals, recovery periods between intervals, and cool-down are all to be included within that 60 minutes.

Tempo (T) Tempo is an excellent workout for developing aerobic power and endurance. The intensity is well below lactate threshold, but hard enough that you are generating a significant amount of lactate and forcing your body to buffer and process it. The intervals are long (15 minutes minimum, and they can be as long as 2 hours for pros), and your gearing should be relatively large so that your cadence comes down to about 70 to 75 rpm. This combination helps increase pedal resistance and strengthens leg muscles. Also, try to stay in the saddle when you hit hills during your T workouts. It Is Important that you try to ride the entire length of the T workout with as few interruptions as possible—T workouts should consist of consecutive riding at the prescribed intensity to achieve maximum benefit. This workout is not used in the TCTP but is featured in the supplemental Endurance Block training in Chapter 10.

> **Training Intensities for Tempo**
>
> RPE: 6
>
> HR: 88–90% of highest CTS Field Test average
>
> Power: 80–85% of highest CTS Field Test average

SteadyState (SS) These intervals are great for increasing a cyclist's maximum sustainable power because the intensity is below lactate threshold but close to it. As you accumulate time at this intensity, you are forcing your body to deal with a lot of lactate for a relatively prolonged period of time. SS intervals are best performed on flat roads or small rolling hills. If you end up doing them on a sustained climb, you should really bump the intensity up to ClimbingRepeat range, which reflects the grade's added contribution to your effort. Do your best to complete these intervals without interruptions from stoplights and so on, and maintain a cadence of 85 to 95 rpm. Maintaining the training zone intensity is the most important factor, not pedal cadence. SS intervals are meant to be slightly below your individual time trial pace, so don't make the mistake of riding at your time trial pace during them. Recovery time between SS intervals is typically about half the length of the interval itself.

> **Training Intensities for SteadyState**
>
> RPE: 7
>
> HR: 92–94% of highest CTS Field Test average
>
> Power: 86–90% of highest CTS Field Test average

ClimbingRepeats (CR) This workout should be performed on a road with a long steady climb. The training intensity is designed to be similar to that of a SS interval but reflect the additional workload necessary to ride uphill. The intensity is just below your lactate threshold power and/or heart rate, and it is critical that you maintain this intensity for the length of the CR. Pedal cadence for CR intervals while climbing should be 70 to 85 rpm. Maintaining the training intensity is the most important factor, not pedal cadence. It is very important to avoid interruptions while doing these intervals. Recovery time between intervals is typically about half the length of the interval itself. This interval is not used as a stand-alone training intensity in the TCTP, but it is used as a component of the OverUnder intervals.

Training Intensities for ClimbingRepeats

RPE: 8

HR: 95–97% of highest CTS Field Test average

Power: 95–100% of highest CTS Field Test average

PowerIntervals (PI) PowerIntervals are perhaps the most important workouts in the entire TCTP. These short efforts are the way you're going to apply the concepts of high-intensity training to your program to make big aerobic gains in a small amount of time. These intervals are maximal efforts and can be performed on any terrain except sustained descents. Your gearing should be moderate so you can maintain a relatively high pedal cadence (100 rpm or higher is best). Two types of PI are used in this program: Steady Effort and Peak-and-Fade.

Training Intensities for PowerIntervals

RPE: 10

HR: 100% max

Power: 101% of highest CTS Field Test average

Steady Effort PowerIntervals (SEPI): Try to reach and maintain as high a power output as possible for the duration of these intervals. Ideally, these efforts should look like flat plateaus when you view your power files (see Figure 4.1). Take the first 30 to 45 seconds to gradually bring your power up and then hold on for the rest of the interval. The point here is to accumulate as much time as possible at a relatively constant and extremely high output. These are the PIs featured in the earlier weeks of the TCTP.

Peak-and-Fade PowerIntervals (PFPI): These intervals start with a big acceleration rather than a gradual increase in intensity. I want you to go all-out right from the beginning and keep your power output as high as possible as the interval progresses. (See Figure 4.2.) Because of the hard acceleration, your power output will gradually fall after the first 40 to 60 seconds of the effort. That's expected and perfectly normal; just keep pushing. Use your gears to keep your cadence high (above 90 rpm) for the entire interval. Don't let fatigue lead you to start mashing gears in the second half of the effort. These intervals generate a great deal of lactate and are reserved for the later weeks of the TCTP.

The rest periods between PIs are purposely too short to provide complete recovery, and completing subsequent intervals in a partially recovered state is a key part of what makes these efforts effective. Typically, recovery times are equal to the interval work time, which is sometimes referred to as a 1:1 work-to-recovery ratio.

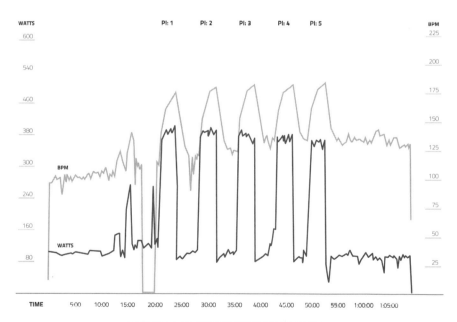

FIGURE 4.1: STEADY EFFORT POWERINTERVAL

This athlete completed five relatively consistent power intervals. Notice the wattage data from each interval forms a mostly stable horizontal line, while heart rate lags behind and continues to rise throughout. This is a good example of why training with power is so useful in providing a picture of actual workload.

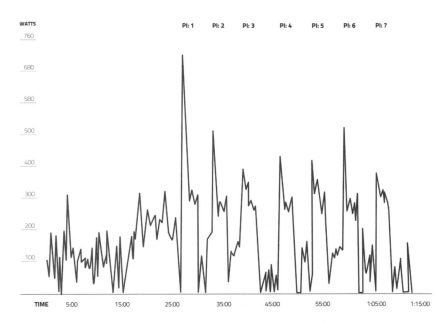

FIGURE 4.2: PEAK-AND-FADE POWERINTERVAL
During a Peak-and-Fade PowerInterval, you should accelerate hard at the beginning
of the interval and continue working as hard as you can throughout. Your power files will
show a sharp spike in power followed by a rapid decline. Your goal is to minimize the
decline and develop the ability to surge again at the end. (Note: heart rate removed for clarity.)

*Note: Aim for your intervals to be well above 101 percent of your field test power.
Many athletes will consistently hit 110–130 percent of field test power, and some may
go higher. The 101 percent level marks the bare minimum. If you can't consistently
exceed this level, you're too tired to complete an effective PI workout.*

OverUnder (OU) Intervals OverUnder intervals are a more advanced form of SS
intervals. The "Under" intensity is your SS range, and the "Over" intensity is your CR
range. By alternating between these two intensity levels during a sustained interval,
you develop the "agility" to handle changes in pace during hard sustained efforts.
(See Figure 4.3.) More specifically, the harder surges within the interval generate
more lactate in your muscles, and then you force your body to process this lactate
while you're still riding at a relatively high intensity. This workout can be performed
on a flat road, rolling hills, or a sustained climb that's relatively gradual (3 to 6 percent grade). It is difficult to accomplish this workout on a steep climb, because the

pitch often makes it difficult to control your effort level. Your gearing should be moderate, and pedal cadence should be high (90 rpm or higher) if you're riding on flat ground or small rollers. Pedal cadence should be above 85 rpm if you're completing the intervals on a gradual climb.

To complete the interval, bring your intensity up to your SS range during the first 45 to 60 seconds. Maintain this heart rate intensity for the prescribed Under time and then increase your intensity to your Over intensity for the prescribed time. At the end of this Over time, return to your Under intensity range and continue riding at this level of effort until it's once again time to return to your Over intensity. Continue alternating this way until the end of the interval.

OverUnder intervals always end with a period at Over intensity. Recovery periods between intervals are typically about half the length of the work interval. (A more

Training Intensities for OverUnders
RPE: 9
HR: 92–94% (Under) of highest CTS Field Test average, alternating with 95–97% (Over)
Power: 86–90% (Under) of highest CTS Field Test average, alternating with 95–100% (Over)

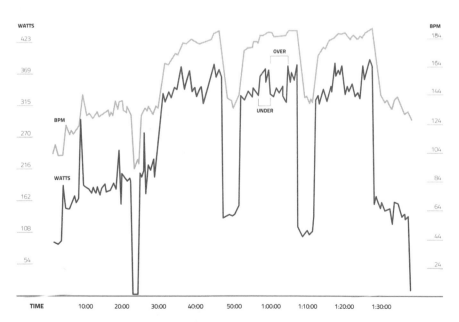

FIGURE 4.3: OVERUNDER

In this particular power file the athlete performed three OverUnder intervals, alternating between "Under" and "Over" twice per interval. Note the high-higher-high-higher pattern in each. This athlete also did a great job riding easy during recovery periods.

advanced version of this interval would alternate between SS and PI intensities instead of SS and CR intensities.)

Note: In the training programs, the parameters of the OU intervals are written as 3 × 12 OU (2U, 1O), 5 minutes RBI. This should be read as follows: Three intervals of 12 minutes. During the 12-minute intervals, the first 2 minutes should be at your Under intensity (2U). After 2 minutes, accelerate to your Over intensity for 1 minute (1O), before returning to your Under intensity for another 2 minutes. Continue alternating in this manner—in this example you'd complete 4 cycles of Under and Over—until the end of the interval. Spin easy for 5 minutes and start the next interval.

ThresholdLadders (TL) This edition introduces a new workout that the coaches at CTS and I developed called ThresholdLadders, which mimic the accelerations and sustained power requirements used in breakaways and at the start of cyclocross races. They begin with a 1- to 2-minute all-out PowerInterval, followed immediately by 3 to 4 minutes at ClimbingRepeat intensity (95–100 percent of threshold power), and end with 5 to 6 minutes at SteadyState power (86–90 percent of power at threshold).

> **Training Intensities for ThresholdLadders**
>
> See Table 3.1 to calculate your training intensities for the PI, CR, and SS workouts that make up the ThresholdLadders

I won't lie: These suckers hurt. But so does racing, where success is the ability to separate yourself from the peloton and then continue hammering away until you open up a significant gap on the rest of the field. ThresholdLadders generate tremendous amounts of lactate in the first segment of the interval, but then there's no recovery period. You go directly to ClimbingRepeat intensity, which is still at or even above your lactate threshold intensity. Your body has to learn how to continue producing power while coping with elevated levels of lactate, and that's what stimulates it to produce more mitochondria to process the lactate faster. This adaptation boosts your power at threshold as well as your ability to attack time after time after time.

Because they're so tough, I've only added two ThresholdLadder workouts to the Commuter plans in the build-up to week 8's weekend race (Chapter 5). Once you start racing each weekend in weeks 9–11, you'll be doing ThresholdLadders without thinking about them because, put simply, that's racing.

The Time-Crunched Training Programs

To better address the various goals and experience levels of individual cyclists, I have included a total of four 11-week training programs in this chapter. Two are designed to prepare you for competitions, and two are meant for riders who are preparing for centuries, cycling tours, or epic weekend rides. For the sake of simplicity, I refer to the two categories as Competitor and Century.

CHOOSING THE RIGHT TRAINING PROGRAM

The Competitor programs focus not only on building greater aerobic fitness but also on preparing you for the repeated high power efforts of racing. You need to be able to accelerate and to handle rapid changes in pace. You need the power for all-out efforts and also the ability to recover from those efforts while still riding at a high speed. As a result, these programs focus more on maximum-intensity PIs that build power for all-out efforts and help your body learn to process and tolerate more lactate.

The Century programs include fewer maximum-intensity intervals and focus more on building power at lactate threshold. The primary goal of these programs is to increase the pace you can comfortably sustain for your long rides, meaning you'll be doing more SS and OU workouts and fewer PIs. The OU workouts are especially important because they will help you handle the changes in pace and power demands that come with riding in pace lines and over undulating terrain.

The categories are further broken down into New and Experienced programs. The differences between them are subtle but reflect the fact that more experienced riders are generally able to handle a higher workload because they have more years and miles in their legs. If you're an experienced cyclist who has been riding for 5, 10, 15 years or more, you'll be happy to know that even if you're currently not riding very much, the training adaptations from all those years of riding haven't completely disappeared. Your current fitness may be quite low compared to what it once was, but riders who have several years of training behind them are able to handle greater workloads when they initially return to more structured training, and they adapt more quickly and regain a greater percentage of their former fitness.

However, it's important to realize that each of the four programs starts with lactate threshold intervals right out of the gate. If you have been riding two to four times a week, participating in group rides or training races, and consider yourself in decent riding condition, you should be able to jump right in and start one of the TCTPs immediately. But if you have been off the bike for a while or have been only riding occasionally, and you can't remember the last time you rode hard enough to go above lactate threshold, you need to spend a week or two just going on 60- to 90-minute rides that include 20, 30, or 40 minutes of time at Tempo intensity (see workout descriptions for info on Tempo) to get back up to speed before jumping into one of the programs in this book.

More detailed descriptions of each program, and the riders they're best suited to, follow.

NEW COMPETITOR PROGRAM

If you've been riding fewer than 5 years and you want to prepare for criteriums, cross-country or short-track mountain bike races, cyclocross races, or road races up to about 60 miles in length, this is the program you should choose. The weekly workload in the New Competitor program (see Table 4.1) is more appropriate for cyclists who have fewer years of miles in their legs, meaning it's slightly lower than the Experienced Competitor program (discussed next). The progression also spends a little more time on lactate threshold workouts before moving on to PIs. Some riders, especially those who have been riding 3 to 4 years, may be able to handle the workload of the Experienced Competitor program, but I encourage you to use the New Competitor program at least once before you decide to complete the harder one. Due to the intensity featured in these programs, it's wise to be conservative with your choice. This is similar to the program CTS coach Jim Rutberg used with John Fallon (read about John in Chapter 11).

EXPERIENCED COMPETITOR PROGRAM

This is the program that riders like Sterling Swaim (see Chapter 1) and Taylor Carrington (see Chapter 2) used because they were experienced racers whose accumulated years of training meant they could handle a high initial workload. Experienced riders also adapt quickly, so the progression in this program is more rapid than in the New Competitor program. If you've been riding and/or racing for 5 years or more, this program is for you (see Table 4.2). That being said, if your current fitness is particularly low because you've done very little training (one or two rides a week) or haven't been training at all in the past 6 months, you may be better off working through the New Competitor program once before moving on to this program (following a 4- to 6-week recovery/maintenance period, of course). If you have any doubt about whether you should use the New or the Experienced Competitor program—perhaps you've been riding for 10 years but you've barely trained or raced in the past 2 years—it's wise to start with the New Competitor program.

NEW CENTURY PROGRAM

The New Century program (see Table 4.3) is the easiest of the four programs in this book and is therefore the best choice for a novice cyclist or a rider who is returning to the sport after several years off the bike. Even though it's the easiest of the programs, it is still quite challenging. For example, the workload is considerably higher than in the easier training program options in my previous training books (*The Lance Armstrong Performance Program, The Ultimate Ride*). This program may even be too difficult for some truly novice cyclists (brand-new bike, just started riding within the past 6 months). I'll explain more about how to determine if you're in over your head a little later. The ideal candidate for the New Century program is a cyclist who has been riding recreationally for a few years, has perhaps completed a century or two, and is looking for improved fitness and higher average speeds on long rides.

EXPERIENCED CENTURY PROGRAM

Of all the programs in this book, I have a hunch the Experienced Century (see Table 4.4) will be the one used most often. There are a lot of new and experienced racers out there, but there are many more of you who have been cyclists for several years and either have no interest in racing or are quite happy being former bike racers. This is the program that will give you the ability to complete your favorite long rides at higher average power outputs,

TABLE 4.1 | **New Competitor**

WEEK	MONDAY	TUESDAY	WEDNESDAY
1	45–60 min. EM	60–90 min. EM with 3 × 8 min. SS (5 min. RBI)	Rest day
2	Rest day	75–90 min. EM with 3 × 10 min. SS (6 min. RBI)	Rest day
3	Rest day	60–90 min. EM with 2 × [3 × 3 min. SEPI (3 min. RBI)] (8 min. RBS)	Rest day
4	Rest day	Rest day or 45 min. easy spinning	Rest day
5	Rest day	60–90 min. EM with 2 × [3 × 3 min. SEPI (3 min. RBI)] (6 min. RBS)	60–90 min. EM with 2 × [3 × 3 min. SEPI (3 min. RBI)] (8 min. RBS)
6	Rest day	60–90 min. EM with 5 × 3 min. SEPI (3 min. RBI)	60–90 min. EM + 3 × [3 × 2 min. PFPI (2 min. RBI)] (8 min. RBS)
7	Rest day	60–90 min. EM with 3 × [3 × 2 min. PFPI (2 min. RBI)] (6 min. RBS)	Rest day
8	Rest day	60 min. EM with 4 × 3 min. FP (3 min. RBI)	Rest day
9–11	Rest day	60–90 min. EM with 6 × 2 min. SEPI (2 min. RBI)	Rest day

RBI: Rest between intervals   **RBS:** Rest between sets
Week 8: End of progression, really good weekend to race   **Weeks 9–11:** Holding on to the fitness

or bump up your average speed for your next century. If you are preparing for a multiday tour, such as a Tour de France camp, this is also the program I'd recommend. The workouts in this program are designed to increase your sustainable power output. Note that even though the Experienced Century program includes a healthy dose of PIs, it is not designed to build a great ability to handle repeated maximal efforts. For that, you need the structure of the Competitor programs.

THURSDAY	FRIDAY	SATURDAY	SUNDAY
60–90 min. EM with 3 × 8 min. SS (5 min. RBI)	Rest day	Group ride or 90–120 min. EM	90–120 min. EM (hilly terrain)
75–90 min. EM with 3 × 10 min. SS (6 min. RBI)	Rest day	Group ride or 90–120 min. EM	90–120 min. EM or group ride
75–90 min. EM with 3 × 9 min. OU (2U, 10) (6 min. RBI)	Rest day	90–120 min. EM with 3 × 9 min. OU (2U, 10) (5 min. RBI)	90–150 min. EM
60–90 min. EM + 2 × [3 × 3 min. SEPI (3 min. RBI)] (8 min. RBS)	Rest day	90–120 min. EM with 2 × [3 × 3 min. SEPI (2 min. RBI)] (6 min. RBS)	120–150 min. EM or group ride
Rest day	Rest day	90–120 min. EM with 3 × 10 min. OU (3U, 20) (6 min. RBI)	90–150 min. EM or group ride
Rest day	Rest day	90–150 min. EM with 3 × 12 min. OU (2U, 20) (8 min. RBI)	90–150 min. EM or group ride
60–90 min. EM with 3 × [3 × 2 min. PFPI (2 min. RBI)] (6 min. RBS)	Rest day	90–150 min. EM with 3 × 12 min. OU (2U, 10) (8 min. RBI)	90–150 min. EM or group ride
60–90 min. EM with 4 × 2 min. PFPI (1 min. RBI); rest 8 min.; 4 × 3 min. OU (2U, 10) (3 min. RBI)	Rest day	90–150 min. EM or group ride	90–150 min. EM or group ride
60–90 min. EM with 4 × 2 min. PFPI (1 min. RBI); rest 8 min.; 4 × 3 min. OU (2U, 10) (3 min. RBI)	Rest day	90–150 min. EM with 3 × 12 min. OU (2U, 20) (8 min. RBI)	90–150 min. EM or group ride

EM: EnduranceMiles   **FP:** FastPedal   **OU:** OverUnders   **SS:** SteadyState
PFPI: Peak-and-Fade PowerIntervals   **SEPI:** Steady Effort PowerIntervals

Knowing When to Say When

As an athlete, listening to your body is one of the most important things you can do to enhance the effectiveness of your training. Even with a perfectly structured training schedule, many factors will influence your ability to complete every workout exactly as it's written. Perhaps you didn't sleep well last night and you're not quite as recovered as you should be from your previous workout. Or maybe a meeting ran long, and you didn't get a chance to eat a

TABLE 4.2 | Experienced Competitor

WEEK	MONDAY	TUESDAY	WEDNESDAY
1	45–60 min. EM	60–90 min. EM with 3 × 10 min. SS (5 min. RBI)	Rest day
2	Rest day	75–90 min. EM with 3 × 12 min. SS (6 min. RBI)	Rest day
3	Rest day	60–90 min. EM with 2 × [3 × 3 min. SEPI (3 min. RBI)] (8 min. RBS)	Rest day
4	Rest day	Rest day or 45 min. easy spinning	Rest day
5	Rest day	60–90 min. EM with 2 × [3 × 3 min. SEPI (2 min. RBI)] (6 min. RBS)	60–90 min. EM with 2 × [3 × 3 min. SEPI (2 min. RBI)] (6 min. RBS)
6	Rest day	60–90 min. EM with 6 × 3 min. SEPI (3 min. RBI)	60–90 min. EM with 3 × [3 × 2 min. PFPI (1 min. RBI)] (6 min. RBS)
7	Rest day	60–90 min. EM with 3 × [3 × 2 min. PFPI (2 min. RBI)] (6 min. RBS)	Rest day
8	Rest day	60 min. EM with 4 × 3 min. FP (3 min. RBI)	Rest day
9–11	Rest day	60–90 min. EM with 6 × 2 min. SEPI (2 min. RBI)	Rest day

RBI: Rest between intervals   **RBS:** Rest between sets
Week 8: End of progression, really good weekend to race   **Weeks 9–11:** Holding on to the fitness

good lunch before your afternoon workout. All athletes experience a workout or a period of time when their bodies are sending them signals that the workload is too high. If you recognize these signals and adjust your workouts accordingly, it's easy to stay on track. On the other hand, if you ignore the signals and blindly plow forward, you'll most likely do yourself more harm than good. There are two times when you really have to know when to say when: during an interval session and between workouts.

THURSDAY	FRIDAY	SATURDAY	SUNDAY
60–90 min. EM with 3 × 10 min. SS (5 min. RBI)	Rest day	90 min. EM with 3 × 10 min. SS (5 min. RBI) or 90–120 min. group ride	90–120 min. EM
75–90 min. EM with 4 × 6 min. OU (2U, 10) (5 min. RBI)	Rest day	90–120 min. EM with 4 × 6 min. OU (2U, 10) (5 min. RBI)	90–120 min. EM
60–90 min. EM with 2 × [3 × 3 min. SEPI (3 min. RBI)] (8 min. RBS)	Rest day	90–120 min. EM with 3 × 9 min. OU (2U, 10) (6 min. RBI)	90–150 min. EM or group ride
60–90 min. EM with 2 × [3 × 3 min. SEPI (3 min RBI)] (8 min. RBS)	Rest day	90 min. EM with 2 × [3 × 3 min. SEPI (2 min. RBI)] (6 min. RBS)	120–150 min. EM or group ride
Rest day	Rest day	90–120 min. EM with 3 × 10 min. OU (3U, 20) (6 min. RBI)	90–150 min. EM or group ride
Rest day	Rest day	90–150 min. EM with 3 × 12 min. OU (2U, 20) (8 min. RBI)	90–150 min. EM or group ride
60–90 min. EM with 3 × [3 × 2 min. PFPI (2 min. RBI)] (6 min. RBS)	Rest day	90–120 min. EM with 1 × [6 × 3 min. SEPI (3 min. RBI)]	90–150 min. EM or group ride
60–90 min. EM with 4 × 2 min. PFPI (1 min. RBI); rest 8 min.; 4 × 3 min. OU (2U, 10) (3 min. RBI)	Rest day	90–150 min. EM or group ride	90–150 min. EM or group ride
60–90 min. EM with 4 × 2 min. PFPI (1 min. RBI); rest 8 min.; 4 × 3 min. OU (2U, 10) (3 min. RBI)	Rest day	90–150 min. EM with 3 × 12 min. OU (2U, 20) (8 min. RBI)	90–150 min. EM or group ride

EM: EnduranceMiles   **FP:** FastPedal   **OU:** OverUnders   **SS:** SteadyState
PFPI: Peak-and-Fade PowerIntervals   **SEPI:** Steady Effort PowerIntervals

WHEN TO STOP AN INTERVAL SESSION

Interval workouts are only effective when you can maintain an intensity level high enough to address the goal of the session. A good example is a PI workout. To be effective, these intervals have to be maximum-intensity, high-power efforts. Ideally, the recovery periods between intervals give you the ability to complete all the efforts at consistent power outputs. However, because they are so strenuous, you're going to fatigue, and you'll be fighting harder to reach that high power output during the final set. The big question

TABLE 4.3 | New Century

WEEK	MONDAY	TUESDAY	WEDNESDAY
1	45–60 min. EM	60–90 min. EM with 4 × 6 min. SS (5 min. RBI)	Rest day
2	Rest day	60–90 min. EM with 3 × 8 min. SS (4 min. RBI)	Rest day
3	Rest day	Rest day	75–90 min. EM with 3 × 10 min. SS (5 min. RBI)
4	Rest day	Rest day	Rest day or 45 min. easy spinning
5	Rest day	60–90 min. EM with 3 × 9 min. OU (2U, 10) (6 min. RBI)	Rest day
6	Rest day	60–90 min. EM with 3 × 9 min. OU (2U, 10) (6 min. RBI)	60–90 min. EM with 3 × 10 min. SS (5 min. RBI)
7	Rest day	90 min. EM with 3 × 12 min. OU (2U, 20) (8 min. RBI)	60–90 min. EM with 3 × 12 min. SS (6 min. RBI)
8	Rest day	45 min. easy ride with 4 × 3 min. FP (3 min. RBI)	Rest day
9–11	Rest day	60–90 min. EM with 3 × 10 min. SS (5 min. RBI)	Rest day

RBI: Rest between intervals   **RBS:** Rest between sets
Week 8: End of progression, really good weekend to race   **Weeks 9–11:** Holding on to the fitness

is, as your power outputs start dropping, how do you tell if you should continue with the next interval or shut down and go home?

I've seen a few methods that attempt to quantify the drop in power output over a series of intervals to provide a clear point at which further intervals are not recommended. One of the better ones is provided by Hunter Allen and Andrew Coggan in *Training and Racing with a Power Meter*. They recommend using the third interval of a VO$_2$max-interval workout as your benchmark. They recommend stopping if your power output in subsequent

THURSDAY	FRIDAY	SATURDAY	SUNDAY
60–90 min. EM with 4 × 6 min. SS (5 min. RBI)	Rest day	90–120 min. EM	90–120 min. EM
60–90 min. EM with 3 × 8 min. SS (4 min. RBI)	Rest day	90–120 min. EM or group ride	90–120 min. EM
60–90 min. EM with 3 × 8 min. SS (4 min. RBI)	Rest day	90 min. EM with 2 × [3 × 2 min. SEPI (3 min. RBI)] (8 min. RBS)	90–120 min. EM or group ride
60–90 min. EM with 3 × 8 min. OU (3U, 1O) (6 min. RBI)	Rest day	120–150 min. EM	120–150 min. EM or group ride
90 min. EM with 2 × [4 × 2 min. SEPI (3 min. RBI)] (8 min. RBS)	Rest day	90 min. EM with 6 × 3 min. FP (3 min. RBI)	120–150 min. EM or group ride
Rest day	Rest day	90 min. EM with 2 × [4 × 2 min. SEPI (2 min. RBI)] (8 min. RBS)	120–150 min. EM or group ride
Rest day	Rest day	120 min. EM with 2 × [4 × 2 min. SEPI (2 min. RBI)] (8 min. RBS)	150 min. EM or group ride
60–90 min. EM with 4 × 2 min. SEPI (2 min. RBI); rest 8 min.; 4 × 3 min. OU (2U, 1O) (3 min. RBI)	Rest day	150–180 min. EM or group ride	90–150 min. EM or group ride
60–90 min. EM with 4 × 2 min. SEPI (2 min. RBI); rest 8 min.; 4 × 3 min. OU (2U, 1O) (3 min. RBI)	Rest day	90–150 min. EM or group ride	90–150 min. EM or group ride

EM: EnduranceMiles   **FP:** FastPedal   **OU:** OverUnders   **SS:** SteadyState
SEPI: Steady Effort PowerIntervals

intervals drops to more than 15 percent below that level. I think that method works best when you're doing one long string of VO_2max intervals, which I prescribe for some advanced athletes, but for most athletes I prefer to break VO_2max intervals (PowerIntervals in the programs in this book) into smaller sets. In the TCTP, for example, most PI sessions consist of three sets of three PIs with a 1:1 work/recovery ratio during the set and 5 to 8 minutes of easy spinning recovery between sets. Breaking the session into sets typically allows athletes to accumulate more total work at high power outputs.

TABLE 4.4 | **Experienced Century**

WEEK	MONDAY	TUESDAY	WEDNESDAY
1	45–60 min. EM	60–90 min. EM with 3 × 8 min. SS (5 min. RBI)	Rest day
2	Rest day	60–90 min. EM with 3 × 10 min. SS (5 min. RBI)	Rest day
3	Rest day	Rest day	75–90 min. EM with 3 × 12 min. SS (6 min. RBI)
4	Rest day	Rest day	Rest day or 45 min. easy spinning
5	Rest day	60–90 min. EM with 3 × 9 min. OU (2U, 10) (6 min. RBI)	60–90 min. EM with 3 × 10 min. SS (5 min. RBI)
6	Rest day	60–90 min. EM with 3 × 12 min. OU (2U, 10) (6 min. RBI)	60–90 min. EM with 3 × 9 min. OU (2U, 10) (6 min. RBI)
7	Rest day	90 min. EM with 3 × 12 min. OU (2U, 20) (6 min. RBI)	Rest day
8	Rest day	60 min. EM with 4 × 3 min. FP (3 min. RBI)	Rest day
9–11	Rest day	60–90 min. EM with 3 × 12 min. OU (2U, 20) (8 min. RBI)	Rest day

RBI: Rest between intervals   **RBS:** Rest between sets
Week 8: End of progression, really good weekend to race   **Weeks 9–11:** Holding on to the fitness

Breaking PI workouts into sets, however, makes it more difficult to provide a clear-cut stopping point based on fatigue. For example, it's possible that the third interval of your second set could be 15 percent or more below your power output from the intervals in your first set. But with 5 to 8 minutes of easy spinning recovery before you begin the third set, you may recover enough to match or even exceed your performance earlier in the workout.

Rather than automatically cutting your workout short if your power outputs are starting to fade, I recommend first adding some time to the recovery

THURSDAY	FRIDAY	SATURDAY	SUNDAY
60–90 min. EM with 3 × 8 min. SS (5 min. RBI)	Rest day	90–120 min. EM	90–120 min. EM
60–90 min. EM with 3 × 10 min. SS (5 min. RBI)	Rest day	90 min. EM with 2 × [3 × 2 min. SEPI (3 min. RBI)] (8 min. RBS)	90–120 min. EM
60–90 min. EM with 3 × 10 min. SS (5 min. RBI)	Rest day	90 min. EM with 2 × [4 × 2 min. SEPI (3 min. RBI)] (8 min. RBS)	90–120 min. EM or group ride
75–90 min. EM with 3 × 12 min. SS (6 min. RBI)	Rest day	120 min. EM with 3 × 9 min. OU (2U, 10) (6 min. RBI)	120–150 min. EM or group ride
Rest day	Rest day	90 min. EM with 2 × [4 × 2 min. SEPI (2 min. RBI)] (8 min. RBS)	120–150 min. EM or group ride
Rest day	Rest day	90 min. EM with 2 × [4 × 2 min. SEPI (2 min. RBI)] (8 min. RBS)	120–150 min. EM or group ride
90 min. EM with 3 × 12 min. OU (2U, 20) (6 min. RBI)	Rest day	120 min. EM with 2 × [4 × 2 min. SEPI (2 min. RBI)] (8 min. RBS)	150 min. EM or group ride
60–90 min. EM with 4 × 2 min. PFPI (2 min. RBI); rest 8 min.; 4 × 3 min. OU (2U, 10) (3 min. RBI)	Rest day	120–180 min. EM or group ride	90–150 min. EM or group ride
60–90 min. EM with 4 × 2 min. PFPI (2 min. RBI); rest 8 min.; 4 × 3 min. OU (2U, 10) (3 min. RBI)	Rest day	90–150 min. EM or group ride	90–150 min. EM or group ride

EM: EnduranceMiles   **FP**: FastPedal   **OU**: OverUnders   **SS**: SteadyState
PFPI: Peak-and-Fade PowerIntervals   **SEPI**: Steady Effort PowerIntervals

period between intervals. This means that if your power output from one PI to the next falls by 15 percent or more, add 1 minute to the recovery period immediately following that effort. If the next interval is no better than the one before it—despite the extra recovery time—then you're done for the day. Don't add more than 1 additional minute of easy spinning between efforts, and don't change the recovery periods between sets. If the added recovery time allows you to get through the end of the workout—or even just a few intervals closer to the end—that's great. Completing the work will help you perform your next PI workout without having to add recovery time.

Even if you don't spend the time or mental effort to figure out if your last interval was equal to or X percent lower than the one before it, PIs are pretty much self-limiting. If you're doing them correctly, meaning that each interval is an all-out effort, then your power output isn't likely to decline gradually and imperceptibly (see Figure 4.4). In my experience, most athletes are pretty

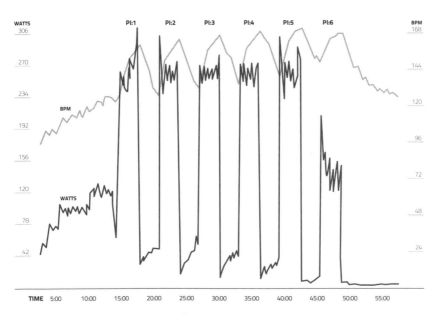

FIGURE 4.4: REACHING OVERLOAD

This rider started with 5 strong Powerlinterval (PI) efforts but quickly ended on the sixth interval when average power dropped by over 100 watts. It was clear to the athlete that the workout was over. He had reached overload and wisely chose to skip interval number 7.

good at telling when the wheels fall off the wagon. Your power won't be just a little lower than before—it will tank. Your legs will feel like bricks, your pedal mechanics will become very ugly, and you'll feel like you're pedaling through wet concrete while breathing through a straw. But as I said previously, there's a difference between recognizing fatigue and making the right decision. When your body tells you it's done, you're done for the day. Grunting your way through one more interval won't make you more of a man or woman, and listening to your body now is going to prevent you from doing more damage to muscles that are already in need of recovery and replenishment.

When it comes to SS and OU intervals, which target improvements in power at lactate threshold, it's not uncommon for athletes to struggle in the final 2 to 3 minutes of an individual interval. After all, these efforts are 8 to 12 minutes long, and they are not that far below the workload from your CTS Field Test (see Chapter 3). However, struggling in the final 2 to 3 minutes of an SS or OU interval is not cause to skip the next effort. More than likely, following several minutes of easy spinning recovery, you'll be able to repeat or exceed your performance in the previous effort. You'll know it's time to stop if you can't reach the prescribed training intensity within the first 60 seconds of an interval, or if the perceived effort to stay at that power output makes the interval feel like an all-out, do-or-die time trial. SteadyState intervals should feel like 7 on a 1-to-10 scale of perceived exertion, with CRs at 8 and OUs at 8 or 9. Only PIs should feel like 10, and if you're not going anywhere, on top of feeling like your eyes are going to pop out of your head, then you're done for the day.

WHEN TO SKIP AN INTERVAL WORKOUT

I can't tell you the number of times I've rolled away from the CTS office in Colorado Springs completely convinced I was too tired to have a good workout, only to return 90 minutes later after hitting every single power output I was shooting for during my intervals. Fatigue can be a tricky thing to judge, especially when you're training on a low-volume, high-intensity program. The interval workouts generate a lot of fatigue even though the work times only range between about 18 and 27 minutes for any individual session. At the same time, there are only 4 workouts scheduled per week, leaving 3 complete rest days. For many athletes, this is enough recovery to have consistently strong performances during their workouts. Nonetheless, the intensity in this program may be enough—especially coupled with your busy work and family schedule—to make you too tired to complete a workout here or there. The trick is understanding whether you need a kick in the butt to get you out the door or an extra day of rest so you can get back to kicking butt on the bike.

Since you have so little time each week to ride anyway, your decision shouldn't be whether or not to ride, but rather whether or not you should complete the scheduled interval workout. You should get on your bike regardless, if for no other reason than to ensure that your already limited training time isn't siphoned away any further. Similarly, although I understand the need to occasionally move workouts around in the schedule due to business trips or family obligations, I'm not a big fan of rescheduling interval workouts that are skipped due to fatigue. If you're too tired to complete a workout on Tuesday and you move it to Wednesday, it's likely you'll then be too tired to have a good workout again when you try to get back on schedule during Thursday's workout. I'd rather see you skip the interval session completely and get back on track with a series of great efforts during the next scheduled workout.

But let's get back to deciding whether or not to complete the day's scheduled interval session. If you're feeling tired when you get on your bike, it's a good idea to start with a focused warm-up and see if that kick-starts your motivation and energy systems. After 5 to 10 minutes of moderate-paced riding, complete the following:

1 minute FastPedal
1 minute easy recovery
1 minute FastPedal
1 minute easy recovery
1 minute SteadyState PowerInterval

By this point you should be about 15 minutes into your ride, and you have completed a few efforts. That should give you enough real information to evaluate whether you're ready to have a high-quality interval session. If you felt like you were really dragging in the SteadyState PI, or your power output for the effort was considerably lower than normal for a 1-minute effort, I recommend skipping the scheduled interval session and instead completing a moderate-paced endurance ride. If you were merely struggling with motivation to get out the door, your body will respond positively to these short efforts, and they will effectively "blow the crap out of the carburetor" (a reference that may be completely lost on athletes too young to remember when cars had carburetors instead of fuel injection; for them let's just say you need to clear out the system to fire on all cylinders). But if your body doesn't come around after these short "openers," you're most likely too fatigued to have a high-quality interval session today.

Adjusting the Programs for Your Personal Schedule

When my coaches and I work directly with an athlete, it's rare that we can go more than 2 weeks without needing to adjust that athlete's training based on a schedule conflict. It's simply a reflection of the complexity of modern life. When you have a full-time career and a family, your schedule changes, and you have to be flexible with your training. After all, when push comes to shove, family and career will come before training.

Because my coaches and I won't be in your living room with you as you try to adjust the training programs in this book to fit your schedule, I have developed the following guidelines to help you.

TWO-DAY INTERVAL BLOCKS ONLY

If you have to rearrange the workouts within a week, it's OK to put two interval workouts back-to-back on consecutive days, but after the second day it's imperative that you take a rest day. A 3-day block would create a workload that is too high, and it's likely that you'll be too fatigued to perform a high-quality interval workout on the third day. Ideally, you should take 2 days of recovery after a 2-day interval block, but if you need to ride Wednesday, Thursday, Saturday, and Sunday, you'll most likely be fine. Be careful to monitor your training the following week, however, and if you struggle in your next workout, you should back off and convert that day to an EM ride rather than an interval workout.

HARDEST INTERVALS FIRST

If you rearrange your schedule to group your workouts into 2-day blocks, always complete the hardest interval workout on the first day of the block. You'll be freshest on this day, so you'll have the power to complete a high-quality training session. For example, if the two workouts in question are a PI session and an OU session, complete the PIs on the first day and the OUs on the second day. The following list of workouts is arranged in order from highest intensity/workload to lowest:

PowerIntervals   ↑ HIGHEST
OverUnders
SteadyState
Tempo
EnduranceMiles
Easy Spinning/Recovery Ride   LOWEST

NO MAKEUP DAYS

If you unexpectedly have to skip a workout, I recommend simply moving on rather than trying to reschedule it. Although you have limited training time and must make every workout count, missing a training session now and then is not going to derail your progress. Constantly rearranging your riding schedule is more likely to cause problems with both your training progress and your work/family/training balance.

INTERVALS TAKE PRIORITY

If you have to cut a ride short, strip it down to the essentials. Complete a short warm-up, complete the interval set, and complete a short cool-down. This may be necessary if you have to cut a 2-hour weekend ride to an hour or a weekday ride to 45 minutes. The intervals are the primary source of training stimulus in these programs, so your primary goal should be to complete as much time as possible at the prescribed interval intensities.

Frequently Asked Questions

In the course of working with our athletes on the TCTP over the years, we've fielded quite a few questions about it, in part because it is so different from the programs they had used previously. Here are answers to the most common questions we've received.

Why 11 weeks?

The TCTP is structured a little differently from most event-based training programs. Many programs are designed with one specific goal event in mind, such as a particular century or criterium. In contrast, the athletes who led the development of these workouts sought to perform at their best for a series of races or a several-week period of time. As a result, the TCTP is designed to deliver peak performance at about week 8, and then provides training necessary for maintaining this level of fitness for another 3 weeks. For racers who are competing in a local criterium series, your best performances are likely to occur during the weekend at the end of week 8 or 9, and you should start racing at about week 6. Depending largely on your fitness level at the beginning of the program, you may find you can maintain race-winning performance levels all the way through week 11, but it's not unlikely for racing performances to start declining at week 10.

The TCTP does not include a longer buildup (say, 12 to 16 weeks to peak performance instead of 8) because we have found that it's difficult for athletes to maintain the focus necessary to complete such a high-intensity training program for 3 to 4 months. These workouts also generate a great deal of fatigue, and extending them to 12 to 16 weeks often leads to a cumulative workload that is higher than most athletes can handle.

Can I complete a Century program and move right into a Competitor program?

No. You can certainly upgrade from using a Century program to completing a Competitor program, but you still need to separate the programs with a 4- to 6-week recovery/maintenance period (see the last question in this section and Table 4.5 for my suggestions on creating a structured recovery period). Even though these are low-volume programs, the high-intensity interval sessions generate a great deal of fatigue, and you need to allow time for recovery before you will be able to benefit from another period of intense training; the same goes for any of the workouts and programs in this book. A recovery/maintenance period is necessary after

*Hi Chris
and Team,
Your program
has proven to be
very successful
for me. I knocked
12 minutes off
last year's time
in a 100-km
participation
ride, finishing in
2:44 [22.7 mph]. I
found the program
to be very hard,
and I missed some
sessions (although
I tried not to miss
the PI sessions)
due to being
tired or family
commitments. No
one said it would
be easy though. I
was using a heart
rate monitor for
my training as I
did not have access
to a power meter,
and although not
as responsive,
I still gained a
great deal from
your program. My
fitness, speed, and
staying power have
improved. I will
be using the
program again.*

—*Jeff Jorgensen*

using any one of the programs. Keep in mind, however, that the periods between being on the TCTP don't have to be weeks of easy spinning. You can—in fact I encourage you to—go on group rides, long rides, training crits, and even epic mountain bike rides. Your fitness isn't going to disappear overnight. It's just important that you back off from doing two or three structured, high-intensity interval workouts per week for a while.

Can I go straight from an Endurance Training Block to the TCTP?

At the very least, you should allow 1 recovery week between the end of an Endurance Training Block (Chapter 10) and the start of the TCTP. If you were to finish an Endurance Block on Sunday and start your high-intensity training program on Tuesday, you'd be coming into the program with a lot of fatigue, and it would be difficult to adequately recover between training sessions in the following weeks.

Should I do my interval workouts in the morning, afternoon, or evening?

In more than 30 years as an athlete and a coach, I've yet to see any compelling evidence that one time of day is any better than another for training. However, there's no doubt that individual athletes are better off choosing times that are the least disruptive to their families and professional schedules. If early mornings work for you because you can get up and be done with your training before helping to get the kids fed and off to school, then mornings are your best training time. If you hate mornings but you're a night owl and you have the energy to train after the kids go to bed, then evenings are your best training time. And if you have the opportunity to train in the middle of your workday. . .

well, I'd take it. Personally, I'd rather go into the office early and ride at lunchtime, because it gives me something to look forward to during the morning, and I often return from my midday rides fired up and ready for a productive afternoon. The most important thing is to find a workout time that fits into your daily schedule and enhances what you're able to accomplish during the rest of the day. If your workout time is disruptive, you're more likely to find reasons to skip workouts.

How can I tell if I should end the program before week 11?

Some athletes will be able to maintain their high-performance fitness longer than others, and some may find that their performance starts to diminish as early as the beginning of week 9. The point at which you're no longer able to adequately recover from the intensity of the workouts in the TCTP will largely depend on your fitness level at the beginning of the program and the amount of prior cycling experience you have before starting it. From week 9 to week 11, the weekly workouts do not progress. The workload remains constant because you are working to maintain the fitness you gained in the first 8 weeks. Ideally your power outputs are going to stay the same for identical workouts in weeks 9, 10, and 11. If your power outputs are a bit low one day, that's not cause for alarm. If they get progressively worse as the week goes on, even if it's in week 10, it's time to start your recovery period.

Do I need to repeat the CTS Field Test each time I start the TCTP?

Yes. Whether you're using the training workouts in this book or you're on a year-round coaching program, your fitness will fluctuate over the course of a year. As a result, your maximum sustainable power output will rise and fall, and it's important to repeat the CTS Field Test at regular intervals to make sure your training intensities are appropriate for your current fitness level. Most often, when cyclists use the TCTP twice in one season (in the spring and once again in the late summer, for example), their field test power outputs are higher the second time. As a result, their training intensities are higher, and they make greater progress. Over the winter, riders' power outputs tend to fall more than during a recovery/maintenance period that covers a portion of the summer. (This is because you're more likely to continue riding more hours during the summer, even if you're between periods of structured training.) As a result, field test results in the spring are often equal to or sometimes lower than field test results from the previous summer/fall. This is why a good winter training program is important;

it's difficult to make progress from year to year if your fitness goes backward for 3 months over the winter.

How can I incorporate training DVDs if I'm doing the Time-Crunched Workouts on an indoor trainer?

Many cyclists have a library of training DVDs and ask about substituting DVD workouts for workouts in the program when they have to use an indoor trainer. This is understandable because in addition to the workouts, the DVDs (whether they're ones CTS has produced or someone else's) provide music and encouragement, which makes indoor trainer time more pleasant and often more productive. The answer to the question is yes, you can substitute training DVDs if you're going to be training indoors. However, I think it's best to limit such substitutions to one workout per week, and it's important to choose DVDs that feature workouts that address the same—or at least similar—goals as the training session that was originally prescribed. For example, if you have a PI workout scheduled, look for a training DVD that features short maximum-intensity intervals, even if the exact number of sets and interval durations are a little different. CTS-produced DVDs that fit this description are Tour of California Workouts 2010 and 2011, Max Power, Race Power, Climbing Speed, Race Simulation, Mountain Biking, Criterium, and Cycling for Power. Similar workouts from other companies will often refer to being race-specific, high-intensity, or just plain hard.

If you have SS or OU intervals scheduled and you're looking for a training DVD to use, find one that focuses on intervals that increase maximum sustainable power or power at lactate threshold. These will likely be longer, sustainable efforts of 6 to 15 minutes, but the key is that the intervals are subthreshold or in or around your SS intensity level. CTS-produced DVDs that fit this description are Time Trial, Epic Climbing, Climbing, Climbing II, and Threshold Power, and titles from other companies will often refer to being applicable to time trials or power at lactate threshold.

Can I use the TCTP even if I don't have any specific racing or touring goals?

Sure. The TCTP will prepare cyclists to achieve greater performances in races, centuries, and tours, but it's also an effective use of limited training time even if you're not preparing for a specific event or series of events. If you only have 6 hours available to train, a high-intensity program is the only kind that's going to significantly improve your fitness for cycling. We have athletes who have used the Century programs two or even three times in a year simply to increase the average speed they can maintain on their weekend rides. As I've said all along, the purpose of training is to give you the opportunity to get greater enjoyment from your rides. For some riders that simply means being able to ride faster rather than slower when they get a chance to go for a substantial ride on the weekends, and you can absolutely use this program to accomplish that goal.

How do I adjust the training schedule if I'm racing on a Saturday or a Sunday?

As you may have noticed, several of the training plans in this book have interval workouts scheduled for Saturdays and endurance or group rides on Sundays. Generally speaking, you can replace the Saturday interval workout with a bike race and continue the rest of the program as is. The intensity and variability of the race will do everything the workout would have, and more. However, if you're going to be racing on Saturday, you might want to go out for 30 to 40 minutes of easy spinning on Friday, and throw in three to five 1-minute PowerIntervals just to stay sharp and primed for Saturday. If you're going to be racing on Sunday, you'll want to lighten up the Saturday workout from what's laid out in the training plan. It's rare for an athlete to see a diminished race performance the day after a 60- to 90-minute endurance ride with three to five 1-minute PowerIntervals and two 3-minute OverUnders (2U, 10). Keep recovery equal to the interval times for both types of intervals. In the first 6 weeks of any of the training programs, I wouldn't recommend racing twice in one weekend. After that, if you have the opportunity to race Saturday and Sunday, go for it!

What's the best plan to follow in the 4 to 6 weeks between two TCTP periods?

Although I don't generally believe you need to incorporate too much structure into this 4- to 6-week "off" period, I've been asked to be more specific about the recommendations for it. So here's a breakdown; note that the outline and terms here will make more sense once you have followed the training program at least once.

First week: The week after completing the program should be a recovery week. That means no riding Monday through Wednesday. Start again on Thursday with a light spin for 45 to 60 minutes. Over the weekend, bring the volume back up to normal but don't add structured workouts until the following week.

Second week: Starting the second week, continue riding Tuesday/Thursday/Saturday/Sunday if you can, or more if you're currently riding more frequently. It's important to retain your training time, lest it be siphoned away to other tasks. In other words, the volume of your weekly training won't go down, but the intensity must decrease. During the first 2 weeks that you're back riding (after the recovery week), your rides should be primarily at EnduranceMiles intensity, with 20 minutes spent near the top of your EM heart rate or power range during a 60- to 90-minute ride, 30 minutes during a ride 2 hours or more.

Third and fourth weeks: Incorporate some efforts at or even above lactate threshold, but there's no need for structure. This would be a good time to jump into local group rides, and go out and hit the gas on a few climbs. Once you get back into the program, there will be a lot of structure and a ton of intervals, so take advantage of this time to avoid following a plan. I've found that athletes are

TABLE 4.5 | Maintenance Program

WEEK	MONDAY	TUESDAY	WEDNESDAY	THURSDAY
1	Rest day	Rest day	Rest day	45–60 min. easy spinning
2	Rest day	60–90 min. EM	Rest day	75–90 min. EM with 15 min. at upper end of EM power or HR range
3	Rest day	60–90 min. EM	Rest day	75–90 min. EM with 20 min. at upper end of EM power or HR range
4	Rest day	60–90 min. EM with 10–20 min. at SS intensity	Rest day	60–90 minutes EM with 6–8 PI-type efforts

EM: EnduranceMiles **PI:** PowerIntervals **SS:** SteadyState more likely to be able to focus on high-quality interval sessions during the program if they've been good about reducing the structure of their rides for a while before they start. Otherwise, the constant focus on intervals and structured training just wears them down.

Fifth and sixth weeks: As I mention in Chapter 2 (see the section on "Foundation/Preparation (Maintenance)"), you don't absolutely have to take 6 weeks off, but you should if you can. During these weeks, continue riding as in weeks 3 and 4. Enjoy your rides, avoid too much planning, and keep your volume up while maintaining EnduranceMiles intensity.

I've also prepared a 4-week program (Table 4.5) that you can use as a guide or starting point.

FRIDAY	SATURDAY	SUNDAY
Rest day	Group ride or 90–120 min. EM	90–120 min. EM in hilly terrain
Rest day	Group ride or 90–120 min. EM with 15–20 min. at upper end of EM power or HR range	90–120 min. EM in hilly terrain
Rest day	Group ride or 120–150 min. EM with 30–40 min at upper end of EM power or HR range	90–120 min. EM in hilly terrain
Rest day	Group ride or 120–150 min. EM with 30–40 min. at upper end of EM power or HR range	120–150 min. EM or group ride

The Commuter's Plan for Race-Ready Fitness

Almost immediately after publishing the first edition of this book, I started getting questions about commuting—which for our purposes refers to riding one's bike to and from work. The questions came from two distinct perspectives: the committed commuter who was already riding to and from work 4 to 5 days per week, and the athlete who was so busy that commuting a few times per week was the only way to fit in any training time whatsoever. For the sake of convenience, I'll call the latter group "occasional commuters."

Committed commuters have always faced a problem when it comes to effective training. Riding 4 to 5 round trips to work each week can generate a significant amount of fatigue, making it difficult to commit to additional training-focused rides. To evaluate the workload of commuting, we put a power meter on a coach's commuter bike in Colorado Springs, Colorado. His commute is 4.5 miles, generally flat (about 100 feet of climbing each way), and 80 percent is on a bike path. On average, he accumulates 170 kilojoules of work during his commute, which means 1,700 kilojoules a week if he commutes all 5 days. Assuming 20 workdays in a month, that's 6,800 kilojoules a month. Remember, kilojoules accumulated on the bike are roughly equivalent to the calories burned to accomplish that work, and 1,700 calories a week—nearly 7,000 calories a month—is lot of energy.

Of course, you can look at the energy expenditure of commuting in two ways. From a training perspective you have to consider that 1,700 kilojoule commuting workload when you plan for your total weekly workload. Too often, committed commuters underestimate the impact that their commute will have on their training. They disregard the commute because it feels too short and too easy. But if you were just training and not commuting, and I put an extra 1,700 kilojoules of work into your training plan every week, there's a good chance your training performance would suffer. That's why it's difficult to just add your training on top of a 4- or 5-day-a-week commuting plan.

The other way to look at the energy expenditure of commuting is from a weight management standpoint. Two pounds of fat contains 7,000 calories, and even though you're only burning them in 170-calorie chunks, the cumulative monthly total can be very significant. There's also something to be said for burning calories on a frequent basis instead of one weekly 3-hour ride that burns 2,000 calories. Short commutes burn energy but are less likely to trigger the pre- or post-workout eating habits that often overcompensate for your actual energy expenditure. In other words, for commutes lasting 20 minutes or less most people just get it done and go on with their day without adding extra calories to their meals and snacks.

Occasional commuters, however, have a much easier time integrating training into their commutes. Since the primary purpose of commuting is to find time for training, their commuting days during the week can be scheduled for maximum effectiveness and optimal recovery. You can essentially follow the training plans in Chapter 4 by commuting on Tuesday and Thursday and driving to work Monday, some Wednesdays, and Friday. Complete the workout for the day by extending one of your commutes if necessary. It doesn't really matter if you do the workout during your morning or evening commute, but if your workout is going to be in the evening, focus on keeping a lighter resistance and a higher cadence in the morning. Think of that ride as a chance to loosen up for the evening workout. If your workout is during the morning commute, treat the evening commute as a recovery ride or an endurance-paced ride.

Should Bike Racers Be Commuters?

For bike racers, there is an argument against commuting that goes something like this: The limited time you spend on your bike should be focused entirely on intensities that will enhance your fitness and performance. Therefore, commuting is a bad option because the intensity level is generally too low and the duration is often too short to lead to any productive training stimulus. As a result, you're better off driving your car to work because you're not wasting energy that you could use the next time you get on the bike for actual training.

When it comes to high-volume trainers, I absolutely agree with the above argument. To take it to an extreme, consider the case of the bike messenger/racer. Electronic documents and other factors have largely gutted the bike messenger industry, but they can still serve as an example. Back in the 1980s and '90s, I knew a lot of up-and-coming bike racers who thought that working as a bike messenger would be the best of both worlds: They'd get to train while earning money! Invariably, after one month they were worthless as bike racers. They were on their bikes all day doing short runs as messengers, and then they'd go training. Some reversed it and trained in the morning and then spent the rest of the day being a messenger. Either way, they ended up exhausted, burned out, and miserable.

A more common example is the Masters or Cat. III racer who trains at least 12 hours a week. For these athletes I don't recommend a commute that's more than 10 minutes. If they live a relatively flat 2 miles from work, then go ahead. But a 30- to 45-minute commute each way, on top of a 12-hours-per-week training load, is frequently too much. The additional workload from the commute takes away from much-needed recovery more than the extra miles enhance training.

On the other hand, time-crunched athletes who have relatively short (under 5 miles) commutes should really consider commuting at least 3 times per week. The additional workload will not be high enough to knock your training out of balance, but the extra time on the bike—and, more important, the increased frequency on the bike—will help you have high-quality workouts when it is time to train.

Assuming you have a safe route to ride to your office and back and a secure place to store your bike at work, you can make commuting work for you. And as gas prices go up and roads become more congested, the financial and stress-relieving benefits of bicycle commuting will become even greater.

The Case for Commuting

According to a U.S. Census report published in 2011, the average American (across all methods of travel) spends a little over 50 total minutes a day (roughly 25 each way) commuting to and from work. That's more than 4 hours a week that these people could be riding their bikes and growing fitter and faster.

Then there's the financial benefit of commuting. It's not like you're going to sell your car and only commute, but calculate how much fuel you'd save by commuting 3 days a week. That tank of gas in your car is going to last a lot longer, right? Gas prices are never going back to the days of $1/gallon, so the surest way to reduce fuel costs is to use less fuel. Fewer miles on the car means fewer maintenance costs, too. About the only way you won't save money is on your taxes. You'll still have to pay the registration on your car, and your insurance, and you'll have a lower annual mileage to put on your tax return as a deduction.

Perhaps the best case to be made for commuting has nothing to do with economics, athletic performance, or cardiovascular fitness. Commuting feels good; it's a blast of crisp morning air to wake you up and a relaxing way to spin away the stress of the day on the way home. That's not to say it's all sunshine and roses—sometimes you get caught in the rain or it's ridiculously hot for the ride home. Then again, there are no traffic jams on bike paths.

Understandably, commuting doesn't make practical sense for everyone. If you normally drive 30 miles each way at highway speeds, your commute could take around 30 minutes door-to-door if traffic is light, but it's going to be 90 minutes each way on the bike even if you can average 20 mph. On a regular basis, 3 hours of bike commuting per day is too much for almost anyone to take on, especially anyone who has a family. For an 8-to-5 workday, you'd have to leave the house before 6:30 a.m. and return after 6:30 p.m. We all have days like that sometimes, but I know my wife wouldn't be very happy to adopt that schedule as the norm.

The Commuting Lifestyle

Once you commit to biking to work, you'll need to be aware that you're making a lifestyle change that affects your family life and your work life. You won't be able to rush out of the office to pick up a sick kid from school, snag some groceries on your way back home, or dash off to a business meeting across town. You'll need to set up fallback options with your spouse or significant other, as well as your boss. I've found that as long as you communicate your plans well in advance, you can make it work.

For instance, you could let your boss know that on Mondays you'll drive to the office, and that you'll schedule your offsite meetings for those days. Or you'll schedule the kid's doctor appointments—or your own—for Fridays when you take the car. The TCTP Commuter plan is flexible like that.

The hardest part about commuting is getting started and setting up the scenario that works for you. There are solutions to almost any perceived obstacle. Here are a few; with luck, you will only have to utilize one or two to make your commute work.

Problem: *I live too far from work.*
Solution: Park-and-Ride (only different). Instead of driving to the train station, drive part way to work, park the car, and ride your bike the rest of the way. Sounds silly, right? Not to people who live far out in the 'burbs. The initial part of the drive is fast; traffic only gets really slow when you get into the city. So drive the fast part, park near a bike path, and ride into the city. You might actually beat your normal commuting time!

Problem: *I'm a professional; I can't show up looking like a bike messenger.*
Solution: Drive to work on Mondays and Fridays to drop off and pick up the work wardrobe you'll need for the week. You can also use these driving days to take care of other errands that are inconvenient on a bike. Another option is to leave 2 or 3 pairs of shoes at the office (they're the bulkiest and heaviest item of clothing to carry) and haul the rest of your work clothes in a backpack.

Problem: *I don't want to start my workday sweaty.*
Solution: Having a shower at your workplace makes commuting a lot easier, and

many career professionals who commute will actually skip shaving before they leave the house (more time saved) and shower and shave at work instead. If you don't have a shower at your workplace, see if there's a gym within walking distance. Some will accommodate commuters with special memberships that are essentially for locker room use only.

Problem: *Where am I going to put my bike?*

Solution: More and more businesses and office buildings are recognizing the need to provide safe parking areas for bikes. In some cities there are bike lockers in parking garages, and there are bike shops that cater to commuters by allowing them space in the shop to store their bikes.

Why go to this much trouble? Because in the big picture, even adding 15 to 20 minutes each way to ride is a better use of your time during the week, and it'll allow you to enjoy more quality time with friends and family in the evenings and on weekends.

How will commuting by bike give you more time to spend with your family? Check out the training plans in this chapter. Because the Committed Commuter is riding to work at least 4 times per week, there's only one weekend training ride instead of two. This may seem counterintuitive because the whole point of training is to enjoy weekend rides and races. In the later portion of the program, around weeks 7 through 11, you'll have the fitness to be racing and participating in events. During this period, by all means ride both days of the weekend if you have the chance (although if you do that you may want to skip your Friday commute). But during the earlier portion of the program, you need the rest in order to recuperate from the workload induced by training and commuting.

During the week, instead of trying to schedule two 60- to 90-minute training sessions before or after work, you're adding 15 to 30 minutes to your commute 3 to 5 times a week. Of course, how much time you save depends on how far you have to ride and what terrain and surface streets you need to navigate. What's great about incorporating the TCTP into a commute is that it works whether you ride 2 miles to work or 20. On training days, you'll simply take the long route to and from work, enough to get in 45 to 60 minutes of riding each way.

Physiologically, bike commuting keeps your body primed to ride all week long and will make your weekend rides or races better. Even a daily 4-mile round-trip commute will produce a difference in your Saturday rides. This is because those midweek miles preserve joint mobility and counter the impact of being sedentary most of the week. By this I mean that the body is always adapting to recent stimuli (or lack thereof). Waking up from a good night's sleep, you're rested but not invigorated, and it can take a strong cup of coffee to wake up your senses. A 20-minute ride to work in the morning gets the blood flowing through the muscles (and the brain), warms up joints, and leaves you firing on all cylinders by the time you fire up your computer. This is your body responding to the stimulus of your ride. The ride home undoes your body's subtle adaptation to sitting in an office chair all day.

Without these twice-daily aerobic efforts, the body will start adapting to a sedentary life of sleeping and sitting. But by riding twice a day, you've elevated the platform from where you'll start your high-intensity workouts. As a result, you'll be able to work harder, go faster, and recover more quickly.

Back in Chapter 2, I pointed out a study (Burgomaster et al. 2008) that found no difference in the metabolic adaptations between cyclists who did 6 weeks of 30-second sprints 3 days a week and those who biked 40 minutes a day for 5 days a week at an easy aerobic pace (kinda like a bike commute, right?). The TCTP commuter programs take the commuter's base mileage and fitness and build on them.

If you've read through this book up to now, you might be scratching your head: "But, Chris, you've told me that the TCTP is so intense that I need to take full days off the bike to recover. Yet here you're saying that it's OK to ride 6 straight days a week." That's true, but remember the original TCTP was designed to produce maximum results with as little riding as possible in a given week. It was for people who couldn't spare more than an hour to an hour-and-a-half, twice during the workweek, to train.

This chapter is for dedicated commuters—and that should be all of us— who want to fold a high-results training program into the task of traveling to and from the office. That work/recovery balance is still very important, however, and to manage it you'll still need at least one day off per week (Sunday and/or one workday), and you'll need to commit to riding very easy on some of your commutes.

The Commuter Bike

Ideally, you'd ride your high-performance road bike to and from work, especially if the bike is the one with a power meter. And you can do that if you live in a relatively warm and dry year-round climate. Throw your work clothes in a backpack, install lights for those pre-dawn or post-sunset rides, and you're good to go.

Those of you who face rain and snow throughout the winter will want a bike with fenders and beefier, knobby tires. Unfortunately, many of today's carbon-fiber racing frames don't have clearances for wider tires or full fenders. This means you'll need to use another bike for your commuter.

There are lots of options, from the hipsters' fixies to the racked-out pannier hauler and everything in between. For cyclists who want to commute and train at the same time, it's helpful for your riding position on the commuter to be as close to your racing position as reasonably possible. You might ride on the tops instead of in the drops, but at least the saddle position should be consistent. Cycling is a very repetitive motion, and if you want to gain power in your race position, you need to ride in that position.

Cyclocross bikes offer a good compromise if you can't or won't ride your primary road bike to work. You can typically set them up in a riding position similar to your road position (although the bars might be a little higher), but the frame allows for larger tires, there's room for fenders, and you might be able to get a rack on the back.

If a new bike isn't in your budget, but you've already got a mountain bike, you can make it work. Swap out your off-road tires for hybrid road/dirt tires, and, at a minimum, make sure your saddle position and height in relation to the pedals, and your handlebar height in relation to the saddle height, are the same as they are on your road bike.

Whether you decide to carry your gear in a backpack or in panniers is a matter of personal preference. The pros to using a backpack: It's the least expensive and most versatile option because you can ride your racing bike. If you have to carry your laptop home with you, it's the safest option because your back offers a smoother ride for fragile electronics. And in the winter, the pack acts like a heat trap on your back and keeps you a little warmer. The cons: Wearing a backpack in a road-cycling position isn't always comfortable, and on hot days the pack prevents heat from escaping, which makes it harder for your body to regulate its temperature.

With panniers, the bags that attach to bike racks, you can shove more gear inside and you don't have to worry about strapping a hot and heavy backpack onto your shoulders. The downside is that racing bikes aren't built for racks, and the added weight over the rear wheel can affect your bike's handling. For the out-of-the-saddle PowerIntervals prescribed in the training plans, you'll need to take more care to control your bike.

Whether you use a backpack or panniers, I recommend a supply of dry bags—if you don't have dry bags, try plastic shopping bags—to protect your clothes, work files, or laptop from sweat, rain, slush, or puddle splashes.

Hydration and Nutrition for Commuters

On days when you're only commuting and not adding workouts to your commute, there is really no dietary adjustment needed. You'll burn a few hundred calories commuting, but it's nothing that requires specific fueling to get through. Personally, I like to eat a very small snack with a cup of coffee before I commute, and then I'll eat something more substantial at the office. It works better for me than commuting with a full stomach. Similarly, in the afternoon I don't change my eating habits if I'm commuting home. After all, I'm going home for dinner.

The times when you might need to account for your commute are when you're going to include a hard workout in the ride to or from work, and when you're commuting in very high temperatures. The individual workouts in this chapter may be short, but they'll still take a lot out of you. For this reason, you'll want to pay close attention to what you eat before and after those rides.

If you're training in the mornings, eat a simple breakfast of fruit, yogurt, and whole-grain cereal or toast and drink a tall glass of water. Eat as soon as you get out of bed to give your stomach time to digest the meal before heading out. Fill a water bottle with an electrolyte drink to suck down during the ride. Once you get to work, mix yourself a bottle of recovery drink and consume it before your first cup of coffee (keep a container of drink mix at your office). The quick calories and electrolytes will help you bounce back from the morning commute and start your day alert.

If you're going to turn your evening commute into a training ride, then at least an hour before your ride home—and especially on hot summer afternoons—down one water bottle full of an electrolyte-rich drink. If it's been a few hours since lunch and you're really hungry, a light snack can be a good choice. It's not so much that you need even more energy than the fact that being really hungry makes it difficult to focus on your training. You can suck down a gel or a small granola bar or something similar right before you change into cycling clothes. Make sure you have a full water bottle of an electrolyte mix for the ride home, and after you walk in the front door, make sure

MONITORING PERFORMANCE WHILE COMMUTING

One thing you'll immediately notice when you start commuting with the weight of your work, clothes, and lunch strapped to your back or bike is that you go slower. That's expected and nothing to worry about. In fact, if you're on your road bike outfitted with a power meter, you'll see that even though you're moving slower, you're still producing the same amount of watts at the same perceived effort. What you don't need to do is redline your power output to maintain what you perceive to be an "acceptable" speed.

Lately I've been using the MOTOACTV from Motorola, and it's a perfect training device for the commuting cyclist. When I'm on my SRM-equipped road bike, the MOTOACTV picks up the ANT+ signal from the power meter and displays and records my workout data. If I want data from a bike without a power meter, the device will pick up heart rate. And if I have nothing else, the GPS and accelerometers in the device provide an accurate picture of the impact my activity had on my caloric expenditure for the day. In any of these scenarios, it provides a reality check and keeps me from overexerting myself to match my weekend/training intensities while commuting. It also syncs to an online portal over a wireless network, so I don't have to tether it to get the data off the device.

to down another water bottle's worth of fluids to rehydrate and speed recovery. Three bottles associated with a 1-hour workout may seem like a lot, but when it's hot outside and you're commuting over multiple days it can be difficult to keep up with the hydration demands.

The Commuter TCTP Plans

The core of the Intermediate and Advanced Commuter training plans in this chapter are the Tuesday–Thursday workouts (see Tables 5.1 and 5.2). Compared to the Competitor programs found earlier in this book, the individual workouts themselves are shorter and somewhat simpler. The main difference is that during the build-up to week 8, when you switch to weekend racer mode, you'll be doing high-intensity work going to work *and* on your way home. This allows you to get in up to 2 hours of productive work in a day, a full 30 minutes more than the longest Competitor midweek workout.

On these days, I'm assuming that you've mapped out a route that'll take you between 45 and 60 minutes to complete. If your commute is always greater than 45 minutes each way, you can skip the rides on Mondays and/or Fridays because you're getting plenty of miles in to set you up for a strong weekend performance. If you do ride on those days, just make sure your riding on Friday is very easy. You'll need to conserve your energy for Saturday or Sunday (the plan lists workouts on Saturdays and rest days on Sundays, but you can flip the order if necessary).

Outside of the prescribed workouts' specific time needs (i.e., 45 minutes), just ride your normal commute even if it's only 2 to 3 miles each way. On some days, you'll take the long way to the office to complete your training, but take the short route home. During the two recovery weeks, weeks 4 and 8, you'll have a couple of days of no riding at all. This is sometimes hard for the committed commuter because it actually breaks up the routine and timing of being a commuter. But the extended recovery is important during the training progression, so the disruption is worth it.

A big part of the strategy behind this mix of workouts and distances is to break up your commute and prevent you from falling into the trap of the "same-ride/same-speed" routine. In short, your body becomes very efficient at traveling the same route to and from work each day and stops adapting.

TABLE 5.1 | Intermediate Commuter

WEEK		MONDAY	TUESDAY	WEDNESDAY
WEEK 1	a.m.	Easy commute	45–60 min. EM commute with 2 x 8 min. SS (4 min. RBI)	45–60 min. EM commute with 3 x 6 min. SS (3 min. RBI)
	p.m.		45–60 min. EM commute with 2 x 8 min. SS (4 min. RBI)	Regular EM commute
WEEK 2	a.m.	Easy commute	60 min. EM commute with 2 x 10 min. SS (4 min. RBI)	45–60 min. EM commute with 2 x 8 min. SS (4 min. RBI)
	p.m.		45–60 min. EM commute with 2 x 8 min. SS (4 min. RBI)	Regular EM commute
WEEK 3	a.m.	Easy commute	60 min. EM commute with 2 x 12 min. SS (5 min. RBI)	60 min. EM commute with 2 x 10 min. SS (4 min. RBI)
	p.m.		45–60 min. EM commute with 2 x 8 min. SS (4 min. RBI)	Regular EM commute
WEEK 4	a.m.	Rest day	Easy commute	Regular commute with 3 x 2 min. FP at 100–110 rpms (2 min. RBI)
	p.m.			Easy commute
WEEK 5	a.m.	Easy commute	45–60 min. EM commute with 5 x 2 min. PI (2 min. RBI)	Easy commute
	p.m.		45–60 min. EM commute with 10 x 1 min. PI (1 min. RBI)	
WEEK 6	a.m.	Easy commute	45–60 min. EM commute with 6 x 2 min. PI (2 min. RBI)	Easy commute
	p.m.		45–60 min. EM commute with 10 x 1 min. PI (1 min. RBI)	
WEEK 7	a.m.	Easy commute	45–60 min. EM commute with 7 x 2 min. PI (2 min. RBI)	Easy commute
	p.m.		45–60 min. EM commute with 10 x 1 min. PI (1 min. RBI)	
WEEK 8	a.m.	Rest day	40–60 min. EM commute	Easy commute with 5 x 2 min. FP (2 min. RBI)
	p.m.		Easy commute	Easy commute
WEEKS 9–11	a.m.	Easy commute	45 min. EM commute with 2 x [5 x 1 min. PI (1 min. RBI)] (5 min. RBS)	60 min. EM commute with 3 x 8 min. SS (4 min. RBI)
	p.m.		45–60 min. EM commute	Easy commute

RBI: Rest between intervals **RBS:** Rest between sets **Week 8:** End of progression, really good weekend to race **Weeks 9–11:** Holding on to the fitness **CR:** ClimbingRepeats

	THURSDAY	FRIDAY	SATURDAY	SUNDAY
	45–60 min. EM commute with 3 x 6 min. SS (3 min. RBI)	Easy commute	120 min. group ride or EM	Rest day
	Easy commute			
	45–60 min. EM commute with 3 x 6 min. SS (3 min. RBI)	Easy commute	120 min. group ride or EM	Rest day
	Easy commute			
	45–60 min. EM commute with 3 x 6 min. SS (3 min. RBI)	Rest day	120 min. group ride or EM	Rest day
	Easy commute			
	Regular EM commute	Rest day	60–90 min. EM	Rest day
	Easy commute			
	45–60 min. EM commute with 5 x 2 min. PI (2 min. RBI)	Easy commute	120 min. group ride or EM	Rest day
	45–60 min. EM commute with 2 x [8 x 30 sec. PI (30 sec. RBI)] (5 min. RBS)			
	45–60 min. EM commute with 5 x 2 min. PI (2 min. RBI)	Easy commute	120 min. group ride or EM	Rest day
	45–60 min. EM commute with 2 x [8 x 30 sec. PI (30 sec. RBI)] (5 min. RBS)			
	45–60 min. EM commute with 5 x 2 min. PI (2 min. RBI)	Easy commute	150 min. EM with 3 x 12 min. TL 2/4/6 (5 min. RBI), or fast–paced group ride	Rest day
	45–60 min. EM commute with 2 x [8 x 30 sec. PI (30 sec. RBI)] (5 min. RBS)			
	45–60 min. EM commute	Easy commute	Race, or fast–paced group ride	Rest day
	Easy commute			
	Easy commute with 3 x 2 min. FP (2 min. RBI)	Easy commute	Race, or fast–paced group ride	Rest day
	Easy commute			

EM: EnduranceMiles **FP:** FastPedal **PI:** PowerIntervals **SS:** SteadyState
TL 2/4/6: ThresholdLadders = 2 min. PI, 4 min. CR, 6 min. SS

TABLE 5.2 | **Advanced Commuter**

WEEK		MONDAY	TUESDAY	WEDNESDAY
WEEK 1	a.m.	Easy commute	45–60 min. EM commute with 3 x 8 min. SS (4 min. RBI)	45–60 min. EM commute with 2 x 10 min. SS (4 min. RBI)
	p.m.		45–60 min. EM commute with 2 x 8 min. SS (4 min. RBI)	EM commute
WEEK 2	a.m.	Easy commute	60 min. EM commute with 3 x 10 min. SS (4 min. RBI)	45–60 min. EM commute with 3 x 8 min. SS (4 min. RBI)
	p.m.		45–60 min. EM commute with 2 x 8 min. SS (4 min. RBI)	EM commute
WEEK 3	a.m.	Easy commute	60 min. EM commute with 2 x 15 min. SS (5 min. RBI)	60 min. EM commute with 2 x 12 min. SS (4 min. RBI)
	p.m.		45–60 min. EM commute with 2 x 8 min. SS (4 min. RBI)	EM commute
WEEK 4	a.m.	Rest day	Easy commute	EM commute with 5 x 2 min. FP at 100–110 rpms (2 min. RBI)
	p.m.			Easy commute
WEEK 5	a.m.	Easy commute	45–60 min. EM commute with 6 x 2 min. PI (2 min. RBI)	EM commute
	p.m.		45–60 min. EM commute with 10 x 1 min. PI (1 min. RBI)	Easy commute
WEEK 6	a.m.	Easy commute	45–60 min. EM commute with 7 x 2 min. PI (2 min. RBI)	Regular EM commute
	p.m.		45–60 min. EM commute with 10 x 1.min PI (1 min. RBI)	Easy commute
WEEK 7	a.m.	Easy commute	45–60 min. EM commute with 8 x 2 min. PI (2 min. RBI)	Easy commute
	p.m.		45–60 min. EM commute with 10 x 1 min. PI (1 min. RBI)	
WEEK 8	a.m.	Rest day	Easy commute	Easy commute with 3 x 2 min. FP (2 min. RBI)
	p.m.			Easy commute
WEEKS 9-11	a.m.	Easy commute	45–60 min. EM commute with 5 x 2 min. PI (2 min. RBI) then 5 x 1 min. PI (1 min. RBI)	60 min. EM commute with 2 x 12 min. SS (4 min. RBI)
	p.m.		45–60 min. EM commute	Easy commute

RBI: Rest between intervals **RBS:** Rest between sets **Week 8:** End of progression, really good weekend to race **Weeks 9–11:** Holding on to the fitness **CR:** ClimbingRepeats

THURSDAY	FRIDAY	SATURDAY	SUNDAY
45–60 min. EM commute with 2 x 8 min. SS (4 min. RBI) _____ Easy commute	Easy commute	120 min. group ride or EM	Rest day
45–60 min. EM commute with 2 x 10 min. SS (4 min. RBI) _____ Easy commute	Easy commute	120 min. group ride or EM	Rest day
45–60 min. EM commute with 2 x 10 min. SS (4 min. RBI) _____ Easy commute	Rest day	120 min. group ride or EM	Rest day
EM commute _____ Easy commute	Rest day	60–90 min. EM	Rest day
45–60 min. EM commute with 6 x 2 min. PI (2 min. RBI) _____ 45–60 min. EM commute with 2 x [8 x 30 sec. PI (30 sec. RBI)] (5 min. RBS)	Easy commute	120 min. group ride or EM	Rest day
45–60 min. EM commute with 7 x 2 min. PI (2 min. RBI) _____ 45–60 min. EM commute with 2 x [8 x 30 sec. PI, (30 sec. RBI)] (5 min. RBS)	Easy commute	120 min. group ride or EM	Rest day
45–60 min. EM commute with 8 x 2 min. PI (2 min. RBI) _____ 45–60 min. EM commute with 2 x [8 x 30 sec. PI, (30 sec. RBI)] (5 min. RBS)	Easy commute	150 min. EM with 3 x 12 min. TL 2/4/6 (5 min. RBI), or fast–paced group ride	Rest day
45–60 min. EM commute with 4 x 1 min. PI (1 min. RBI); 6 min. recovery, then 9 min. TL 1/3/5 _____ Easy commute	Easy commute	Race, or fast–paced group ride	Rest day
Easy commute with 3 x 2 min. FP (2 min. RBI) _____ Easy commute	Easy commute	Race, or fast–paced group ride	Rest day

EM: EnduranceMiles **FP:** FastPedal **PI:** PowerIntervals **SS:** SteadyState
TL 1/3/5: ThresholdLadders = 1 min. PI, 3 min. CR, 5 min. SS
TL 2/4/6: ThresholdLadders = 2 min. PI, 4 min. CR, 6 min. SS

We're adjusting the workload of the commutes to focus some rides on being hard enough to stimulate adaptation, and others easy enough to allow those adaptations to take place.

In some of the higher-intensity weeks, I'll have you doing three hard workouts on three consecutive mornings with the afternoon commutes serving as easier recovery or EM rides. The key to these blocks of training is that afternoon ride. Having the opportunity to spin the legs out, increase your heart rate slightly, and increase circulation to fatigued muscles is actually an advantage you have over cyclists who train but don't commute. You get to benefit from an active recovery activity while they are sedentary.

The difference between the Advanced and Intermediate Commuter plans is in the number of intervals assigned on a given day. The timing of the two plans is pretty much equal, but the Advanced plan has more workload because of the increased number or duration of intervals. I recommend new commuters start with the Intermediate plan, as should experienced commuters who are new to bike racing or serious training. Experienced commuters who have already been racers for more than two seasons will probably want to start out with the Advanced plan. Similarly, racers who are Cat. III or higher and/or have many years of racing experience can typically handle the workload in the Advanced plan.

And do yourself a favor on mornings that call for high-intensity workouts by starting the interval sets right after you complete a 10-minute warm-up. This way you'll give yourself a few miles to cool down before you reach the office and stop sweating. Nothing's worse that steamrolling to the office, still out of breath from your last SteadyState interval, and quickly changing into your work clothes only to soak them through because you're still overheated from the ride in.

CHAPTER

6

Cyclocross: A Perfect Application of the TCTP

As you read in Chapter 2, the solid results of Taylor Carrington at the U.S. Cyclocross National Championships proved to me that the TCTP worked and could be shared with a wider audience. And in fact, many 'cross racers now use the Competitor program to great success during the short racing season each fall and early winter. But ever since we began using the TCTP with more racers who are very focused on cyclocross, we have made some subtle but important tweaks to the program to make it more specific to the unique demands and opportunities of cyclocross. It's for that reason I have added this chapter, to take a great training program and dial it in for the specifics of this unique type of bike racing. For Carrington, the plan in this chapter has continued to pay dividends: He used it to ride to a ninth-place finish at the Masters World Championships.

If you live in a region with an active cyclocross scene, consider yourself lucky. You've got a built-in reason for staying on your bike deep into the year and enjoying the rush of competition without burning yourself out. Since 'cross races are short—30 to 45 minutes on average for the majority of amateur events—they provide a great training stimulus that hits your high-end energy systems, and you can be surprisingly competitive with only a few hours of training each week.

The Cyclocross plan has its roots in the Competitor plan; the biggest difference between the two is that you will ramp up more quickly to the point where PowerIntervals become the mainstay of your training. You will also do more of them in a given workout, often in 1 long set instead of split among 2 to 3 sets. Part of the reason is that you'll likely be coming off a summer season of riding. If you were on the TCTP in the summer, you'll have that fitness to build on. If you were on another program or just riding when you could, you're still likely to be more fit in the fall than you were coming out of last winter.

The other reason to concentrate on PowerIntervals is that 'cross events are raced all-out from the starting gun to the finish line. There are no breaks, no times where you can settle in for a few laps or miles and catch your breath. You'll be at your lactate threshold intensity during the *easy* parts of the race; everywhere else you'll be cross-eyed in the midst of lung-busting VO_2 efforts. The races are incredibly hard, but also very short. They are a lot of fun and take a lot of focus, and to prepare your body for that kind of stress you'll need to spend time pushing your body to VO_2max.

Spending more time at VO_2max intensities in training has a few important impacts on your race-day performance in cyclocross races. You may not substantially increase your absolute VO_2max (in terms of the maximum amount of oxygen your body can take in and use in a given period of time). If you start the training program with a VO_2max of 55 milliliters/kilogram/minute (ml/kg/min.), with a little weight loss and some improvement in fitness you might get to 57 or 58 ml/kg/min. But the more important adaptation is the amount of time you can spend at VO_2max and the amount of power you can produce while you're at that intensity. That's what you're after, and that's what the specificity in this program delivers.

The Cyclocross Training Plan

Unlike the other programs in this book, you have the green light to start racing as early as week 4 in this program. Now understand, you won't be in prime shape by then, but in cyclocross racing, you quickly learn that the fittest man or woman on the course isn't always the fastest. The barriers, run-ups, sand pits, and even the weather throw so many variables at competitors that it becomes apparent how valuable racing experience is for success. 'Cross practice is great and is incorporated into the plan, but there's no substitute for racing.

Another reason: 'Cross season is short and only comes around once a year. With almost all other cycling disciplines, there are plenty of races to choose from and you can time the start of your training program to be ready for the specific races you want to be fastest for. With 'cross season, I want you to be able to race as many races as you can get to, because there's not much point in doing cyclocross-specific training and then skipping a bunch of the available races. As I said earlier, the events are short, and the experience you pick up will serve you well once you reach the peak competition during weeks 9 through 11.

For many of the training rides, you can use your road bike to complete the workouts. Of course, if you've been training with a power meter for most of the year, you should be on your road bike so that you can continue to monitor your power readings. If it's relatively easy to swap your power meter onto your 'cross bike, you may want to consider doing more of your training sessions on it because you'll be able to accurately target the appropriate power ranges prescribed for a workout. In the case of OverUnder intervals or ThresholdLadder intervals, a power meter will enable you to lock in on the exact yet subtly different efforts required to produce the most benefit.

Whether your interval sessions are on the 'cross bike or the road bike, there are cyclocross practice sessions in weeks 4 through 7 if you're not racing. During these rides, the idea is to spend 30 to 45 minutes on your cyclocross bike practicing your skills (mounts, dismounts, run-ups, sand, turning at high speed on wet grass, etc.) and then going for a 60- to 90-minute road ride on either that bike or your road bike. In Colorado we have a lot of dirt roads, and many cyclocross racers will spend their long autumn rides on those dirt roads with their 'cross bikes. If you also have dirt roads nearby, I recommend that you get out on them at least once in a while to hone your skills and become more familiar with the way your 'cross bike handles and feels.

TESTIMONIAL

During my first season of 'cross, I couldn't break the top 30. After training with the Time-Crunched Cyclist Program, I placed second overall in the series—and the leader was only one point ahead of me! This year, I've even decided to try road racing. Thanks for the book. It's changed how I do everything on my bike, as well as teaching me about nutrition and the science of how my body functions. Thanks!

—JUSTIN BURTON

Once you hit your prime block of racing, let it all out every time you step to the line. There's no reason to hold back in week 8 versus week 11. The midweek workouts don't ask much of your body, so you'll have plenty of time to recover. Besides, the only thing following the 'cross season is winter and some well-deserved time off. I'd rather see you finish the season on a completely empty tank, and truth be told, so will you.

The Workouts

Cyclocross is a sport that you need to practice. You need to learn how to dismount, lift your bike, flow quickly through a series of barriers, and remount the bike smoothly at full speed. You need to learn how to maintain power and control through sand, mud, and gravel as well as over grass and, sometimes, ice and snow. You'll notice, however, that there isn't a lot of time spent here on specific skill instruction for cyclocross. As with the other programs in this book, my focus is on the physiological adaptations you need to be successful in your races. I'm making the assumption that you are already experienced with cyclocross racing, or that you will utilize resources such as local 'cross clinics and group cyclocross practices to gain hands-on skills instruction. Another good reference for cyclocross skills polishing is Simon Burney's book *Cyclocross Training and Technique*.

On specific training days, you'll ride your 'cross bike to complete PowerIntervals with a dismount and run at the end or doing laps on a makeshift 'cross course you've mapped out. The key word I want you to remember here is "practice." These days are to build skills first, fitness second (see Table 6.1).

PowerIntervals Three types of PIs are used in the Cyclocross plan.

Steady Effort PowerIntervals: With these you take the first 30 seconds of the PI to build up to max power and then hold that effort to the end of the interval. PIs scheduled for Tuesdays, Wednesdays, and Saturdays follow this format.

Training Intensities for PowerIntervals
RPE: 10
HR: 100% max
Power: 101% of highest CTS Field Test average

Peak-and-Fade PowerIntervals: Put your bike in a big gear, stomp on the pedals as hard as you can, and hang on until the end. Your peak power will come in the first 15 to 20 seconds and drop off a cliff for the last 15 seconds.

PowerIntervals with Run-ups: PIs with Run-ups have to be done on your 'cross bike. First, find a stretch of pavement, grass, or dirt (something relatively solid, not sand) leading to a small steep hill (grass or dirt is fine) or a staircase. Start your PI on the bike, following the Steady Effort format, and head toward the hill or staircase. Time your approach so that it does not take longer than 45 seconds to reach the hill/stairs. When you reach the bottom, dismount and shoulder the bike, and then run up the hill/stairs as fast as you can. At the top, remount the bike and take a couple pedal strokes to finish the PI. Take a minute to spin back down to the start and repeat. These are very hard, but effective at making you quicker on your feet when it comes to race-day run-ups.

Skills Practice

On skills practice days, map out or create your own cyclocross loop in a neighborhood park that takes you 3 to 5 minutes to complete. Use sandy playgrounds, hills, staircases, little bits of singletrack, logs, homemade barriers—whatever you can find—to construct a reasonable course. Except for the last 10 minutes, complete your laps at a moderate pace that allows you to focus on technique. Use this time to work on being smooth through a section of barriers, on practicing a variety of inside- and outside-lines through corners, and so on. You might discover that shouldering your bike is unnecessary in some instances. Don't be afraid to try unconventional lines through corners or sand/mud sections. Test the limits of your handling skills and your comfort zone; better now than during the race. During the last 10 minutes or

TABLE 6.1 | **Cyclocross**

WEEK	MONDAY	TUESDAY	WEDNESDAY
1	Rest day	60–90 min. EM with 3 x 8 min. SS (4 min. RBI)	Rest day
2	Rest day	60–90 min. EM with 3 x 9 min. TL 1/3/5 (5 min. RBI)	Rest day
3	Rest day	60–90 min. EM with 3 x 9 min. TL 1/3/5 (5 min. RBI)	Rest day
4	Rest day	Rest day, or 30 min. easy 'cross practice	Rest day
5	Rest day	60–90 min. EM with 8 x 2 min. PI (2 min. RBI)	60–90 min. EM with 15 x 1 min. PI (1 min. RBI)
6	Rest day	60–90 min. EM with 5 x 2 min. PI (2 min. RBI), then 8 min. easy, then 5 x 1 min. PI with Run-up (1 min. RBI)	60–90 min. EM with 15 x 1 min. PI (1 min. RBI)
7	Rest day	Rest day, or 30 min. easy 'cross practice	Rest day
8	Rest day	60–90 min. EM on 'cross bike with 10 x 1 min. PI (1 min. RBI)	Rest day
9	Rest day	60–90 min. EM with 8 x 1 min. PI (1 min. RBI); Run-up optional	Rest day

RBI: Rest between intervals   **Run-up:** During last 15 sec. of PI dismount, run up a hill or stairs, remount to complete PI   **CR:** ClimbingRepeats   **EM:** EnduranceMiles   **FP:** FastPedal last two laps, go all out, hitting the course at race pace. This way you'll test the skills practiced earlier in the workout and see how they work at full speed.

Of course, there are several other types of workouts used in the plan, but here I've only outlined the workouts that are unique to this program. For explanations of training intensities used elsewhere in the book and here, refer to the Index.

THURSDAY	FRIDAY	SATURDAY	SUNDAY
60–90 min. EM with 3 x 8 min. SS (4 min. RBI)	Rest day	Group ride or 90–120 min. EM	90–120 min. EM over hilly terrain
75–90 min. EM with 3 x 10 min. SS (5 min. RBI)	Rest day	30–45 min. 'cross practice PLUS group ride or 90–120 min. EM	90–120 min. EM, or group ride
60–90 min. EM with 3 x 9 min. TL 1/3/5 (5 min. RBI)	Rest day	90 min. EM with 3 x 12 min. SS (5 min. RBI)	30–45 min. 'cross practice PLUS group ride or 90–120 min. EM
60–90 min. EM with 3 x 2 min. PI (2 min. RBI)	Rest day	Race or 30–45 min. 'cross practice PLUS 60–90 min. EM with 8 x 2 min. PI (2 min. RBI)	120–150 min. EM, or group ride
Rest day	Rest day	Race or 30–45 min. 'cross practice PLUS 90 min. EM with 3 x 12 min. OU (1 min. O, 1 min. U), 6 min. RBI	90–150 min. EM, or group ride
Rest day	Rest day	Race or 30–45 min. 'cross practice PLUS 90–120 min. EM with 3 x 12 min. TL 2/4/6 (6 min. RBI)	90–120 min. EM, or group ride
60–90 min. EM with 5 x 2 min. PI (2 min. RBI), then 8 min. easy, then 5 x 1 min. PI with Run-up (1 min. RBI)	Rest day	Race or 30–45 min. 'cross practice PLUS 90–120 min. EM with 3 x 12 min. TL 2/4/6 (6 min. RBI)	120–150 min. EM, or group ride
60–90 min. EM with 5 x 1 min. PI (1 min. RBI), then 8 min. easy, then 3 x 6 min. OU (1 min. O, 1 min. U), 3 min. RBI	Rest day	Race	120–150 min. EM with 3 x 12 min. OU (1 min. O, 1 min. U), 6 min. RBI
60–90 min. EM with 5 x 1 min. PI (1 min. RBI), then 8 min. easy, then 3 x 6 min. OU (1 min. O, 1 min. U), 3 min. RBI	Rest day	Race	90–120 min. EM with 2 x 12 min. TL 2/4/6 (6 min. RBI)

OU: OverUnder   **PI:** PowerIntervals   **SS:** SteadyState   **TL 1/3/5:** ThresholdLadders = 1 min. PI, 3 min. CR, 5 min. SS   **TL 2/4/6:** ThresholdLadders = 2 min. PI, 4 min. CR, 6 min. SS

Race Day

The warm-up for a cyclocross race is critical. Since there's no time to settle in to a manageable pace as in a road race, you need to be primed to go right from the start. The only way that's going to happen is to do a proper warm-up. The 13-minute one laid out for the CTS Field Test in Chapter 3 works very well for cyclocross since it's designed to activate all your energy systems, starting the process of lactate production and—most important—lactate processing. One change: If it's brutally cold, add 5 minutes of EM spinning to the beginning of your workout. I've found that the colder it is, the longer it can take to feel ready to start the harder efforts of the warm-up routine. That extra 5 minutes of spinning can make a world of difference in how your body feels. Obviously, you can't complete the warm-up and roll right into the race, but you do want to complete it as close to your start time as possible.

Since it's going to be cold, bring a jersey, jacket, hat, and gloves that are specifically for the warm-up. You'll start sweating during this time and soaking your clothes, and in the minutes between the end of your warm-up and the start those wet clothes will make you cold, forcing blood to leave your muscles and move toward your core. That's not going to happen to you, though, because after your warm-up you'll change out of most of your wet gear and pull on your warm and dry racing kit. I say "most" because many riders will warm up wearing the skinsuit they'll race in (with the top rolled down), or at least the shorts. It's much easier to swap out tops and accessory items such as skull caps, gloves, arm/leg warmers, and so on than it is to get into a new chamois in the minutes between your warm-up and your race start.

Of all the clothing you're going to wear during a race, pay special attention to your gloves. Keeping your hands warm and dry is critical because if they go numb, everything goes to hell. You'll run into trouble braking, shifting, and steering. Unfortunately, there's no magic answer for what type of glove works best—some of the top racers have gone with scuba gloves or the gloves used by deckhands on fishing boats—but you'll need to figure out which gloves work best for you in the conditions and temperatures you race in. Another reason gloves matter is that your hands are like your body's thermostat. If they're comfortable, the rest of your body is comfortable, and it can focus on powering your muscles instead of fending off the chill.

A great aspect to the short nature of cyclocross races is that if you're mainly doing your local race series you don't really need to focus too intently on race-day nutrition. You're not going to drink or eat during a race because the intensity is so high. Plus, your bike won't have a bottle on it anyway. You might get a hand-up of a water bottle, but at most that'll net you half a bottle of intake. And you don't want to start a race on a full stomach because, again, the intensity is so high. If anything, shoot to start the race on a somewhat empty stomach. It's a bit of a balancing act. You want to be feeling a bit hungry, but not anywhere near bonking. Here's how it works: If you're racing in the morning, have a simple breakfast such as a serving of yogurt, berries, and a banana right after you wake up. Wash it down with a water bottle of fluids, and you should be good to go. This is the same strategy used by runners for shorter distances such as 5K and 10K races. They know their muscles have stored all the energy they need to run a strong race. Same goes for cyclocross.

After the race, well, have at it. The culture of cyclocross is perhaps the best reason to sign up in the first place. Whereas criteriums can be somewhat up-tight affairs, the beer tends to flow freely at 'cross races. You'll probably get heckled, there will be plenty of bells ringing, and perhaps dollar bills stuck in the mud (or other places) that you can try to grab on your way past. That's not to say that racers don't take the training and competition seriously; it just means they know well enough to not take it *too* seriously.

Ideally, grab a bottle of water and a bottle of recovery drink after your race, especially if you plan on racing again the next day. Because of the cold weather and the fact that you didn't eat much before the race, meals such as hearty soups, rice and beans, or breakfast foods (oatmeal, waffles, eggs) will deliver the warmth and fullness you'll be craving. And if someone offers you a good Belgian-style beer—well, that might be a well-earned reward.

Training for Endurance Mountain Bike Races

I will never grow tired of seeing how people experiment and tinker with the training plans outlined in this book. The origins of the TCTP have their roots in bike racing—criteriums and cyclocross races, specifically. And I've heard from many athletes who have used the New Century and Advanced Century training plans to set themselves up for enjoyable 50- to 100-mile event rides or week-long cycling vacations. What I didn't expect was the flood of people who asked for tweaks to the TCTP to train for endurance races such as La Ruta de los Conquistadores in Costa Rica and the 200-mile Dirty Kanza gravel road race in east-central Kansas.

In the years before and since the first edition of this book came out, our coaches have worked with and successfully guided hundreds of mountain bikers through some of the toughest races in the world, including the Leadville 100, La Ruta de los Conquistadores, and the Trans Andes Challenge in Chile. In a growing number of cases we had to utilize the same low-volume/high-intensity training principles employed by the TCTP. We did it because our athletes asked us to try to make it work. We did it because it was a challenge! Most of all, we did it because we wanted to open up opportunities for time-crunched athletes to pursue ambitious goals.

I added this program to the book to fill a need for an efficient training program that can be folded into a hectic work week, splits the all-day weekend ride into two more manageable chunks, and yet still prepares you for the wide range of challenges presented by ultraendurance races.

Be aware that this is not an off-the-couch program that takes you from a life of no exercise to the finish line at Leadville. Before commencing this plan, you should have cycled through either the TCTP Competitor or Century programs and biked through a 4-week recovery and maintenance block (see Chapter 4). The people who achieve the best results with this plan are those who are already experienced cyclists and can leverage some of the long-term aerobic fitness they've accumulated over the years. This program was designed for those looking to tackle a new challenge, one that keeps them riding and enjoying the sport throughout the year.

The Endurance MTB Program

There's a massive difference in the physical demands of racing a mountain bike up and down 10,000 vertical feet over the course of 9 to 10 hours and being able to stay competitive in hour-long criterium races on the weekend. Unlike the weekend racers, competitive endurance mountain bikers are usually logging at least 10 hours a week on the bike. Many riders are more in the 16 to 20 hours a week category. So keep in mind that like the Century plans, this plan isn't likely to produce race-winning fitness for ultraendurance events; there's simply not enough time on the bike prescribed here for a rider to dominate a 7-plus-hour race, much less a mountain bike stage race. Of course, if you prove me wrong, be sure to let me know about it.

To match your expectations to the reality of the program in this chapter, I'm confident that a reasonably experienced mountain biker who follows the plan closely has a good shot at a finishing the Leadville 100 in around 10 hours. Is a sub-9 hour finish possible? Yes, it's been done, but it's a stretch for the program, and the CTS athletes who have accomplished that feat came into the program very fit. Those results assume that you have good weather, no equipment failure, no crashes, and a smart nutrition-and-hydration strategy on race day.

The biggest departure from the other plans in this book is that the Endurance MTB plan (see Table 7.1) requires significantly more weekly training hours. That, of course, leads to the question: How can it still be called a Time-Crunched Training Plan? In essence, the program relies on the same science and utilizes most of the same weekday training structure. That's the part that targets metabolic improvements: an increase in your ability to produce energy from carbohydrate and fat, and an increase in your ability to deliver oxygen to working muscles and process lactate before it starts building up. But then there are the unique challenges associated with long days in the saddle, and there's no other way to prepare for those than with long days in the saddle. The Endurance MTB plan requires no fewer than 7 hours a week throughout its 12-week schedule and maxes out at 13.5 to 14.5 hours of training during week 10. However, the weekday workouts can be completed in as little as 90 minutes.

BACK-TO-BACK TRAINING

The bulk of this plan's training time is devoted to back-to-back multihour rides on the weekends. These aren't overly intense or structured rides, they're what I call "ass-in-the-saddle" rides where you prepare your body for the rigors of 10 hours of riding. By splitting up, say, the 8 total hours of weekend rides in week 8, you're logging a huge chunk of saddle time within 24 hours. When you get on the bike on Sunday, you'll be fatigued, your back and joints will be a bit stiff, and your sit bones (the ischial tuberosities) may be a bit tender. Riding through the soreness and fatigue is an important part of preparing yourself for the final third of long endurance races.

Midweek rides are short—less than 90 minutes—but still intense, and placed on back-to-back days. I planned them on consecutive days to increase the cumulative workload and better replicate the training stimulus from a longer ride. On these longer rides, I'd have a rider completing several 20-minute SteadyState intervals, longer ThresholdLadders, or more Over-Under sets (see Chapter 4 for details on these workouts). When there isn't time to put all that work into one interval session, you can achieve a very similar overload with back-to-back interval days.

Because back-to-back training days serve as the foundation of the Endurance MTB plan, Monday and Friday rest days are even more critical. You

TABLE 7.1 | **Endurance MTB**

WEEK	MONDAY	TUESDAY	WEDNESDAY
1	Rest day	60–90 min. EM with 3 x 8 min. SS (5 min. RBI)	60–90 min. EM with 3 x 8 min. SS (5 min. RBI)
2	Rest day	60–90 min. EM with 3 x 10 min SS (5 min. RBI)	60–90 min. EM with 3 x 10 min. SS (5 min. RBI)
3	Rest day	45 min. easy spinning	75–90 min. EM with 3 x 12 min. SS (6 min. RBI)
4	Rest day	Rest day	Optional: 45–60 min. EM
5	Rest day	60–90 min. EM with 3 x 12 min. OU (1 min. O, 2 min. U), 6 min. RBI	60–90 min. EM with 3 x 12 min. OU (1 min. O, 2 min. U), 6 min. RBI
6	Rest day	60–90 min. EM with 3 x 12 min. OU (1 min. O, 1 min. U), 6 min. RBI	60–90 min. EM with 3 x 12 min. OU (1 min. O, 1 min. U), 6 min. RBI
7	Rest day	60–90 min. EM with 3 x 12 min. OU (1 min. O, 1 min. U), 6 min. RBI	90 min. EM with 3 x 12 min. SS (6 min. RBI)
8	Rest day	60 min. easy spinning	Rest day
9	Rest day	60–90 min. EM with 3 x 9 min. TL 1/3/5 (5 min. RBI)	60–90 min. EM with 3 x 9 min. TL 1/3/5 (5 min. RBI)
10	Rest day	60–90 min. EM with 4 x 9 min. TL 1/3/5 (5 min. RBI)	60–90 min. EM with 4 x 9 min. TL 1/3/5 (5 min. RBI)
11	Rest day	Rest day	60–90 min. EM with 8 x 2 min. PI (2 min. RBI)
12	Rest day	60–90 min. EM with 4 x 2 min. PI (2 min. RBI)	60 min. easy spinning

RBI: Rest between intervals **RBS:** Rest between sets **CR:** ClimbingRepeats
EM: EnduranceMiles **MTB EM:** Mountain climbing rides; see text

THURSDAY	FRIDAY	SATURDAY	SUNDAY
Optional: 45–60 min. EM	Rest day	120–150 min. EM	120–150 min. EM
Optional: 45–60 min. EM	Rest day	150 min. EM	150 min. EM
60–90 min. EM with 3 x 10 min. SS (5 min. RBI)	Rest day	180 min. EM	150 min. EM, or group ride
75–90 min. EM with 3 x 12 min. SS (6 min. RBI)	Rest day	150 min. EM with 3 x 12 min. OU (1 min. O, 2 min. U), 6 min. RBI	150 min. EM, or group ride
Optional: 45 min. easy spinning	Rest day	180 min. EM with 4 x 15 min. SS (8 min. RBI)	180 minutes EM, or group ride
45–60 min. EM	Rest day	4 hrs. MTB EM with climbing	120–150 min. road or MTB EM, or group ride
60–90 min. EM with 3 x 10 min. SS (5 min. RBI)	Rest day	4 hrs. MTB EM with climbing	3 hrs. road or MTB EM, or group ride
60–90 min. EM with 1 x 9 min. TL 1/3/5	Rest day	5 hrs. MTB EM with climbing	3 hrs. road or MTB EM any terrain
Optional: 45–60 min. EM	Rest day	5 hrs. MTB EM with climbing	4 hrs. MTB EM any terrain
90 min. EM with 3 x 12 min. SS (6 min. RBI)	Rest day	6 hrs. MTB EM with climbing	4 hrs. MTB EM with climbing
60–90 min. EM with 4 x 2 min. PI (2 min. RBI), 8 min. recovery then 4 x 3 min. OU (1 min. O, 2 min. U), 3 min. RBI	Rest day	3 hrs. MTB EM with climbing	2 hrs. MTB EM any terrain
60 min. EM with 5 x 1 min. PI (1 min. RBI)	30 min. easy spinning, with 3–5 5 sec. accelerations	Race	Rest day

OU: OverUnder   **PI:** PowerIntervals   **SS:** SteadyState
TL 1/3/5: ThresholdLadder = 1 min. PI, 3 min. CR, 5 min. SS

need them to recover from the training block and give your body time to adapt so you go into the weekend or week feeling fresh and fitter. Don't skip these rest days. Don't use them to make up a workout. If you can't ride on a given day, especially during the middle of the week, skip it and move on. Just try to keep the skipped workouts to a minimum.

If you have time to get in the optional 45- to 60-minute EnduranceMiles (EM) ride in the middle of the week, great. But remember, the intensity for an EM ride ranges from 45 to 75 percent of your threshold power and 50 to 91 percent of your threshold heart rate. Do your body a favor and keep your power and heart rate at the lower end of the EM range for these rides. All I want you to do here is get more time in the saddle and add more miles to your legs.

CLIMBING RIDES

Half of the Saturday rides in the plan call for climbing on your mountain bike. This doesn't mean you have to do climbing repeats up the same trail or dirt road for 4 hours. Aim to spend 40 to 60 percent of your overall ride time (not distance!) going uphill. That means at least 90 minutes of climbing in a 4-hour ride or up to 3 hours of climbing in a 5-hour ride. Now, I understand that it's easy for me to find routes that will accomplish those goals in my hometown of Colorado Springs, while in some areas of the country it's not realistic at all. If rolling hills are what you have, then use them well. And if you live in a truly flat region, you'll have to make do riding into the wind or somewhat over-geared.

WEEK 10

Week 10 is the most demanding week in the program—in this entire book, for that matter. It calls for around 14 hours of saddle time dominated by a 6-hour ride on Saturday and a 4-hour ride on Sunday. Besides the physiological challenges of this weekend block, the stretch of time on your mountain bike—and the long weekend blocks before it—will uncover any issues you have with your gear and with your nutrition-and-hydration strategy. For example, you may discover that your stomach doesn't tolerate sweet gels or sports drinks after 5 hours of riding. If that's the case, you'll need to ensure you have salty or bland food options available for the last half of the race. During my multiple races at the Leadville 100, La Ruta, Trans Andes, and other epic events, I've consumed every GU Energy flavor and product; chomped through baked potatoes covered in salt, breakfast burritos, and other foods; and downed Cokes because the variety helped settle my stomach, provided me with something I was craving, or kept me interested in eating.

Although it is important to keep eating during long training rides and long races, you still have to adjust your consumption based on your energy expenditure. During a hard 2-hour road race, you could burn 850 calories per hour or more, but during a 10-hour mountain bike race your burn rate falls sharply because of your pacing. You're going slower, spending more time at aerobic intensities and less time at intensities at or above lactate threshold. So instead of 850 calories per hour, you may be at 500 to 600 per hour. And you're still only going to want to replenish 20 to 30 percent of those calories (probably closer to 30 percent) by eating and drinking on the bike.

The biggest thing to remember on your long training rides, and even in your race-day nutrition strategy, is that you can come back from a calorie crisis in minutes, but it can take several times as long to recover from a hydration crisis. Calories get to their destination very quickly, so if you get behind with eating and you catch the problem in time you can make a pretty rapid recovery. But it takes a lot longer for fluids to replenish the areas they were pulled from as you become more and more dehydrated or overheated.

With regard to gear, pay attention to the fit of your shoes, gloves, bike shorts, and helmet. Things you don't even notice on a 2-hour ride are annoying at 5 hours, painful at 7 hours, and excruciating at 9. If your apparel or gear is causing discomfort during the long weekend blocks starting on week 8, find solutions to those problems as quickly as possible. You want to have time to get used to new equipment before the race.

Quick tip: After you shower off the grit from Saturday's long ride (or any long ride), apply some Aquaphor to your inner thighs, groin, the area around your sit bones, and anywhere else you've experienced chafing. It's a great product for preventing and treating chafed and irritated skin, especially when you need something to work overnight. Apply more in the morning before you get into your riding shorts.

Quick tip: Pay attention to your bike fit and setup as well. An aggressive position that works great for short track and cross-country races might lead to back, neck, and hand pain during a 10-hour race. You may also want to seek suspension tuning and tire pressure advice from riders experienced with the particular course you'll be racing. The right setup can dramatically improve your levels of comfort and control, which in turn help you go faster!

Road Biking to a Better Mountain Bike Race

You're going to want to do the bulk of your training on your road bike unless you're fortunate enough to have a mountain range out your back door that's riddled with singletrack or forest roads featuring long, sustained climbs that take well over an hour to ride. And if your road bike has a power meter but your mountain bike does not, then you'll definitely want to use it over your mountain bike for the midweek interval workouts. There are a few reasons for this:

- **Time:** It's much faster to roll out of your driveway and start your warm-up at the end of the block on your road bike than ride or drive to a trailhead to get on your mountain bike. You can also knock out a workout on an indoor trainer in the predawn hours if necessary.
- **Terrain:** Even with great off-road options, it's rare to find a trail that allows you to climb all-out for at least 12 minutes. Switchbacks, technical sections, or short downhills can throw off your momentum and wreak havoc with the work you need to do. On the road, you can still reach the intensities outlined in the program even if it's pancake flat.
- **Weather:** When I was a kid I loved to ride in the mud (who didn't?), but now I know that riding muddy trails leads to more erosion, means I have to spend a lot of time cleaning my bike, and increases the wear and tear on my drivetrain. I don't have time for the cleanup and I can't make my training dependent on trail conditions *and* weather conditions, so when time is short I often find I can train more consistently by focusing my interval workouts on my road bike.

Comparisons of data from road bike and mountain bike power meters also provide valuable insight into the pros and cons of dividing time between the mountain and road bikes. We have several elite-level mountain bike racers training and racing with mountain-bike SRM power meters, and one interesting finding is that overall workload and pedaling time (total ride time minus the time when cadence equals zero) is very often lower on the mountain bike compared to the road bike for rides of equal duration. There's a lot more coasting in mountain biking, whereas road cyclists pedal more on descents.

On the other hand, the high-power spikes during mountain bike rides are more frequent and reach higher power outputs. It's not uncommon to see 800- to 1,000-watt spikes in a mountain bike power meter file, and the distribution of points in a cadence/force scatter plot is more spread out for a mountain bike ride.

This means that even if workload is constant between a road and mountain bike ride, the workload was accumulated across a wider range of power outputs and cadence ranges on the mountain bike. There are more high-power, low-cadence efforts (accelerating out of a sharp switchback) and instantaneous power spikes (popping the front wheel over a log).

From a training specificity standpoint, mountain bikers have to ride their mountain bikes. But from an energy system standpoint, you can maintain consistent efforts at the appropriate power levels more easily on the road bike. The crossover point sometimes occurs on forest service roads, if you live in a place where they are prevalent. Living in Colorado Springs, Brevard (NC), Santa Ynez (CA), and Tucson, my coaches are fortunate to have dirt-road climbs that provide the opportunity to maintain road-bike-like consistency for anywhere from 25 minutes to 3 hours. There are other parts of the country, though, where mountain biking is pretty much restricted to laps in a park, and it can be difficult to achieve consistent training efforts in that terrain. If that's the case, I recommend focusing your longer SteadyState, ClimbingRepeat, and ThresholdLadder workouts on the road bike. You can do PowerIntervals on the mountain bike, and you can modify the Over-Unders to be less structured and more like runners' Fartlek intervals on your local trail system.

Until week 10, you have the option of doing one of the weekend rides on your road bike. From week 10 to race day, all your Saturday/Sunday rides should be done on your mountain bike. This gets your butt, back, hands, shoulders, and neck used to your mountain bike's fit.

Using the Endurance MTB Plan for Multiday Events

I developed this plan with a focus on one-day endurance mountain bike races, but it also works for those of you looking to get the most out of a multiday cycling vacation or mountain bike race like the Trans Andes. The volume of back-to-back miles over the weekend closely matches—and in many cases exceeds—the amount of daily saddle time most people face on a cycling vacation.

You can also use it to plan your own epic adventure. In a follow-up to Jim Rutberg and Grant Davis's 2-day, 200-mile weekend in northern New Mexico mentioned in Chapter 9, the two of them set out in September of the following year with Grant's brother-in-law Jeff Klem on a 3-day jaunt along the San Juan Skyway, a 235-mile loop connecting the southwestern Colorado mountain towns of Durango, Ouray, and Telluride. The route rolls through some of Colorado's best scenery, crosses four spectacular 10,000-foot high passes, snakes through tight canyons, and includes a fast downhill that goes on for an unbelievable 50 miles. The area's known as the "Switzerland of the Rockies" for good reason.

To prep for the ride, Grant had used a hybrid modification of the New Competitor TCTP plan with his thrice-weekly bike commute while Jim used the first inklings of the training ideas and workouts outlined in this chapter to get ready for the Leadville 100 race. Jim got through Leadville just fine, took a week off to recover, and then turned his sights to this trip.

During their ride through the San Juans, Grant was pleasantly surprised that his roughly 6 to 8 hours of riding a week had given him just enough fitness to see him through the tour. Jim rode strong over all three days and thoroughly relished every mile. Like his time in New Mexico, the ride in Colorado cemented Jim's love of cycling. Being able to spin up and over towering mountain passes day after day was what the sport is all about.

If you do decide to build your own epic, make sure days 1 and 2 are relatively easier rides. Your "queen stage," a bike racing term for the hardest day in a stage race, should come no sooner than day 3. By then, you'll have settled into the routine of riding long hours each day. Your queen stage will still be hard, but your body will bounce back from it sooner and leave you in shape to face the next day. If you'd put the hardest ride on day 1 or 2, you'd likely ride well but wake up the next day feeling completely thrashed and suffer through that day's miles. And if you try to finish off your week-long trip with a big finale, you're likely to be too exhausted to have fun all the way to the final miles.

High-Speed Nutrition

If I've learned anything over the past 20 years of being a coach, it's that nothing will derail a training program or race strategy faster or more devastatingly than poor nutrition choices. Fortunately the opposite is also true: Making the right nutritional choices will enhance the effectiveness of your workouts and give you the energy to perform at your best on race day. And just as you need to change your training in light of your time constraints, you also need to change your nutritional choices to optimize your performance during the TCTP. As an athlete it's likely that your diet is already substantially healthier than the average American's, but making some changes to the "standard" endurance athlete's diet will help you meet the unique demands of this high-intensity program.

Key Concepts in Sports Nutrition

After publishing an entire book on sports nutrition and nutrition periodization (*Chris Carmichael's Food for Fitness*) and writing extensively on the importance of proper nutrition in optimizing health and fitness (*5 Essentials for a Winning Life*), it's difficult for me to resist the temptation to write an exhaustive treatise on sports nutrition for this book as well. But because this is a book for athletes who are short on time, I'm going to do my best to cut to the chase.

Just to make sure we're all on the same page, let's quickly review the basics. First of all, all the calories you consume come from three macronutrients: carbohydrate (4 calories per gram), protein (4 calories per gram), and fat (9 calories per gram). (Note: To avoid confusion, I use the more common spelling of food calories, using a lowercase *c*, even though the scientifically accurate terminology would either be kilocalories or Calories with a capital C.) These macronutrients directly and indirectly provide all the energy you use to build and maintain your body, perform all your normal bodily functions, and complete all your voluntary tasks, including exercise.

On top of these macronutrients, there are three other items you need to consume to stay alive and healthy: water, vitamins, and minerals. Despite delivering zero calories, water is sometimes referred to as a fourth macronutrient because of its overwhelming importance. In fact, water is probably more important than anything else you consume, because dehydration can kill you in days, whereas you can survive without food for much longer. Vitamins and minerals, known as micronutrients, also deliver zero calories but are necessary in varying amounts for completing the biochemical reactions that keep your body functioning properly.

Your body burns calories every minute of every day, and you are constantly deriving that energy from a mixture of carbohydrate, protein, and fat. The relative percentage of energy coming from each depends on many factors, but for the purposes of this book, I concentrate most on the impact of exercise intensity on fuel utilization. Of the three macronutrients, you rely on protein for a relatively low and constant amount of energy during exercise. Protein is still an important component of an athlete's nutrition program and performance, but under normal conditions a healthy individual derives 10 to 15 percent of his or her exercise calories from protein, regardless of exercise intensity. As a result, and for the sake of simplicity, I will remove protein from the equation and focus on the relative contributions from carbohydrate and fat during exercise.

As I explained in Chapter 2, during exercise your muscles process carbohydrate and fat to produce energy using aerobic metabolism and glycolysis.

Your exercise intensity and fitness directly affect the relative amount of energy being produced by each method. At rest, your body relies on fat for 80 to 90 percent of its energy needs (breathing, digestion, pumping blood, etc.). At very low exercise intensities (20 to 25 percent of VO$_2$max), you're still relying on fat for about 70 percent of your energy. As you reach 40 to 60 percent of VO$_2$max, your fuel utilization reaches about a 50–50 balance between fat and carbohydrate. Athletes with greater aerobic fitness will reach and maintain this 50–50 balance at a higher relative workload than will athletes who are less fit. As your exercise intensity increases from 60 percent of VO$_2$max, the relative contribution from carbohydrate increases dramatically because of the increased reliance on glycolysis. But remember, even when you're burning a lot of carbohydrate at higher exercise intensities (glycolysis burns carbohydrates exclusively), you are still processing fat and carbohydrate using aerobic metabolism. Once you exceed your lactate threshold intensity (70 to 90 percent of VO$_2$max, depending on your fitness level), more than 80 percent of your energy is being derived from carbohydrate.

To put this in perspective, at 90 to 100 percent of VO$_2$max, a 160-pound athlete's caloric burn rate may reach 20 to 24 calories per minute, which means you could burn up to 5 grams of carbohydrate per minute. That might not sound like much, but if you could maintain that intensity for an hour, you would burn close to 300 grams of carbohydrate, and your power meter would show that you produced around 1,200 to 1,400 kilojoules (Kj) of work. At a solid Tempo pace, the same cyclist would burn 9 to 10 calories per minute and produce 550 to 600 Kj/hr. Even during a 1-hour hard interval, that number would only increase to 750 to 850 because of the increased energy expenditure during the intervals. The point is, high-intensity exercise burns a lot of carbohydrate very quickly, and because the TCTP features short, high-intensity workouts, it's important to understand the nutritional implications of relying on so much carbohydrate for energy.

High-Intensity Training Calls for High-Octane Fuel

I often listen to National Public Radio, and that means I've learned a lot from Click and Clack (Tom and Ray Magliozzi, the hosts of *Car Talk*). Over the years, they have answered many questions about the difference between regular and premium gasoline, particularly who needs it and who's wasting money purchasing it. My interpretation of their advice is that it basically comes down to the engine in your car. High-performance cars are built with engines that create higher levels of compression in the cylinders, which produce a bigger bang (literally) every time the cylinder fires. That in turn leads to greater horsepower and more speeding tickets. High-compression engines perform better on high-octane fuel because the fuel burns better at higher temperatures and pressures. Most cars, though, are designed with lower-compression engines that run well on regular gas and don't really benefit from premium fuel.

In some ways, you can look at your body as having two engines that power your training. Your aerobic engine is the smooth and steady automatic you'd find in the family minivan, and your glycolytic system is the turbocharged, smoke-the-tires, 500-horsepower motor in your sports car. Ideally, you'd take great care of both, but the minivan will be more forgiving of poor fuel while the sports car needs premium fuel to deliver top performance. Because the high-intensity efforts in the TCTP rely heavily on the glycolytic system, your success using the program depends on providing your muscles with clean-burning, high-octane fuel.

Carbohydrate is your body's high-performance fuel. There are some people who push protein as the preferred fuel, because high school biology taught us that muscle is made of protein, and therefore you must need to eat protein if you want to use your muscles. Protein is indeed necessary for building and maintaining muscle tissue, but it's not a very good fuel for intense exercise. For the most part, it has to be transported to the liver and be converted into carbohydrate (a process called gluconeogenesis, literally "creating new glucose") so it can be transported back to muscles and be burned as fuel. Protein plays important roles in sports nutrition (muscle maintenance, immune function, enzymes, etc.), but those roles don't include being a primary fuel source for high-intensity, high-performance efforts.

Some people say fat is the best fuel for endurance performance, and they'd be correct if your goal were to ride very slowly all the time. Fat is a great fuel for steady, low- to moderate-intensity exercise, but if you were to take this idea to its extreme and rely solely on fat for energy, the hardest efforts you'd be able to sustain would be at about 60 percent of your VO_2max. Because it can only be burned through the aerobic system, relying entirely on fat would mean that you wouldn't be able to take advantage of the glycolytic system's tremendous capacity for producing energy that contributes to higher speeds and rapid accelerations. In fact, the aerobic system requires a small amount of carbohydrate to burn fat in the first place, so you really wouldn't be able to fuel exercise entirely with fat anyway. From a nutritional standpoint, even the leanest cyclist has fat stores that are sufficient to supply the aerobic engine with the fuel it needs, so although some fat is essential in an athlete's diet, a high-fat diet is not a high-performance nutrition program.

Carbohydrate is your high-performance fuel because it can be used to power aerobic metabolism and is the primary fuel for high-intensity efforts. When you hit the throttle and demand energy for accelerations, attacks, strenuous climbs, or hard pulls at the front of the group, you call on the glycolytic system for a little or a lot of that energy. The glycolytic system only burns carbohydrate, which means you'd better have it on board if you want to continue pushing the pace.

In general, an endurance athlete's diet should be rich in carbohydrate and moderate in protein and fat. I wrote extensively about "nutrition periodization" in *Food for Fitness*; it's the process of matching your nutrition program to the energy demands of your training. Rather than rehash that information here, I'll just say that for the TCTP, endurance athletes need to get 60 to 65 percent of their total calories from carbohydrate, 13 to 15 percent from protein, and 20 to 25 percent from fat.

Your overall carbohydrate intake should be relatively high so that you can replenish the carbohydrate you burn during your workouts. This is crucial because you want to begin each training session with full stores of glycogen (the storage form of carbohydrate in muscles and your liver). Starting training sessions with full glycogen stores increases your time to exhaustion, which is to say that you'll be able to exercise longer before fatigue significantly hurts your performance. Within the context of the relatively short workouts in the TCTP, this means you'll be able to complete more high-quality efforts before you fatigue to the point that you should stop. Completing more efforts at higher power outputs leads to a greater training stimulus and bigger performance gains.

ADJUSTING CALORIC COMPOSITION

My affinity for carbohydrate in nutrition programs for endurance athletes is based on its proven ability to improve workout quality and race-day performance. But there can be a downside to consuming 60 to 65 percent of your calories as carbohydrate; many sources of carbohydrate are not very filling or satisfying, so some athletes end up feeling hungry quite frequently. Choosing low-glycemic carbohydrate sources (carbohydrates that lead to smaller increases in blood glucose or insulin production, like those found in fiber-rich vegetables and fruits, whole-grain breads and cereals, nuts, and some dairy products) can go a long way to solving this problem, but some athletes benefit from taking steps to change the overall composition of their diet.

If you're consuming 60–65 percent of your calories as carbohydrate and you're experiencing frequent hunger between workouts, increased irritability, and notable sleepiness well before bedtime, you may benefit from reducing your carbohydrate intake and increasing the amount of protein you consume. Another sign to watch out for is regularly feeling like you're coming down with a cold the day after a hard workout, even if that feeling goes away later in the day or by the following morning.

If you are going to make this change to your diet, it's important to reduce your carbohydrate intake at the same time as you increase your protein intake; don't just add protein to the diet you're already consuming, because you will end up with a cumulative increase in total daily calories. Aim to bring your carbohydrate consumption down to about 50–55 percent of your total calories while bringing your protein intake up to between 20 and 25 percent. Fat intake should remain around 20–25 percent of your total caloric intake. For most athletes, a shift like this is only a matter of increasing protein intake by 3 to 5 ounces of protein per day (with a relatively equal reduction in carbohydrate intake), but the impact on your lifestyle can be much more significant. And as long as you make sure to follow the carbohydrate recommendations for nutrition before, during, and after workouts, your training performance should remain high and your physiological adaptations will progress normally.

In addition to a diet that's rich in carbohydrate, your nutritional habits directly before, during, and after your training sessions will have a significant impact on the quality of your training sessions, and hence your success with the TCTP.

Pre-workout Nutrition

If you're getting set to complete a difficult training session—a PowerInterval workout, let's say, that's going to include 16 to 20 minutes of effort way above your lactate threshold power output—you're going to want to make sure you're properly fueled up. There are two steps: your pre-workout meal and your pre-workout snack. The differences between the two are how big they are and when they're consumed.

PRE-WORKOUT MEAL

The most important thing about the last full meal you eat before a training session is that it's out of your stomach and digested before you start training. This is especially important for hard interval workouts, because high-intensity efforts tend to be downright unpleasant on a full stomach. A relatively light meal that's rich in carbohydrate (preferably about 70 percent of total calories) is a good choice, because meals that contain a lot of fat or protein stay in the stomach longer and are digested more slowly. That's a good thing if you're trying to feel full longer, but not good if you're about to go out for a hard workout. Table 8.1 lists examples of good foods to choose before a workout.

A good rule of thumb, revised from the first edition of this book to reflect the latest research in this area, is to consume 1–1.5 grams of carbohydrate per

TABLE 8.1	Choosing the Right Pre-workout Food	
GOOD FOODS FOR PRE-EXERCISE MEALS	**LESS DESIRABLE FOODS FOR PRE-EXERCISE MEALS**
High carbohydrate, moderate protein, low fat: pasta, rice, potatoes, sandwiches (roast beef, turkey, peanut butter and jelly), oatmeal, breakfast burrito with eggs and potatoes, pizza (with reduced-fat cheese or less cheese), fruit	High fat and/or protein, low carbohydrate: steak, bacon, sausage, ice cream, chili dogs, cream sauces Low carbohydrate, low calorie: salads (garden, tuna, or chicken), diet soft drinks

kilogram of body weight about 2 to 3 hours before your ride (see Table 8.2). You want to be closer to 1.5 g/kg if you're eating 3 hours before training, and closer to 1 g/kg if you're going to train within 2 hours after your last significant meal. And just as this isn't the time for a high-fat or high-protein meal, you shouldn't try to fill your daily fiber requirement just before a workout, either. The American Heart Association recommends 25 to 30 grams of fiber a day to reduce levels of LDL cholesterol (the bad kind) and reduce the risk of heart disease, but fiber also slows digestion, so it's better saved for other meals.

PRE-WORKOUT SNACK

There is perhaps nothing more important to the quality of your training sessions than what you eat and drink in the hour immediately prior to getting on your bike. Eat the right things, and you'll feel strong, invigorated, and energized. Eat the wrong things, and you'll feel bloated, sluggish, and nauseated. It's difficult to have a great workout when you feel like you're carrying a bowling ball in your gut.

The key here is to choose foods that will get out of your gut and into your blood quickly. There are many choices available, and it's important to experiment with various combinations until you find a solution that doesn't come

TABLE 8.2 | **Recommended Grams of Carbohydrate in Pre-exercise Meals**

BODY WEIGHT, KG (LBS)	3–4 HOURS PRIOR	2–3 HOURS PRIOR	1–2 HOURS PRIOR	0–60 MINUTES PRIOR
	(1.5–2.0 g/kg)	(1.0–1.5 g/kg)	(0.5–1.0 g/kg)	(0.25–0.5 g/kg)
55 (121)	83–110	55–83	28–55	14–28
60 (132)	90–120	60–90	30–60	15–30
65 (143)	98–130	65–98	33–65	16–33
70 (154)	105–140	70–105	35–70	18–35
75 (165)	113–150	75–113	38–75	19–38
80 (176)	120–160	80–120	40–80	20–40
85 (187)	128–170	85–128	43–85	21–43

back up halfway through your workout. Your best options, from both the sports nutrition and practical standpoints, are carbohydrate-rich gels and sports drinks. That's not to say you can't have a great workout on a peanut-butter-and-jelly sandwich or a granola bar, but you're more likely to fully

CAFFEINE AND STIMULANTS

Any discussion of pre-workout and during-workout sports nutrition generates questions about using caffeine and other stimulants as ergogenic aids. I'll keep this simple: Caffeine, in amounts normally found in foods, coffee, and tea, is fine and effective. Furthermore, I haven't seen any markedly better stimulant that's not on the World Anti-Doping Agency's list of banned substances or that doesn't come with a federal prison term for possession. In other words, caffeine works. It's generally safe in reasonable quantities (200 milligrams or less per dose), and its effects and side effects are well-known and predictable. People keep coming out with new additives and claim all manner of performance enhancements for them, but the truth is, plain old caffeine is hard to beat.

The impact of caffeine on athletic performance is twofold. The more important effect is that it improves motivation, alertness, concentration, and enthusiasm. Considering that the workouts in this program are relatively short and decidedly challenging, adding a little caffeine to your pre-workout snack wouldn't hurt. This is especially true if you find yourself struggling to generate the enthusiasm necessary to start a hard workout after 8 to 10 hours at your day job. Caffeine's second impact on performance is that it may help your body liberate more fat for use as energy during exercise. This isn't a bad thing, but it's also not going to have a very significant influence on the effectiveness of your workout.

Interestingly, there's some evidence that caffeine may help accelerate glycogen replenishment when it's consumed immediately after a workout. This opens up the possibility of caffeinated recovery drinks but also means you may have a good excuse for your coffee shop stop after the hard part of your local group ride.

digest the carbohydrates in a gel or sports drink and have all that energy available for your muscles.

I've also found that using specifically designed sports nutrition products makes it less likely that athletes will experience an upset stomach during a hard workout. These products are simply easier to digest; they get out of the stomach and gut faster than conventional foods. To aid in the digestion and absorption process, make sure you consume at least 8 ounces of fluid whenever you eat a gel or bar. Just to show that there is some variability in what works best for individual athletes, my tried-and-true recipe before 2-hour rides is a bit higher in carbohydrate than the standard recommendations. I consume a bottle of sports drink 30 to 60 minutes before training and a gel 10 to 15 minutes before I get on my bike. With a bottle of sports drink and one gel packet, that adds up to about 50 grams (g) of carbohydrate, or 0.65 g of carbohydrate per kilogram (I weigh about 170 pounds, or 77 kilograms). When I get the chance to go out for 3- to 5-hour rides, like those featured in the Endurance Mountain Bike training plan in Chapter 7, I typically choose lower-glycemic-index carbohydrates and foods containing a bit more fat and protein to help me avoid feeling hungry or having a quick spike in energy early in a long ride.

As you can see in the following list, many other snack combinations provide 50 to 75 g of carbohydrate and would work in the hour leading up to training, and you can easily bring this down to 30 to 50 g by consuming smaller portions. Regardless of the option you choose, it's imperative that you consume 16 to 24 ounces of fluid in the hour before training, be it water, fruit juice, or a sports drink.

- 1 cup vanilla yogurt + ½ cup grape nuts + 2 tablespoons raisins
- 1 cup vanilla yogurt + 1 cup fresh fruit
- 1 cup juice + 1 banana
- 1 slice banana nut bread + 1 cup skim milk
- 1 energy bar + 8 ounces sports drink
- Smoothie: 2 cups skim or soy milk + 1½ cups mango or berries + 2 tablespoons soy protein
- 1½ cups multigrain cereal + 1½ cups skim milk
- 1 bagel + 1 banana + 1 tablespoon nut butter
- 1 cup cottage cheese + 8 whole-wheat crackers + 1 apple

Nutrition During Workouts

Short, high-intensity workouts can have a significant impact on your willingness, ability, and need to consume food and fluids while you're on your bike. In particular, hard workouts inhibit your desire and your opportunities to consume either food or fluids, which is part of the reason that your preworkout snack is so important. Fortunately, because of the amount of glycogen you can store in your muscles and the fact that you can only process and utilize about 1 gram of ingested carbohydrate per minute anyway, there is little need to consume any calories during a 1-hour workout.

Before you call or e-mail me to point out the discrepancy between that last sentence and recommendations (my own included) to eat early and often during rides, let me make an important distinction: If you're planning on having a good ride that lasts more than about 75 minutes, you need to consume carbohydrate within the first 30 minutes that you're on your bike. If you're going to be done with your hard efforts and either off your bike or into your cool-down within 60 to 75 minutes, you can complete a high-quality training session without consuming a single calorie while you're on the bike. Will your ride be even better if you use a sports drink or a gel during a 1-hour workout? Maybe, but it depends less on the calories themselves and more on what you can tolerate.

Water is the one thing you can't do without during even a 1-hour training session. Depending on the temperature, humidity, and your personal sweat rate, you can lose up to 1.5 liters of fluid in a 1-hour workout. To make matters worse, high-intensity workouts increase core temperature more than low- to moderate-intensity rides, especially if you're riding indoors, and sweat evaporating off your skin is your body's primary cooling system. Sweating out up to 1.5 liters of fluid and failing to drink will absolutely hinder your performance, resulting in lower power outputs for your intervals and a shortened time to exhaustion.

You also lose electrolytes as you sweat (primarily sodium, but also some potassium and traces of other minerals), so you'd ideally consume a sports drink during even short workouts, but again we have to go back to the concept of tolerance. Studies, including one published in 2004 by Dr. Ed Coyle, have shown that as exercise intensity and core temperature increase, athletes gradually lose their drive to drink and eat. Anecdotal evidence not only

FUELING EARLY-MORNING WORKOUTS

Early morning is a great time for busy professionals to squeeze in a workout. You can be up, on your bike, done with your workout, and showered before your kids wake up or your BlackBerry starts buzzing. A lot of people prefer starting their day with a workout because it's their time for themselves and allows them to begin the day with a positive accomplishment. You may not be able to control much of what happens in the hours afterward, but at least you can go into the day having already checked something valuable off your list.

Fueling early-morning workouts is a challenge, because you haven't eaten for 8 to 10 hours and you burned through about 80 percent of your liver glycogen overnight. All the same, you don't have time to eat and wait around for an hour or more before getting on your bike. So, what can you do to ensure you have a great morning workout?

Keep it simple and small: Your muscles are full of glycogen and ready to go; it's your blood sugar that's low because your liver glycogen stores are mostly depleted. Low blood sugar means less fuel for your brain, and a hungry brain has trouble staying focused on completing intense inter-

supports this but also shows that many athletes experience an upset stomach when they consume calories during very hard workouts. At the same time, adding carbohydrate and sodium to the fluid increases an athlete's motivation to drink and increases the amount of fluid you consume every time you lift your bottle to your lips. And the American College of Sports Medicine recommends consuming 500 to 700 milligrams of sodium per hour of aerobic exercise.

I recommend trying to find a compromise that works for you. Many athletes can tolerate electrolyte solutions and lightly flavored carbohydrate/electrolyte sports drinks, but you shouldn't dilute sports drinks, because that changes the carefully designed concentrations and negatively affects absorption rates. Few athletes have any desire to consume energy gels or solid foods. For short workouts, caloric replenishment may not be much of a necessity, vals at high power outputs. You just need something light that delivers simple and complex carbohydrates, and maybe a little protein to make it more satiating. A sports drink or a gel would work, as would any of the aforementioned pre-workout snacks. If you normally consume caffeine, a shot of espresso or a small cup of coffee isn't a bad idea, but make sure you also consume about 16 ounces of plain water or fruit juice.

Eat first: It always takes a little time to get dressed and set up for your ride, so eat before you start that process. This means eating as soon as you get out of bed, and then going about the business of getting ready to train.

Get started: Early-morning workout time disappears fast, so get started even if it means doing a slightly longer warm-up spin to let your food settle. If you find you really need a little more time to digest your snack before you work out, be careful not to get too engaged in something like reading the paper or checking your e-mail. One athlete I talked to had a good solution: To ensure that he wouldn't get sucked into reading the newspaper, he only brought the first section into the house, leaving the rest of it on the porch for later.

but the need for electrolytes and fluids means that a sports drink is a good idea for high-intensity workouts as long as it doesn't upset your stomach.

Ideally, while riding you'll consume enough fluid to replenish at least 80 percent of the water weight you lose by sweating. That's often not a problem during moderate-intensity Tempo rides, but it becomes difficult when you're in the throes of repeated sets of PowerIntervals. That's OK, and the relatively short nature of your workouts should be taken into consideration. The fluids (and electrolytes) you consumed before your workout will help ward off dehydration during short workouts.

The bottom line is that if you consume nothing else during your hard interval workouts, make sure you drink water. Aim for at least one full bottle over the course of an hour. And as I'll cover in more detail in the next section, good post-workout hydration habits will help you, too.

During longer workouts, events, and races, your nutrition requirements are somewhat different. When you're going to be on the bike for more than 75 minutes, it's important to start consuming carbohydrates, electrolytes, and fluid early on and continue to do so all the way through the end of the ride. The standard guidelines for carbohydrate consumption during endurance exercise call for 30 to 60 grams of carbohydrate per hour, more toward the high end of the range as intensity increases. From watching athletes train for more than 20 years, I can tell you that 50 to 60 grams of carbohydrate in an hour is good for racing and hard group rides, but riders on moderate-intensity group rides and centuries tend to gravitate more toward 35 to 40 grams per hour. And if you're wondering if body weight has an impact on the guidelines, the answer is yes and no. The 30- to 60-gram range is pretty large, and both small and large riders tend to fit within it, but smaller riders often do well at the lower end, and larger riders sometimes need to be at the higher end. That said, a smaller rider who is working hard may need to consume 50 grams of carbohydrate an hour while a bigger rider who is just cruising along may only need 30 to 40 grams.

Another way of gauging calorie consumption during longer rides is as a percentage of your hourly workload in kilojoules. Remember that you start your rides with about 1,600 calories of stored carbohydrate, and you can make that stored energy last longer by adding exogenous carbohydrate in the form of a sports drink, energy bar, or gel while you're riding. But when you see 600 kilojoules on your handlebar display after the first hour, don't make the mistake of thinking you should be consuming anywhere near that number of calories. Instead, you want to consume 20 to 30 percent of your hourly caloric expenditure, which in this case would be 120 to 180 calories or 30 to 45 grams of carbohydrate. And 600 kilojoules an hour is a good ballpark figure for most amateur cyclists. During a hard interval workout you might get up to 800 kj/hr, and at a moderate cruising pace with a group you might be down at 450 to 500 kj/hr.

What do numbers like 35 to 50 grams of carbohydrate per hour mean in terms of items you can hold in your hand? Most energy gels contain about 25 grams of carbohydrate per packet. There is more variation in the amount of carbohydrate found in sports drinks per serving. GU Electrolyte Brew, for example, contains 26 grams of carbohydrate in a 16-ounce serving, or 39 grams in a 24-ounce serving (equivalent to a large water bottle). If you use other brands, you may consume anywhere from the high 30s to nearly 60 grams of carbohydrate in a 24-ounce serving. Most energy bars targeted at endurance athletes contain 30 to 45 grams of carbohydrate per bar. Throughout your training, it's best to diversify your sports nutrition, in terms of type and texture, so you can fuel yourself properly as product availability and your taste preferences change.

Here's a tip for everyone who prefers to use energy gels: You have to drink about 6 to 8 ounces of water with the gel for it to work properly. You're consuming a concentrated, viscous source of carbohydrate, and a few slugs of water will help your body break it down, get it out of the stomach, and absorb it from the gut more quickly. A gel plus water means you'll get to use more of the carbohydrate you just consumed. If you just down the gel and skip the water, you'll absorb most of the carbohydrate, but you'll absorb it more slowly, and some will just keep going toward the other end of the system without any benefit.

In terms of hydration on longer rides, you still want to consume enough fluid to replace at least 80 percent of the fluid you're losing from sweat. The bare minimum is one standard bottle (24 ounces or 500 milliliters) per hour, but that will only be adequate for low-intensity rides on cool days. In warmer conditions, or for any moderate- to high-intensity ride, shoot for two bottles an hour. And if it's a particularly hot day, you may need to add a third bottle. I recommend consuming a carbohydrate-rich sports drink in at least half the bottles you drink during rides longer than an hour. Not only will the taste and sodium increase your drive to drink, but sports drinks are an easy way for athletes to get fluid, electrolytes, and carbohydrates all in one place.

One of the changes we've seen in sports nutrition since the first edition of this book was published has been moving away from all-in-one nutrition to the current trend of separating nutrient sources. The best example of this is the idea of having your hydration on the bike (bottles) and your calories in your pocket (gels, bars, food). This shift has partly come about because of the development of low-calorie electrolyte-rich drinks and effervescent tablets. The benefit to separating fluid/electrolyte intake from carbohydrate intake is that your fluid and electrolyte intake may need to increase significantly based on heat and humidity, but your caloric needs in those conditions won't rise as quickly. Consuming more of an all-in-one sports drink in those conditions sometimes means you're meeting your hydration and electrolyte needs but over-consuming calories to the point where you're at higher risk of gastric distress. If that's happening to you, try separating your sources, putting electrolytes in your bottle and carbs in your jersey pocket.

Post-workout Nutrition

Your nutrition and hydration choices immediately after your rides play important roles in preparing you for successful training sessions in the following days. This is true whether you're on a high-volume, moderate-intensity training program or a high-intensity, low-volume plan, but low-volume trainers have some additional challenges to overcome.

It's likely that you will finish your hard interval workouts having only consumed one bottle of plain water. In my experience, some of you will have chosen an electrolyte drink instead, fewer will consume a carbohydrate-rich sports drink, and very few will have eaten a gel or any solid food. We can talk about guidelines and recommendations all we want, but the reality is, athletes consume fewer calories during high-intensity interval sessions. You can compensate for this somewhat with your pre-workout snack, but after your training session is done, it's very important to focus on nutrition and hydration so you can replenish what you've depleted and give your body the nutrients it needs to recover and adapt. Remember, physiological improvements come during recovery, not exercise, so it is important to fuel your recovery properly.

Start with a carbohydrate-rich recovery drink. These specially formulated mixtures contain the three components you need most: carbohydrate, sodium, and fluid. Perhaps most important, these drinks are easy to consume so that you start getting nutrients into the system faster. Your body is primed to replenish muscle glycogen stores most rapidly within the first 30 to 60 minutes following exercise, and the sooner the better. This period is known as the "glycogen window," and quite literally there are more gates or "windows" open to allow sugar to enter muscle cells during this time. (In recent years some studies have suggested that post-workout recovery drinks or carbohydrate feedings within the first 30 to 60 minutes following exercise aren't

SAVING YOURSELF

Every cyclist has felt it: a sudden emptiness in your gut, a twitch in a calf or hamstring muscle, or a momentary bout of light-headedness. You didn't eat enough or drink enough, and now you're about to bonk, cramp, or both. Your body is telling you it needs food and/or fluids right now, and if you refuse to listen, your body will begin to shut down. You screwed up and you know it, but it's still possible to save yourself and continue to have a good ride or race.

Time is of the essence, and desperate times call for—or at least excuse—desperate measures. If you're bonking, you need carbohydrate fast. That means simple sugars and a lot of them. Down two energy gels right away (with at least half a bottle of water), or try to consume a full bottle of carbohydrate-rich sports drink. If you're out of sports drink or you've already eaten all the food in your pockets, it's time to hit the candy aisle of the convenience store. Everyone has favorite emergency foods; some go for chocolate chip cookies and Mountain Dew while others go for Little Debbie Oatmeal Cream cookies and Coke. My personal favorites are a Snickers bar and a Lipton Iced Tea (sugar and caffeine equal to a Coke but no carbonation). Obviously, these options are not the preferred choices for sports nutrition—they almost always put too much sugar into your belly—but they'll do the trick in a pinch. You'll get a boost from the sodium, sugar, and caffeine, and buy yourself enough time to get back on track with your nutrition.

If you're starting to cramp, you need to look for electrolytes, primarily sodium and potassium. Not all cramps are caused by a lack of electrolytes, but it's very difficult to pinpoint exactly what's causing the situation in your calf while it's happening, and there's an above-average chance that consuming electrolytes will help solve the problem. If it works, you get to keep going. If it doesn't, you'll still have to deal with the cramp, but at least you'll have more electrolytes onboard. In other words, as soon as you feel a pre-cramp twinge in your calf, hamstring, or quadriceps, try to immediately consume 200 to 400 milligrams of electrolytes. Depending on the products available, this can mean one or two energy gels and/or

CONTINUED

CONTINUED

a full bottle of sports drink. Often this will mean consuming more carbo-hydrate than you ideally want at one time, but without the electrolytes you're going to cramp, and right now that's going to harm your perfor-mance a lot more than overconsuming carbohydrate.

Even after more than 30 years as a cyclist, I had to save myself the second time I rode the Leadville 100. It was hot that year, and I made some nutritional mistakes in the first 2 hours of the race because I was too focused on staying with a fast group of riders. About halfway up the 10-mile climb to the turnaround at the Columbine Mine, I felt my right calf twitch. Crap. I had more than 5 hours left to ride, and if I started cramping that far out, it was likely I wouldn't make it to the finish. Over the next 10 minutes I pounded three gels and consumed a full bottle of sports drink, way more carbohydrate and sodium than I or any sports dietitian would recommend. But the reasons we don't recommend such rapid consumption are that absorption rates slow down and there's a significant risk you'll end up with an upset stomach.

In my opinion, when the building is on fire you dump as much water on it as you need to put the fire out, and you worry about the possibility of water damage later. I needed sodium, and if that meant consuming too much carbohydrate to get it, then so be it. If you cramp or bonk it's all over, so if you screwed up and put yourself in a bad nutritional po-sition, eat and drink a lot in an attempt to bring yourself back from the brink. You might have to deal with an upset stomach later (fortunately, I didn't), but the alternative is cramping or bonking right then and there. In other words, you're avoiding an immediate certainty in exchange for a future possibility.

necessary for replenishing. My view is a little different; see the section "Fo-cused Fueling" on page 183 for more about this.)

Sodium helps replenish sodium lost in sweat, but it also plays an impor-tant role in transporting carbohydrate out of the gut and into the blood-stream (part of the reason you rarely see sodium-free sports nutrition products). And, of course, fluid is important for replacing the water that evaporated off your skin to keep you from overheating.

In terms of total amounts, your goal within the first 2 hours after exercising should be to consume 500 to 700 milligrams of sodium and enough water to equal 1.5 times the water weight you lost during the exercise session. In other words, if you lost 2 pounds (32 ounces) during your ride, you should drink 48 ounces of fluid in the 2 hours after you get back. Within 4 hours after training, you should consume 1.5 grams of carbohydrate per kilogram (g/kg) of body weight. For a 170-pound (77-kilogram) athlete, 1.5 g/kg means 115 g of carbohydrate. That can be quite a challenge, especially when you add in the protein and fat calories that come with that carbohydrate, and obviously it becomes even more challenging for heavier athletes. That's why this recommendation is over a 4-hour period. Ideally you should consume the first 50 to 60 grams of that carbohydrate within the first 30 to 60 minutes so you can take advantage of the glycogen window, but the rate of glycogen replenishment doesn't magically go to zero after 60 minutes. Stuffing your face to eat 115 to 135 grams of carbohydrate in an hour isn't fun, nor is it necessary to fully replenish your glycogen stores in time for tomorrow's training session.

Managing Your Total Caloric Intake

One of the greatest aspects of being an athlete is being able to eat like one. When you were on a high-volume training program, you may have burned an average of 600 calories an hour for 12 to 14 hours, meaning you churned through approximately 7,200 to 8,400 calories each week. When you dropped down to 7 hours a week of training without increasing its intensity, your weekly caloric expenditure declined by more than 3,000 calories. More than likely that led to some weight gain, because most athletes are relatively slow to reduce their caloric intake as their training level diminishes.

So, although your primary goal in starting the TCTP may be to improve your cycling performance, you probably wouldn't mind losing a few pounds in the process. That's where your total caloric intake comes into play. The math is simple: You will lose weight if you expend more calories than you consume. However, if you consume too few calories, you will fail to provide your body with the fuel necessary to complete high-quality workouts, recover from them, and adapt to them.

CALCULATING CALORIES

Cyclists place a premium on being lean, especially those who live or compete in hilly or mountainous areas. This presents a significant challenge to coaches and athletes, because it can be difficult to consume enough calories to support training while simultaneously attempting to create a caloric deficit that leads to weight loss. Although I don't recommend attempting to exactly match your caloric intake and expenditure on a daily basis, athletes working with power meters can use the kilojoule information from their workouts to obtain a more precise view of how training affects their total daily caloric expenditure. The kilojoules of work you perform during a cycling workout are approximately equal to the number of calories you burned during that time. Sports dietitians and coaches have long used equations and estimates to calculate an athlete's total daily caloric expenditure, and kilojoule data from power meters allow us to replace an estimate with a real measurement, which leads to a more accurate result.

COMPONENTS OF CALORIC EXPENDITURE

Your total caloric expenditure for a day has three main components: resting metabolic rate (RMR), lifestyle, and exercise. Your RMR can be measured directly in a lab, but it is more often derived from one of several calculations. The energy requirement for your lifestyle (work, daily activities) is calculated by multiplying your RMR by a lifestyle factor, and the calories you expend during voluntary exercise can either be estimated or measured directly, depending on the exercise and the equipment available.

Use the following steps and equations to calculate your total daily caloric expenditure:

1. **Determine your resting metabolic rate (RMR):** Resting metabolic rate (sometimes called basal metabolic rate) represents the number of calories your body needs every 24 hours to complete basic bodily functions and keep you alive. At CTS we prefer the Mifflin-St. Jeor equation, which is a little complicated to calculate but has been shown

to be more accurate than other equations. To find your RMR using this equation, you will need to know your weight in kilograms (1 kilogram = 2.2 pounds), your height in centimeters (1 inch = 2.54 centimeters), and your age in years. Input your data into the appropriate equation below:

Male: RMR = (10 × weight) + (6.25 × height) − (5 × age) + 5
Female: RMR = (10 × weight) + (6.25 × height) − (5 × age) − 161

2. **Lifestyle factor:** Take the number from your RMR above and multiply it by the appropriate lifestyle factor from Table 8.3. Example: A 37-year-old, 5-foot, 10-inch, 150-pound male has an RMR of 1,612 calories. He works at a desk all day and drives to and from the office, so his lifestyle factor is 1.25. Thus his minimum daily calorie needs are 2,015 (1,612 × 1.25).

3. **Exercise calories:** This is where you get to apply the kilojoules displayed on your power meter. If you're not using a power meter, you can use Table 8.4 to estimate how many calories you burn during your workouts. Once you determine your caloric expenditure from exercise, add that number to the total of your RMR times your lifestyle factor to determine your caloric expenditure for the day. Using the example

TABLE 8.3 | **Lifestyle Factors**

ACTIVITY FACTOR	DESCRIPTION	MULTIPLY RMR BY
Very light	Most of workday is sitting or with some standing—relatively little physical activity.	1.25
Light	Work involves some sitting, mostly standing and walking—for example, retail sales—light recreational activity.	1.55
Moderate	Work involves sustained physical activity with little sitting—for example, UPS or mail delivery person—active recreational pursuits. Walk or bike to work.	1.65
Heavy	Occupation is physical labor—very active recreationally. Few jobs fall into this category.	2.0

above, our 150-pound male with a minimum daily calorie total of 2,015 exercises roughly 1 hour a day. Thus he'd need to add 750–800 calories to his diet, for a total of 2,765–2,815 calories burned each day.

It is important to know that the process of calculating total daily caloric expenditure is not perfect. The Mifflin-St. Jeor equation is more accurate than others, but calculations are often less accurate than direct measurements. The lifestyle factor provides a good way to account for the energy demands of your lifestyle, but it's a multiplier, not a direct measurement. Even the one direct measurement you can get from your power meter, kilojoules, doesn't provide a truly accurate accounting of the number of calories you burned, because, as I explained previously, the conversion between kilojoules and calories is close but not perfect. Nevertheless, the process described here, using data from your power meter, is one of the most accurate available outside a laboratory.

KEEPING TOTAL CALORIC EXPENDITURE
IN PERSPECTIVE

Total daily caloric expenditure calculations are most helpful for making sure an athlete's caloric intake is in the right ballpark. The calculations are usually accurate to within a few hundred calories, and an athlete's recollection or tracking of caloric intake is often off by a similar amount. As a result, it's difficult—and typically unproductive—to consider either number exact. Rather,

TABLE 8.4 | **Calories Burned During Workouts**

FEMALE BODY WEIGHT, KG (LBS)	CALORIES BURNED PER HOUR OF AEROBIC EXERCISE	MALE BODY WEIGHT, KG (LBS)	CALORIES BURNED PER HOUR OF AEROBIC EXERCISE
54 (120)	572	63 (140)	731
63 (140)	668	72 (160)	835
72 (160)	762	82 (180)	940
82 (180)	857	91 (200)	1,044
91 (200)	953	100 (220)	1,148

these calculations are best used to reveal, and correct, major disparities between an athlete's perceived caloric expenditure or intake and his or her actual expenditure or intake.

A power meter is a great tool for helping cyclists manage caloric intake. The kilojoules of work you produce are roughly equal to the calories you burned to produce them, so your power meter provides you with a pretty accurate accounting of your daily exercise caloric expenditure. Now, does that mean you should attempt to match your caloric intake to your training session every day? No. First of all, you'd drive yourself—and your spouse and kids—crazy in the process. Second, your body doesn't have a counter that resets to zero at midnight, so there isn't a useful way to match caloric intake and expenditure on a strictly daily basis.

It's better to think about balancing average caloric expenditures and intakes over a 3-day period. The information from your power meter may tell you that right now you're burning 700 calories during your hard interval workouts and 1,500 calories during your slightly longer weekend rides. After you've gained fitness, these numbers may go up to 900 and 1,800, which may mean a slight adjustment to your caloric intake.

For endurance athletes, the desire to become and remain lean sometimes approaches the level of obsession. The TCTP can make weight management even trickier, and in order to get or stay lean—and improve your fitness—as a time-crunched athlete, there are two main concepts you need to keep in mind: focused fueling and caloric overcompensation.

FOCUSED FUELING

When athletes in high-volume training programs are preparing for rides and runs of 3-plus hours, those training sessions impact the size and composition of several meals before and after the workout. The vast majority of the workouts in the Time-Crunched Training Program, however, are 90 minutes or shorter, which means you can be optimally fueled by focusing primarily on good nutrition habits during your rides and in the hour before and the hour after training.

For many athletes, this may mean consuming more sports nutrition products than you do right now. And from both a weight-management and a performance perspective, especially for workouts lasting 2 hours or less, it's better to consume calories you specifically want to use for training as close as possible to the times when you will need them. A small (25 to 35 grams of carbohydrate) snack in the hour before a 60-minute workout staves off hunger and keeps you alert and focused, while the carbohydrate you have stored in muscles takes care of the actual fuel for training. For workouts that are 90 minutes to 2 hours, a 100-calorie energy gel eaten during your workout will enhance the quality of the efforts you perform as little as 10 minutes after that. In these cases, your pre-workout snack and the calories you ingest during exercise have a direct and acute impact on the quality of your training session.

When you focus on fueling immediately before and during your workouts, you can avoid consuming more calories than you need. In thousands of dietary analyses, one pattern that emerges is that many athletes consume more food than necessary prior to relatively short workouts. They increase the size of their meals and the frequency of snacks in anticipation of a workout, but the total caloric increase over a nontraining day can easily be out of proportion to the actual demands of the day's exercise session.

Focused fueling helps eliminate overeating for time-crunched athletes by reinforcing the notion that you don't need to change your baseline eating habits; just add training-specific calories in the hour before training and fuel up early during your longer workouts with high-carbohydrate gels and sports drinks. Because gels are typically only about 100 calories, it's difficult to gorge yourself on them, and you'll be in better shape than if you had downed a 600-calorie treat at a coffee shop.

Following a high-intensity training session, even a short 60-minute workout, I think a recovery drink is a good idea. Strictly speaking, you will completely replenish your muscle glycogen stores within 24 hours of a hard workout whether you take advantage of the glycogen window or not, and some people use that fact as an argument against specific post-workout nutrition products and recommendations. More specifically, there's debate as to whether any specific sports-nutrition guidelines are necessary following workouts that are 60 to 90 minutes in length. In my view, recovery nutrition is still a worthwhile component of your overall nutrition plan, especially since the majority of the athletes reading this book or working with CTS coaches are expending a minimum of 600 calories per interval workout (and many are expending much, much more). At these intensities, the 200 calories from a post-workout recovery drink is fuel that will be used for replenishment, not stored as fat. The sodium in the drink will be used for replenishment, not merely excreted in urine, and there's no downside whatsoever to some additional post-workout fluid replenishment.

The caveat that's missing in the typical argument against post-workout nutrition is that it's probably not necessary for entry-level exercisers and the low-workload or low-intensity general fitness crowd. The need for post-workout nutrition should be based more on the workload and energy demand of the workout, not only its duration.

CALORIC OVERCOMPENSATION

When you're in the Time-Crunched Training Program, one thing to watch is the difference between perceived exertion and actual caloric expenditure. Depending on the training you were doing before you started this program, you may experience a significant change in your total weekly caloric expenditure. If you are coming down off a higher-volume program, you may experience a decrease in your weekly energy expenditure from training. However, if you are transitioning from a training program of relatively equal hours each week, you may experience an increase in caloric expenditure due to the increased intensity found in this program.

As a starting point, I recommend using the calculations listed earlier in this chapter to evaluate your caloric needs on typical training days. Many athletes find they can arrive at some broad generalizations about the caloric demands of different types of training. For instance, after making the calculations several times for lactate threshold workouts, you may find that the numbers always fall within a 50- to 75-calorie range (like 700–750 calories/hour). Going forward, you can then use that range as a general guideline for at least a few weeks, rather than making the calculations day after day.

But regardless of your actual caloric expenditure, you must be careful to avoid a particular trick of the mind that is especially troublesome for endurance athletes: caloric overcompensation. The previous discussion of focused fueling touches on the problem of caloric overcompensation, in that it sometimes manifests as eating too many calories in anticipation of an upcoming workout. But the more insidious aspect of caloric overcompensation occurs after workouts, particularly after training sessions that are difficult. An interval workout that felt really hard may not have cost you as many calories as you think, and the harder the workout, the greater this discrepancy between perceived and actual caloric expenditure.

In interval workouts you work hard during the efforts, but you also recover at low-intensity levels between efforts. The cumulative time at high intensity may be only 16 to 24 minutes out of an hour on the bike. The workout will feel very difficult and will provide the stimulus necessary to improve your fitness, but the actual total caloric expenditure may be relatively low. If you base the size of your post-workout meals on the perceived exertion from your workout, you may very well consume a lot more calories than you need.

Caloric overcompensation is common following strenuous workouts, and it may be even more of a problem when it's cold outside. Hunger is one response to a low core temperature, and it's not uncommon to get pretty cold—and hungry—as you spin your way home after a high-intensity workout outdoors on a cold day. Your body craves calories when you're cold because breaking food down into usable energy creates heat. Triathletes notice the same phenomenon after runs in cold weather, and swimming in general, and there can be a real and additive effect from your body working to stay warm (actually burning more calories) as you're exercising in really cold conditions. As simple as it sounds, a hot shower and getting into warm clothes after a training session can help to reduce this core-temperature-driven desire to overeat.

Overall, I'm not recommending that you match your post-workout meal to the kilojoule number on your power meter or the calorie counter on any other training device; I am only saying that you want to use the data to get a sense of how many calories you're actually burning during workouts.

In my experience, the best way for time-crunched athletes to manage caloric intake, make great training progress, and lose some weight at the same time is to eat as you normally do during most of the day and only make small adjustments to your nutritional habits immediately before, during, and after your training sessions. So while you certainly want to consume sufficient calories to support your training, when you're following a low-volume or lower-frequency training program, it's best to let your pre-, during-, and post-workout sports nutrition habits take care of a significant portion of the calories you burned during your exercise session.

Being an athlete should have a positive impact on your diet, and everything in your diet affects the quality of your training and recovery, so don't take the recommendations above to mean you can gorge on greasy fast food for breakfast and dinner as long as you consume high-quality fuel before, during, and after your training sessions. I'm trusting you to eat a diet that's suitable for an athlete—one that's rich in whole grains, lean proteins, and fresh fruits and vegetables, and relatively low in both total and saturated fat. And if you do that, you'll need to make only minor adjustments to optimally support your training in the Time-Crunched Training Program.

Making the Most of Your Fitness

The point of the TCTP is to enable you to have more fun and achieve greater accomplishments on your bike. You're going to endure a lot of difficult workouts, so it's important that you take advantage of your hard-earned fitness when you get to your goal events or long-awaited epic ride. I want you to go out and win criteriums, power your way through cyclocross races, enjoy a warm summer century, or escape into the backcountry wilderness on your mountain bike. I want those rides to be the best days you have on your bike all year, so fun and fulfilling that they remind you why you're a cyclist.

Jim Rutberg had one of those rides the fall after the arrival of his second child, Elliot. Between the stress of work, a newborn, and the germs his 19-month-old son brought home from day care, he endured a seemingly endless series of summer colds. His training was haphazard at best, and he was lucky if he strung together two rides in a week's time. Yet in the spring he'd used the TCTP as preparation for riding in a four-man team at the 24 Hours of Elephant Rock mountain bike race in Castle Rock, Colorado, and he was hoping to build on that fitness to have a good ride at the Leadville 100 in August.

The 24 Hours of Elephant Rock was a great place for Jim to experiment with the TCTP's application for longer events, because lap times averaged about 40 minutes each. His team decided that each rider would do two to four laps per rotation. Between the short laps and the 4 to 6 hours of recovery between riding sessions, Rutberg came away from the event with lap times that were consistently equal to those of his teammates, who were on higher-volume training programs.

The 24 Hours of Elephant Rock took place in the first week of June, one week after Elliot was born but a week before he was due, and Rutberg's training went off the rails within a week after the race. In late July I asked him to come out to Leadville, Colorado, for a reconnaissance ride of the Leadville 100 mountain bike race course.

I wanted Rutberg along because he'd raced Leadville three times already, but I didn't know he had barely ridden his bike in the previous two months. There were about a dozen people on the ride, and it was a good thing Jim knew the course better than any of the rest of us, because he was off the back on the first climb and didn't see another soul until he reached the Twin Lakes Dam, almost 40 miles later. Surprisingly, he rolled in only about 5 minutes behind the group, but he'd obviously dug very deep in the process. While we continued for another 20 miles up to and back from the race's turnaround point at 12,600 feet of elevation, he wisely chose to stay at Twin Lakes with the cars and support crew we'd brought along for our little adventure.

Two weeks later, despite knowing he was woefully unprepared, Rutberg raced his fourth Leadville 100. The year before, he had beaten me by about 20 minutes and earned a big rodeo-style belt buckle for finishing in fewer than 9 hours. That year it was my turn to finish in fewer than 9 hours and earn my big buckle, whereas Rutberg rode about half an hour slower than his previous best time, to cross the line in 9:13:56. Like all riders who finish in fewer than 12 hours, he earned a smaller buckle for his efforts, but it had clearly been an excruciating effort for a pretty disappointing result.

Immediately following the Leadville recon ride on July 30, Jim had put himself back on the TCTP. He rode the Leadville 100 during week 2 of the program, even though he knew it was too early to see significant improvements in power output, because he was on a mission. He knew things would settle down at work and at home in August, and he decided he needed to do something to salvage his season. The 24 Hours of Elephant Rock had gone OK, but it was stressful because he'd commuted 40 minutes each way between Colorado Springs and Castle Rock during the race so he could help his wife with their newborn and 19-month-old sons. The Leadville recon ride and the race itself were both sufferfests. As he had seen happen with several of the athletes he'd been coaching, cycling was losing its appeal because his efforts weren't being rewarded with fun, powerful, and affirming experiences on the bike.

Grant Davis, a friend and freelance writer who also lives in Colorado Springs, suggested that Jim join him for a weekend of riding in New Mexico. Grant was going because he had a travel piece to write about the Angel Fire Ski Resort, and he was planning on riding the Enchanted Circle Century course on Saturday and the longer Southern Loop the following day. More than 200 miles in 2 days, including several significant mountain passes, would be quite a challenge, but Jim decided it would be a good opportunity to see how he'd do with 6 weeks of time-crunched training in his legs.

Coincidentally, as Grant and Jim started along the Enchanted Circle Century course from Angel Fire, the 31st edition of that ride was starting in Red River, New Mexico. About 50 miles into their ride, the two started picking up stragglers at the back of the century. As Jim, who found he had good legs that day, rolled at 21 to 25 mph along the valley roads and rolling hills toward Taos, a long line of riders joined Grant on his wheel. He felt great, and even though he figured his good legs would disappear on the 20-mile climb out of Taos, he just kept going.

Because they'd started at Angel Fire instead of Red River, Jim and Grant were about 70 miles into their ride when they reached Taos. All that remained was the 20-mile climb out of town and a few miles of descending and valley roads back to the resort. As they turned onto the climb, there was a tailwind, and Jim decided to just keep riding the steady power output he'd been holding and see how long it took for his legs to give out. Within 2 miles, there was no one on his wheel, and he was streaming past the mid-pack century riders. Deciding not to question where the power was coming from, he just kept going and waited to see where he would finally crack. A little more than an hour later, he rounded one final bend, and there was the summit! It was the best climb—in terms of average power output and personal satisfaction—that he'd had all year. He waited for Grant, and the two blasted down the curvy descent and cruised back to Angel Fire.

The following morning, Grant and Jim hit the road again, this time for the 106-mile Southern Loop. Jim struggled badly in the first 20 miles and figured he was in for a long day of suffering, especially when the two reached the bottom of a 10-mile mountain pass that immediately preceded another 20-mile pass. Somewhere on the first climb Jim found his legs again, and he scorched the second pass. Still not knowing where the power was coming from, he pulled along the long valley on the way back to Angel Fire so fast that Grant had little choice but to stay in his draft. Though neither man felt fresh as a daisy during the final 2 hours of the ride, they rolled back into Angel Fire after 106 miles and 6,200 feet of climbing in just under 7 hours.

Jim had had the weekend he was looking for: He rode with the power to enjoy long climbs instead of just survive them. He was the one pulling over valley roads and rolling hills instead of praying to hold on to the wheel ahead of him. Even the weather was perfect, with tailwinds in all the right places. He'd had two rides that salvaged an entire season, 206 miles that justified the thousands he'd put in since January, and one weekend that reaffirmed his identity as a cyclist.

You don't have to win the Tour de France or become a national champion to have achieved something valuable as a cyclist. It's not the event, but what you take away from it, that sticks with you and provides the memories and motivation to continue training.

Taking full advantage of the fitness you'll gain from the TCTP is a matter of using your power wisely. Jim was able to ride back-to-back centuries and have the best weekend of his season because he understood how to adjust his riding habits to his fitness. Likewise, the first season Sterling Swaim used the TCTP he finished in the top 10 of almost every criterium he entered, by basing his tactics and decisions on his understanding of both the strengths and limitations of his training.

To put it simply, the TCTP will give you the fitness to accomplish great things, but not the luxury to waste your efforts. One frequently used analogy in cycling equates hard efforts in races or long rides with matches: You start out with a finite number of matches, and once you burn them all, you're done for the day. This is actually a pretty accurate illustration of what happens. The more times you push yourself over lactate threshold, the faster you burn through your limited carbohydrate stores, and the closer you get to the point where you'll be forced to ride at a relatively slow and steady pace for the rest of your ride. If you burn all your matches three-quarters of the way through a criterium, you won't have any power left for the sprint or to either create or follow the winning breakaway. Burn them all in the first half of the race, and you may not even reach the finish.

When you have the giant aerobic base provided by a high-volume training program, you start a race or long ride with a bigger pack of matches. And although that doesn't mean you *should* waste those matches with frivolous attacks, it does give you the luxury of being able to make mistakes and still recover from them. Riding with time-crunched fitness means you get to start with matches that burn just as bright and hot as everyone else's; you just have fewer of them. You'll have the power to stay with and beat riders who train two and three times as many hours as you do, but you're going to have to pick your battles carefully.

Time-Crunched Tips for Top Performance

When I was 9 years old, I rode my first race, and although I was in the top three coming out of the final corner, I hesitated because I wasn't sure what to do, and finished third. After the race a coach told me, "You can't win if you don't sprint." The statement stuck with me throughout my athletic career and has been very influential in the way I coach. But when I was still a young racer, I simply took it to mean that to win I needed to give 100 percent. Years later I realized the statement had a second, yet equally important, meaning.

With Olympic Trials approaching in advance of the 1984 Olympics in Los Angeles, a lot of motivated athletes were trying to win races in 1983 and the spring of 1984 to get noticed by the U.S. Cycling Federation. I remember there was one rider whom I kept seeing at races; he was a tremendously strong sprinter who had to be considered a threat to win any race that was going to come down to a mass acceleration to the finish line. But neutralizing him was also incredibly easy, because he was a sucker. He was so afraid of missing out on his chance to sprint that he'd chase down every acceleration and potential breakaway in an effort to keep the pack together. Knowing this, the rest of us would launch dummy attacks and watch him burn matches shutting them down. By the time the pace really picked up in the final 20 miles or 20 laps of the race, he was cooked and no longer a threat for anything better than 20th place. He helped me realize that "you can't win if you don't sprint" also means that before you can sprint for the win you first have to *make it to the finish*.

Being a low-volume rider on a high-volume training program means you lack both the endurance to reach the finish and the power to win if you do manage to get there. The TCTP changes that by providing greater performance gains from fewer training hours and giving you the opportunity to not only reach the finish but get there with enough energy to achieve the results you want.

You've been an underdog ever since your priorities shifted to activities like building a career, maintaining a loving relationship with your spouse or significant other, and raising your kids. As your training time diminished, so did the advantages you had over other riders who are still devoting most of their time to riding. I've experienced this firsthand; I see it every time I go out on a road ride with the 20-something-year-old coaches in my office or compete in our local Wednesday-evening mountain bike races, but I don't question for a single moment that I chose the right priorities. The TCTP will help you even the odds and get you back to riding strong and racing for the win, but to be successful you're going to have to ride smarter than you ever have before.

This is going to be guerrilla warfare, in which you're the stealthy and underestimated freedom fighter battling against tyrants who are heavily favored and even more heavily armed. You're going to have to be crafty to conserve energy whenever you can and only display your strengths when they'll do the most good. For those of you who have been cyclists for many years, this may mean some significant changes in the way you act in the pack, but in the end those changes will be essential to getting what you want out of those rides and races. These tips can be divided into two categories: conserving your energy and using your power.

CONSERVING YOUR ENERGY
Learn to Pedal Less

One of the things coaches noticed once we started more advanced analyses of power files was that some athletes spend less time pedaling than others, and often riders who pedal less end up performing better in races. Pedaling takes energy, and if you can save yours while those around you burn theirs, you can gain an advantage over riders who started out with greater endurance. Several of the following tips will help you reduce the time you spend pedaling while still ensuring that you stay with the group, but the basic key is not to pedal unless you have to, and to make each pedal stroke count.

Stay Near the Front of the Pack

Repeated accelerations cause your power outputs to spike, and every time you rev your engine far above your threshold power, you're forcing your glycolytic system to burn through a chunk of carbohydrate. That's material you have to protect, because it's the high-octane jet fuel that powers extreme efforts such as attacks, sprints, and bell-lap-all-or-nothing flyers. If you light the fuse and there's nothing left in the tank, you're going to sputter and flame out instead of rocketing to the win. In any pack-riding situation, the pace is steadiest at the front and gets increasingly variable as you move toward the back. This is most noticeable in a criterium on a tight course, in which riders at the front barely use their brakes, whereas folks at the back of the pack are forced to brake hard before every corner and then accelerate like a dragster just to stay with the field. Fifteen laps of that is enough to spit most amateurs out the back, no matter how strong they are.

The best place to be is about 10 to 25 riders deep in the field, a position often called the "sweet spot." You're close enough to the front that the pace is very steady, and you're able to see and anticipate accelerations and attacks. At the same time, you're deep enough in the field that you're safely tucked into the draft. Staying in this position is important, because maximizing your time in the draft and minimizing the hard accelerations you have to endure will help reduce the total amount of time you spend pedaling.

Take Short Pulls

I understand you want to be a conscientious member of the group and do your share of the pacemaking, but it's also important that your contribution serve your interests as well as the group's. The most important thing you have to do when you hit the front of a large pack or small group is keep the pace steady. If the group is rolling along a flat road at 21 mph, when the rider ahead of you pulls off, you have to pull through at 21 mph. But you don't have to spend 5 or 10 minutes pushing through the wind at that pace just because the four riders before you did. Stay up there for 30 seconds or a few minutes, and then pull off. If this hurts your ego, consider this: How's your ego going to take it if you match the others pull for pull for an hour and then get dropped completely? Or to put it in a more positive light, riding strong on the way home and sprinting for the city limit sign will be a great reward for riding smarter rather than harder.

The idea of taking short pulls brings up the concept of etiquette in pack-riding situations. When you're in a race, I don't care if the rider behind you resents the fact that you're pulling for 30 seconds when he or she is sitting on the front for 2 minutes at a turn. You have every right to be selfish and ride to your strengths, and he has to make a tactical decision about how he wants to deal with it. On the other hand, when you're out with half a dozen buddies on a Sunday morning, it's time to play nice.

The truth is, your riding buddies want you to stay with the group and be an active participant in the ride, and if that means you're going to take shorter pulls, so be it. For them, you taking shorter pulls is a lot better than having to wait for you later or having to ride home slower just so you can keep up.

Choose the Right Partner

A lot of group rides are conducted with a two-by-two pace line, meaning there are two lines of riders led by two pacesetters riding side by side at the front. When it's time to pull off, the right-hand rider moves right and the left-hand rider moves left, and then they back off their pace so the entire group passes between them. Eventually they reunite at the back. Unlike in a rotating pace line, the amount of time you spend at the front isn't entirely up to you. If you're in a group of riders you know well, it shouldn't be too hard to pair up with another rider who will be more than happy to take a relatively short pull with you. If you don't know anyone in the group, you're just going to have to do your best to size up your options as the group leaves the parking lot or coffee shop. If you guess wrong and end up next to a diesel engine of a rider who wants to take 30-minute pulls, remember that it's in your best interest to do the ride that's right for you. Tell him or her you're going to pull off, and do it. The rider will be either fine with it or will find a new partner the next time the group shuffles a bit.

Cruise in a Big Gear

When you're in the draft and cruising down the road, there are many times when a relatively low power output will be all that's necessary to hold your current position. Rather than spin at 120 rpm to put out 100 watts, shift into a bigger gear and bring your cadence down to 60 to 70 rpm. You're basically coasting and just turning your legs over with enough force to keep from decelerating. Your heart rate will come down, your breathing will slow, and you'll burn fewer calories per minute.

When you employ this technique, it's imperative that you pay attention to what's going on around you. One of the greatest benefits to pedaling fast is the ability to respond rapidly to changes in pace or power demand. When your cadence is low, it's much more difficult to suddenly increase your speed in response to an acceleration. Similarly, if you hit a hill you didn't see coming, you'll find that you have to pedal very hard to keep from immediately losing momentum and decelerating into the rider behind you. It's always important, whether you're cruising in a big gear or riding in any other situation, to look far ahead to anticipate stoplights, hills, and changes in pace or wind conditions. Some advance notice will give you the opportunity to shift gears and bring your cadence up so that you're better prepared for the upcoming challenge.

During their rides in New Mexico, Jim Rutberg used this technique to conserve energy whenever he was drafting behind Grant Davis. Instead of the 90 to 95 rpm cadence he maintained while he was pulling at 220 to 240 watts, he shifted into a bigger gear and brought his cadence down to 70 to 75 while maintaining 120 to 130 watts in Grant's draft. Yes, the work (kilojoules) would be the same whether he was producing 120 watts at 90 rpm or 70 rpm, but the aerobic cost of producing that work went down.

Skip Some Pulls

There's a difference between skipping some pulls and sitting at the back of the group all day (otherwise known as "sucking wheels"). Skipping the occasional pull will help you conserve energy but not draw the ire of the group. And if you only sit out every third, fourth, or fifth pull, your fellow riders may barely notice. Better yet, if you're riding with a group you know well, just tell them that's what you're going to do. If they're like most cyclists, they'd rather you contribute a little less frequently for 4 hours instead of taking pulls for 3 and then sitting on the back for the last hour.

To skip a pull, you simply rotate through the pace line until you reach the very back and then let a small gap open instead of moving over into the line that's advancing toward the front. The rider ahead of you will see no one passing and will move over into the advancing line. You move over as that rider does and rejoin the advancing line on his or her wheel. If you're in a fast-moving group in which people are just staring at the rider in front of them, you may be able to make this barely noticeable by dropping back and a little to the opposite side of the advancing line. In other words, if the retreating line is on the left and the advancing one is on the right, you'd move slightly to the left once you reach the back of the retreating line. The rider ahead of you is less likely to see you lingering back there because his focus is entirely on the right side. I've actually seen athletes ride in this position for miles, completely unnoticed, on the tail of a hard-charging group.

On the other hand, in a breakaway group during a race, sitting on or skipping any pulls will certainly be noticed, and you have to be careful not to take advantage of the group's goodwill. If you decide to skip the occasional pull in a breakaway, your companions are more likely to tolerate that if the pulls you do take are good ones. If you're both soft-pedaling your way through pulls and skipping them, it won't be long before someone launches an acceleration to get rid of you. If that doesn't work, someone will take you off the back of the group to open up a sizable gap. Then that rider either will make you accelerate to close the gap (while he or she sits on your wheel) or will jump really hard so he or she rejoins the group and leaves you behind. You don't want to be in any of these situations, because your efforts to conserve energy will inadvertently force you to burn every last match you have. In a breakaway, your best bet is to take short high-quality pulls to contribute to the group's success, and only start skipping pulls if you think it's the only way you're going to get a chance to contend for the win.

USING YOUR POWER

The reason you want to conserve your energy on a ride or in a race is so you can use it to devastating effect later. You need to dispel any notion that riding to conserve energy is somehow less honorable than taking long pulls or launching a dozen attacks. We all see pros bury themselves to set a fast tempo on the front of the peloton, and we admire their strength and dedication, their sacrifices for the team and peloton. But behind them, riders use every one of the aforementioned techniques to save their energy.

In training books and magazine articles, we talk about maximizing your sustainable power output, enhancing your ability to perform repeated maximal efforts, and improving your tolerance for lactate. The message that's often missing is that although you have to ride hard in training to gain these improvements, no matter how strong you become, performing your best in a race, group ride, or long day with your friends comes down to using your power only when you absolutely need to.

Wait

You have the power to match any rider, but you don't have the endurance to go 10 rounds. This means you're going to have to be patient and uncork your best efforts close to the finish. In a criterium, this means saving your power for the final 10 laps, but it doesn't mean you have to just sit on wheels and then sprint. Any move you want to pull, from a 5-lap breakaway to a last-lap flyer or a field sprint, is well within your capabilities. In contrast, launching a solo breakaway from the starting gun is probably not the best use of the kind of fitness you've built.

If you're out for your epic day in the saddle, ride conservatively early on so you have power for the final hour, but then make the decision that it's time to go to work and drain the tank. At CTS we have weekly Coach Rides in which six to eight coaches and I go out for a 3- to 4-hour ride. At different times of the year, some coaches are riding more than others, and we rotate the pacemaking accordingly. I like it when the riders who are only training a few hours a week are smart enough to take short pulls early on and then strong enough to go to the front and rock a few good hard efforts on our way back into town.

Be Smooth

Racing with a power meter is always a good idea, because races provide some of the best information you can use to guide your training. But there are times to look at the power meter and times to ignore it. When you're attacking or jostling for position near the front of the peloton in a race, just focus on getting the job done and look at the data later. On the other hand, when you're out on your own or taking pulls in a breakaway, you can use your power meter to enhance your performance. You want to avoid hard accelerations that force your power output to skyrocket, because these power spikes lead to fatigue quickly. If you're in a criterium, this means taking good lines that minimize the need for braking in the corners. If you have to slow down significantly, shift into an easier gear so you can accelerate using a higher cadence and gradually shift back into harder gears as you get back to top speed. This is less fatiguing than slowing down and then generating a lot of torque by pushing slowly against a bigger gear. Similarly, when you hit a hill, shift into easier gears to keep your cadence up. When riders are in breakaways, the temptation is to pound up a short climb rather than shift gears, but you can see the difference in training: When you muscle your way up a 30-second hill at 70 rpm, your power output is often lower than when you pedal 85 rpm up that same incline, even though perceived exertion may make you feel that the 70 rpm effort was harder.

Special Tips for Century Riders

If you've been a cyclist for 15 years, you know you can get through a 100-mile ride pretty much any day of the week, if you have to. But there's a big difference between being able to complete the distance and having an enjoyable, satisfying, and fun day on the bike. Regardless of how long you've been a cyclist, you will be able to enjoy a 100-mile ride by using the TCTP as preparation. To have a good day, though, it's important to consciously ride a conservative pace for the first 50 miles so you burn your stored energy more slowly and minimize the energy contributions from your glycolytic energy system. Put another way, you want to aim for a "negative split," in which your effort level—and quite possibly your average speed—is greater in the second half than in the first. Interestingly, your average speeds and overall ride times often turn out to be faster when you start out conservatively and finish strong, and that's been shown to be equally true for marathon runners and Ironman triathletes. The other benefit of this strategy is that you finish feeling strong instead of shattered, and riders tend to feel smarter and better about their accomplishment when they finish strong. So, if you're going to be out there for at least 5½ hours, measure your efforts so you come away with a positive experience.

Increase Your Caloric Intake

The rate at which you burn through stored carbohydrate is affected by the amount of carbohydrate you consume before and during exercise. This is important for racers and recreational riders because the longer you can hold on to that stored carbohydrate, the longer you'll have fuel for big efforts. Riding aggressively, either in competition or just during a challenging group ride, you can burn through all your stored carbohydrate in 2 hours or less if you're not replacing energy by eating. Once your muscle glycogen is gone, you're dependent on ingested carbohydrate to deliver enough carbohydrate to working muscles (and your brain). The problem with that is that you can only digest about 1 to 1.5 grams of carbohydrate per minute, depending on the mixture of sugars in the foods you're eating.

When you started your ride, you may have had 400 grams of glycogen (1,600 calories' worth) in your muscles, all of which was available for use as fast or slow as you wanted to burn it. But once the glycogen is gone or running low, you can only partially refill the tank. It would be like starting a long drive with a full tank of gas but only being able to fill the tank a quarter of the way each time you stopped for gas. This is not a perfect comparison, because your aerobic engine also burns fat, but remember, carbohydrate is your high-performance fuel. The more carbohydrate you have onboard, the greater your potential for maintaining higher power outputs, faster average speeds, and more successful attacks.

The CTS coaches and I have found that athletes would benefit from consuming carbohydrate-rich foods and sports drinks sooner than they often do. The adjustment is subtle, however. I'm not suggesting that you overload on calories; you're still limited by the body's ability to digest and process in-gested carbohydrate. The reality is that, despite recommendations to start consuming energy gels and sports drinks in the first 30 minutes of long rides and races, most athletes wait 45 to 60 minutes to start consuming calories. In my experience, this is even more true of veteran athletes who have been rid-ing and racing for many years, and it's not uncommon for some riders to go 90 minutes before eating for the first time.

So, to optimize your performance during long rides and races, follow the guidance provided by Brent Mann, the director of research and development at GU Energy: Consume a carbohydrate/electrolyte gel 15 to 30 minutes be-fore you start your ride, and every 30 to 45 minutes thereafter. This means your first during-ride gel would be consumed about 15 to 30 minutes after you start pedaling. Because an energy gel only contains around 25 grams of carbohydrate, it's also important to consume a bottle of carbohydrate-rich sports drink each hour—or a second gel if you're only drinking water—to bring your hourly carbohydrate intake closer to 60 grams. These subtle changes in the way you fuel your rides will help preserve your stored carbo-hydrate longer and increase your chances of having high-performance en-ergy when you want and need it.

Attack Wisely

Whether you train 6 hours a week or 20, you have to choose the most oppor-tune moments to launch your attacks. The advice in this section is obviously targeted more to racers than to recreational riders, but the tactics I include can also be used to improve your performance at the local group ride. I've written and spoken about launching effective attacks innumerable times over the past 20 years, so some readers may have seen some of the material in this section in magazine articles or *The Ultimate Ride*.

Attack hard and quick: Timid and hesitant attacks don't win races, and you can't afford to burn energy with ineffective, halfhearted moves. If you hold something back when you attack, you're still burning a tremendous amount of energy and generating a ton of lactate. However, you're less likely to be rewarded for your efforts. You're not saving that much energy by at-tacking at 90 percent, so you're better off putting your full effort behind your move and improving your chances of success. Ideally, start your acceleration in the draft from somewhere in the first 10 positions in the pack. If you start from farther back, the riders at the front have enough time to react to your acceleration before you pass them. Your attack should be sharp and violent so that a substantial gap immediately opens behind you. When you create a big gap in the first 15 to 20 seconds, your competitors will think twice about coming after you. If your initial acceleration only nets you 20 meters, though, the gap will look temptingly easy to bridge. The training you've done with this program will give you the power necessary for the explosive efforts that lead to big initial gaps, as well as the endurance for relatively short solo break-aways. I encourage you to launch all-or-nothing solo flyers anywhere in the final 3 miles of a road race (or the final 3 to 5 laps of a criterium). To extend your range, try to get a few other riders to come with you, or use your attack to bridge up to a small breakaway.

Attack when the pace is at its highest: This is a painful proposition be-cause your legs and lungs are already burning, and I'm telling you to hit the throttle even harder. Remember, if you are hurting, so is the rider next to you. There are many instances when one more acceleration is all it will take to make the decisive selection. When riders are already struggling to keep up, they won't be able to accelerate and catch you. The reason riders hesi-tate to execute this tactic is the knowledge that they can't sustain such a high speed for long. But you don't have to. Once the selection is made, the pace of the breakaway and the main peloton usually fall to a fast but sustainable level. You are attacking to cause the selection, and the riders you leave behind are there because you pushed them beyond their limits. They may be able to come after you once they recover, but by that time the gap will have grown, and bridging may again push them past their limits.

Choose the best location: Where you choose to leave the peloton behind influences your chances of success. The general rule of thumb is to attack in a place where your effort will quickly result in a significant gap and maximize the effort required to bring you back.

- **The steepest pitch:** Probably the single most effective place to attack is on the steepest pitch of a climb. You can put meters between yourself and your nearest competitor with every pedal stroke, and chasing you down takes an enormous effort from all involved. This is where a high

Power-to-Weight Ratio (PWR) really pays off, because it gives you the ability to accelerate a lot faster than a rider who has a lower PWR. The steeper the pitch, the greater the impact of gravity, hence the greater your advantage. Bigger riders with big diesel-type engines can sometimes generate tremendous wattage and climb very fast, but they tend to struggle with rapid accelerations because their size limits their PWR. Simply put, push the pace on the climb, then put the final nail in the other riders' coffins with a decisive attack at the hardest point.

- **Into a corner:** Sometimes not slowing down works better than working to go faster. Make a hard and quick acceleration off the front of the peloton in the straightaway shortly before a turn (50 to 75 meters). The sharper and tighter the turn, the better this will work. The idea is to get out front so you can take the absolute fastest route through the turn. You're hoping the peloton will be more cautious through the turn, giving you a critical few seconds to establish a gap. This is a risky move because you are pushing your cornering skills and the laws of physics to their limits. If it works, you can win. If it doesn't, you may end up in the barriers. Again, this also works best when the corner's exit is uphill. You're carrying more momentum into the climb, and the pitch makes it harder for anyone to accelerate up to you.

- **Tight terrain:** When the peloton can see you dangling just in front of them, they are motivated to come after you. If you're out of sight, you're out of mind, and there's less motivation to chase you. On a long, straight road you have to be almost a minute ahead to be out of sight, so use a curvy or technically demanding section of road to establish your lead before emerging back onto open roads. Besides the factor of being out of sight, it is harder to organize an efficient chase through corners and urban areas. By the time the peloton gets organized, you're gone. If you're in a criterium, you need a lead at least as long as the longest straightaway. Tight courses are best for these breakaways because the corners help to diminish the pack's momentum. On open courses, the pack's collective strength gives it a big advantage over a small breakaway group, but narrow criterium courses with tight turns level the playing field and sometimes swing the advantage to the break.

Bridge the gap: Bridging a gap is really a form of launching an attack; it's just an attack in response to an earlier one. Ideally, you'd always be near the front when an attack happens so you can accelerate with it if you choose, but we all know you're not always going to be in the perfect position. If you miss it by a few seconds, still go for it, but realize you're going to have to dig deep because you have some ground to make up. If you miss the attack completely, wait until the gap is small but established before your attempt to cross it. If the gap is too small, you may merely fill the hole between the fledgling breakaway and the peloton and inadvertently pull the entire field up to the break.

If the gap has already grown to more than 20 seconds, your initial acceleration probably won't take you all the way across. Attack as if you are initiating a move of your own and then quickly settle down into a pace higher than your normal time trial pace. You will only reach the breakaway if you are going faster than it is, so for a period of 1 to 2 minutes you have to sustain a speed higher than that of the field and the breakaway.

Bridging gaps of more than 1 minute is very challenging. To be successful you have to commit to a sustained, all-out effort lasting several minutes, and as a rider on a low-volume training program, it's important to realize that as a solo effort this may be an all-or-nothing proposition. Bring along some help and essentially create a second breakaway group chasing the first.

However and whenever you decide to bridge a gap, there is a chance you will get stuck in no-man's-land. When you realize you are not gaining on the breakaway, you have to quickly assess the chances of successfully reaching it. Right or wrong, make the decision quickly, because sitting 30 seconds in front of the peloton and 30 seconds behind the break for 5 minutes is a huge waste of energy.

Don't Be Afraid to Light Your Last Match

When it's time to burn matches, do it with confidence and conviction. You have worked hard for your fitness, it's there and it's real, and unlike athletes on high-volume training programs, you don't have the luxury of having big power for months at a time. Now, more than ever before, you have to leave everything out there on the road or trail. These are the days and experiences that become part of your "highlight reel" for the year—the rides you joke about with friends over cold beers on the back porch, and the races that make you smile and dig a little deeper when you're on an indoor trainer in January. Above all, honor the work you've done by riding with intelligence and courage. Dare to go for the win instead of sitting in the pack, charge up the hard climb to feel the exhilaration of the effort, and attack to leave them all behind.

"It took me a few races to really get the confidence to lay it all on the line," Sterling told me during a visit to our Colorado Springs training facility. "I had this idea I was more fragile than before, that I had to be extremely cautious with my efforts. Over a period of weeks, though, I started riding more and more aggressively and found I had more than enough power and endurance to race the way I wanted to. In truth, the experience showed me that I should have been riding smarter all along."

Supplementing Your Training: Endurance Blocks

Every once in a while, the Fates converge and provide you with an opportunity to pack a lot of high-volume rides into a reasonably short period of time. Perhaps your spouse takes the kids to his or her parents' house for 2 weeks, or you get assigned a weeklong business trip in a prime riding area like Tucson, Arizona, or Asheville, North Carolina. Funny as it sounds, athletes who become accustomed to following training plans sometimes get confused about how to approach such a training windfall. The big question is: Do you change your program, or stick to the schedule you're already on?

Unless you're in the middle of the TCTP, with a series of races or an important goal event coming up in a few weeks, I recommend taking advantage of an unexpected increase in available training time by completing an Endurance Training Block. Although research and anecdotal evidence support the use of a low-volume, high-intensity training program for developing superior cycling fitness, there is also much to be gained from moderate-intensity endurance rides if you have the time to complete them. And honestly, even if there weren't, you'd be a fool to pass up the chance to spend more time out on your bike. After all, the whole point of training is to enable you to get out there and enjoy as much time as you can riding.

There are two approaches to an Endurance Training Block: You can use it for focused training, or you can just go ride your bike. Fortunately, the two approaches are very similar in execution. The key is to remember that as volume increases, intensity should decrease. When you have the opportunity to ride 2 to 5 hours a day for several days in a row, you need to be conscious of the fatigue that will accumulate and build from day to day. If you get too excited and go out and throttle yourself on day 1, you'll be cooked by day 3. Rides after this will become progressively slower, more difficult, and less fun.

In working with a wide variety of cyclists, CTS coaches have discovered that it's not uncommon for riders to find themselves, at least once a year, with a 2-week period in which they have almost unlimited training time. In response, I have developed a 2-week Endurance Training Block that incorporates longer rides, a few structured workouts to build deeper aerobic conditioning, and plenty of "free time" for exploring new routes and generally taking advantage of your short-term freedom to ride as much as you want.

Two-Week Endurance Training Block

The Two-Week Endurance Training Block (see Table 10.1) is structured so you have 2- to 3-day blocks of back-to-back long rides, and then 1 to 2 days of recovery before the next series of back-to-back longer rides. You'll also notice that the week before the Endurance Block begins should be predominantly a recovery week. Your final hard interval workout should be on Tuesday, or Wednesday at the very latest. Your weekly training volume during the block is likely to be double what you normally do—if not more—and it's very important that you be rested and fresh at the beginning.

The first week of this Endurance Training Block is the more difficult of the two, which is fitting because you'll be fresher and able to complete the work. There's a 3-day block (Tuesday, Wednesday, and Thursday), including two Tempo interval workouts (see Chapter 4 for a description of this interval). Tempo intervals are long, but the intensity level is not very high, and your goal should be to complete the interval with as few interruptions as possible. I have scheduled "free rides" on the weekends so you can choose anything

TABLE 10.1 | Two-Week Endurance Training Block

MONDAY	TUESDAY	WEDNESDAY	THURSDAY	FRIDAY	SATURDAY	SUNDAY
Rest day	Last hard interval workout before Endurance Block	Rest day or 1 hr. EM	Rest day or 45 min. easy spinning	Rest day or 45 min. easy spinning	3 hrs. EM or group ride	2–3 hrs. EM with 30 min. T
Rest day	3 hrs. EM with 40 min. T	2–4 hrs. EM	3 hrs. EM with 40 min. T	Rest day or 45 min. easy spinning	3–5 hrs. free ride	3–5 hrs. free ride
Rest day	1.5–2 hrs. EM, light gearing, higher cadence	4 hrs. EM with 40 min. T	3 hrs. EM	Rest day	3–5 hrs. free ride	3–5 hrs. free ride
Rest day	Rest day	45 min. easy spinning	1–1.5 hrs. EM	Rest day	2 hrs. EM	2 hrs. EM or group ride
			Return to normal training			

▓ : Endurance block   **EM:** EnduranceMiles   **T:** Tempo

from an epic ride with your buddies to doing the local group ride and then adding on a few hours afterward, or jumping into a local century. If you're a mountain biker, remember that a daylong epic into the backcountry certainly counts as an endurance-building workout.

During the second week of the block, Tuesday's ride is perhaps the most important. If you are really wiped out from the previous week's training volume, it would be a good idea to either take Tuesday as an additional rest day or make this ride a 30- to 45-minute recovery spin. Even if you feel pretty good, I want you to ride conservatively and limit your ride to a maximum of 2 hours. If these 2 weeks of training were included as a normal part of a high-volume trainer's program, this Tuesday would definitely be a rest day because of the two back-to-back periods of training the previous week. The only reason I've made this an optional EnduranceMiles ride (see Chapter 4) is that your Endurance Block is only going to last these 2 weeks.

PREPARING YOUR BODY FOR ENDURANCE BLOCKS

Doubling or tripling your weekly training volume by embarking on an Endurance Training Block affects you in ways that go beyond workload and fatigue. You're going to be spending a lot more hours outdoors, in your cycling clothes and on your saddle, and it's important to consciously help your body deal with the increased stress.

Use sunscreen: A lot of time-crunched cyclists ride early in the mornings or after work, when the sun's rays are weaker. Then they go to a cycling camp or start on an Endurance Training Block and end up looking like a lobster or a raccoon halfway through the first week. Sunscreen is important, not only to help you avoid getting a sunburn but also to protect your skin from the damaging effects of UV radiation. After riding countless miles without sunscreen as a younger man, I have had to have several spots examined and removed from my skin. Fortunately, none was cancerous, but I know there's a significant chance that one of these days one of them is going to be skin cancer. Use a sunscreen with an SPF rating of at least 15, and apply it liberally. And when checking your skin for suspicious spots, keep in mind that skin cancer can occur anywhere, even on areas that are not frequently exposed to sunlight.

Protect your skin: The more time you spend riding outdoors, the more you need to protect your skin from drying out. Windburn is a common problem for cyclists, especially on the face. Using skin protectants and moisturizers is an important way to keep your exposed skin healthy. I recommend using a product like Aquaphor before outdoor activities and again after your post-workout shower.

Protect your crotch: Athletes rarely suffer from chafing problems during short rides; it's when you're on the bike for 3-plus hours that you start dealing with raw skin and pressure sores. Applying Aquaphor or chamois cream to your skin or the pad in your shorts is a good habit to get into if you're susceptible to chafing. If you start to get saddle sores, it may be time to invest in new shorts or a new saddle. Improper saddle position or tilt can also contribute to both chafing and saddle sores, so you may want to consider a bike fit if the problems persist.

Nutrition for Endurance Blocks

When you embark on any of the Endurance Training Blocks described in this chapter, it's important to remember that your nutrition and hydration choices are going to largely determine your ability to ride well in the final few days of the block. We know this, not only because it makes good sense from a sports nutrition perspective but also because we've seen firsthand the impact of sports nutrition on cyclists' performances at our weeklong spring training camps, like the ones held every year in Santa Ynez, California. We close the week of riding with an adventure we call "The Stinger"—a long day in the saddle that includes El Figueroa, a narrow and nasty climb that would be a Cat. I ascent if judged by the standards used to rank climbs in the Tour de France. Without fail, athletes who follow the nutritional guidance below fare better on The Stinger than athletes who don't.

EAT A HEARTY BREAKFAST

During an Endurance Training Block is not the time to skimp on breakfast. A reasonably large portion of cereal (about 3 cups when you might normally eat 2), toast, fruit, and plenty of fluids would be a minimal breakfast. Even better, include some protein from eggs and/or yogurt. One option that seems to agree with many cyclists is an omelet with veggies and cheese, a few slices of toast with butter or a bagel with cream cheese, a large glass of orange juice, and a cup of strong coffee. Other options to consider are oatmeal, granola, pancakes, or potatoes, but I'd stay away from greasy breakfast options such as hash browns, bacon, sausage, or ham.

START YOUR RIDE WITH TWO BOTTLES
OF SPORTS DRINK

Some riders go to the trouble of carrying drink mix so they can consume a sports drink after their first two bottles of the day, and athletes at training camps or bike tours can typically get sports drinks from support vehicles. If you're out doing your own Endurance Block, however, it's likely you'll be filling up with plain water. If that's the case, start your ride with two bottles of sports drink, and use bigger (24 ounce) bottles instead of normal (21 ounce) bottles if you have them. This will help you consume a steadier supply of carbohydrate during the early portion of your ride, which will make the later hours better and reduce your post-ride recovery demands.

BE VERY CONSCIOUS ABOUT EATING
DURING YOUR RIDE

During your shorter rides, and especially when you have a full day of recovery between workouts, you will pay less for underconsuming carbohydrate calories while you ride. But when you're doing back-to-back days of long rides, it becomes increasingly difficult to overcome nutritional mistakes. Carry plenty of sports nutrition products, such as energy bars and chewables, and at a minimum eat something every 45 minutes (if you're only consuming water, eat something at least every 30 minutes). Make sure you have some variety in flavors and textures, because your tastes and cravings will change as your ride gets longer. You're more likely to continue eating if there's something you like and want in your jersey pocket.

USE A RECOVERY DRINK

Post-ride recovery nutrition is crucial for continued success during an Endurance Training Block, training camp, or cycling tour. Most times you're going to be back on your bike less than 24 hours after you finish your current ride, so you want to do everything you can to ensure that you start tomorrow's adventure with fully stocked carbohydrate stores. A carbohydrate-rich recovery drink should be the first thing you look for after your ride, followed within about an hour by a full meal that's rich in carbohydrate and contains a moderate amount of protein. Remember the guidelines from Chapter 8: 1.5 grams of carbohydrate per kilogram of body weight within 4 hours after your ride, and about one-third to one-half that amount of protein. And drink fluids equivalent to 1.5 times the amount of weight you lost during the ride; if you lost 2 pounds (32 ounces) during the ride, drink 48 ounces of fluid during the 2 hours after the ride.

RELAX AND GRAZE

When you're in the midst of a higher-volume Endurance Training Block, it's not a good time to also commit to heavy-duty yard work, hours of sightseeing, or a full round of golf. When you're done with your long ride, relax, take a nap, watch a movie, or sit by the pool. And it's a good idea to continue snacking throughout the afternoon and evening, a habit known to many as "grazing"—grabbing a handful of nuts, trail mix, a piece of fruit, or a granola bar here and there, and of course continuing to drink plenty of fluids. Generally speaking, at a stage race it's rare to see a pro rider without a water bottle or a piece of food in hand in the afternoon and evening after a stage. The same should be true of cyclists at training camps and cycling tours, or during Endurance Training Blocks (which can be thought of as your own private training camp).

One-Week Endurance Training Block

Not everyone has the luxury of being able to complete a full Two-Week Endurance Training Block, but you can still do yourself a lot of good if you happen to find 1 week when you can put in a lot of training hours. Ideally, you'll be able to ride during the weekends on both ends of your "free" week, and the schedule in Table 10.2 is a good way to structure your time. In this schedule you'll start out with a 4-day block of training, take a complete rest day, and follow that up with a light endurance ride before embarking on a 3-day series of big rides. If you're tired on Thursday, I'd recommend cutting this shorter ride to a recovery spin or taking it as a complete rest day. As in the 2-week block, recovery is important to preserve the quality of your rides later in the week.

TESTIMONIAL

I'm midway through The Time-Crunched Cyclist's 11-week program, already seeing massive gains in power and endurance. My only problem is I love the program so much that I don't want to stop training.

—TIM RANDALL

TABLE 10.2 | **One-Week Endurance Training Block**

MONDAY	TUESDAY	WEDNESDAY	THURSDAY	FRIDAY	SATURDAY	SUNDAY
Rest day	Normal interval workout	Rest day or 1 hr. EM	Last hard interval workout before Endurance Block	Rest day	3 hrs. EM or group ride	2–3 hrs. EM with 40 min. T
3 hrs. EM with 40 min. T	2–4 hrs. EM	Rest day	1.5–2 hrs. EM, light gearing, higher cadence	3–5 hrs. EM	3–5 hrs. free ride	3–5 hrs. free ride
Rest day	Rest day	45 min. easy spinning	1–1.5 hrs. EM	Rest day	2–3 hrs. EM or group ride	2 hrs. EM
Return to normal training						

■: Endurance block   **EM:** EnduranceMiles   **T:** Tempo

Working Cyclist's Endurance Training Block

Can't put your job on hold for 1 or 2 weeks? That's understandable, but it doesn't mean you can't benefit from an Endurance Training Block. In your case you're going to have to get a little more creative. The Working Cyclist's Endurance Block (see Table 10.3) consists of two weekends and the week between them, and uses a total of 2 or 3 days of your personal vacation time. That shouldn't pose much of a problem, considering that a June 2008 report from Leisure Trends found that fewer than half of American workers use all their vacation time each year anyway. This training block calls for a few half days and one or two long weekends, time you likely have coming to you, especially as many companies are eliminating the option of rolling unused vacation time from one year to the next.

The Working Cyclist's Endurance Training Block was originally published in my column in *Bicycling* magazine in April 2008, although in that column it was called the "Spring Break Endurance Block" because of the time of year. As in the other Endurance Blocks, you should consciously reduce your training load in the week preceding the Working Cyclist's Block. It starts with a

TABLE 10.3 | Working Cyclist's Endurance Training Block

MONDAY	TUESDAY	WEDNESDAY	THURSDAY	FRIDAY	SATURDAY	SUNDAY
Rest day	1–1.5 hrs. interval ride	1 hr. EM	Rest day	2.5–3 hrs. EM *Work half day*	3–4 hrs. EM	3–4 hrs. EM
1 hr. recovery ride	2 hrs. EM with 30–45 min. T	2–3 hrs. EM with 30–45 min. T *Work half day if possible*	1 hr. EM	4 hrs. EM *Personal day or half day*	4–5 hrs. ride (may include group ride)	4–5 hrs. EM with 45–60 min. T
4 hrs. EM *Personal day*	Rest day	Rest day	1 hr. EM	1 hr. EM	2–3 hrs. EM	2–3 hrs. EM
Return to normal training						

■**:** Endurance block   **EM:** EnduranceMiles   **T:** Tempo

2½- to 3-hour ride on Friday, and I recommend working a half day, whether that means riding in the morning and going in to work for the afternoon or vice versa. That's followed by 2 back-to-back 3- to 4-hour rides over the weekend.

The following week will likely be a different routine than your normal training week, with EnduranceMiles rides on Tuesday, Wednesday, and Friday and 1-hour rides on Monday and Thursday. Typically, cyclists are able to complete Tuesday's ride without having to take time off from work, but I recommend taking off a half day on Wednesday and either a half day or full day on Friday. This second weekend of the block is the big push: 16 to 18 hours on the bike in 4 days. You're going to be tired when you're done, but the training stimulus you get from these 2 weeks will do you a lot of good.

There are a few things you need to remember if you decide to embark on the Working Cyclist's Endurance Block:

1. **Consult your family:** This training block can be perceived as being extremely self-centered if you don't communicate your rationale clearly. From my experience, families tend to be supportive of a block like

this when you point out that this kind of plan allows you to focus on your training for a relatively short period of time without incurring the higher cost of attending a training camp or cycling tour, without leaving home for a week or longer, and without burning a lot of vacation time that you'll be able to use to go away on a family trip (and you should follow through on that pledge).

2. **You will need a recovery week:** After you finish the Working Cyclist's Endurance Block on Monday, it's important to take 2 complete rest days and then gradually return to training. Your rides on Thursday through Sunday should be moderate-paced endurance rides, with perhaps a group ride on the weekend. Wait until the following week to return to hard interval workouts.

Case Study:
Mick Hitz Goes Long

CTS athlete Mick Hitz is a Cat. III racer and owner of Big Wheel Productions, a video production company in North Carolina. Like many small-business owners, Mick devotes almost all his time to his work and family, and though he enjoys racing, his training is typically limited to fewer than 7 hours a week. As luck would have it, his wife went on a trip for almost 2 weeks just as he wrapped up a big project, and he had some downtime before his next editing job was due. He called his coach, CTS Pro coach Colin Izzard, who recognized that the situation was perfect for a big Endurance Block.

Mick rearranged his work schedule so he could take 2 back-to-back 4-day weekends, and arranged for his assistant editor to come in to cover the phones and keep the office running on the Wednesday and Thursday of the week between them so he could take off half days on those 2 days as well. Mick wrote down some of the long loops he rarely had a chance to ride from his hometown, and also went online to look up some of the great rides to be had in the Appalachian Mountains, a few hours away in western North Carolina.

To make the most of his opportunity, Mick then called his friends and shared his schedule. Though no one else was able to commit to all of the rides he had planned, he was joined by at least two buddies—and as many as eight—for each one. The second weekend he traveled west to Boone, North Carolina, for three epic rides in the mountains.

When he was done, Mick was exhausted and happy. About 2 weeks later, Colin started ramping up Mick's training for a fall series of criteriums, using many of the Time-Crunched Training Program concepts found in this book. To start out, Mick completed a CTS Field Test, and his power numbers were about 5 to 10 watts higher than the previous time he had started a race-focused training period. That, however, was pretty normal—we often see such incremental improvements when we use relatively short-term, high-intensity buildups. What was remarkable to Colin was a change in Mick's attitude about training and the extent of his recovery between rides.

The Endurance Training Block was a refreshing challenge for Mick, and he found that it boosted his enthusiasm for training in the weeks and months afterward. He looked forward to the next time he could string together several days of big, long rides with his friends. And there were some physiological benefits as well. The cumulative training stimulus of just 10 days of high-volume riding deepened his aerobic fitness to the point where he could maintain his normal cruising pace at a lower level of effort. He was able to recover a little faster from hard interval workouts, which in turn improved the quality of his individual training sessions (especially on the second day of 2-day training blocks).

CHAPTER

11

Strength Training
on Limited Time

For many years, coaches and sports scientists have debated the merits of strength training for endurance athletes. Having read the research, talked to the experts on both sides of the debate, and used various forms of resistance training with athletes throughout the spectrum of ability, age, and experience, I still cannot decisively agree with either side. That is to say, I'm not entirely convinced that a cyclist needs to engage in strength training to be stronger and faster on the bike, nor am I completely convinced that strength training won't improve a cyclist's performance. What I do know, without a doubt, is that strength training plays an important role in the overall health and vitality of an athlete. It is for this reason that I am including a chapter on strength training in this book.

Cycling, for all its benefits, is very one-dimensional. For the most part, your upper body stays in a relatively static position while your legs move in only one plane. As a result, devoted cyclists can become prisoners to the bike. Just take a look at professional cyclists; they have among the most highly developed aerobic engines in sports but are virtually crippled by a pickup game of basketball. It's something I refer to as the Cyclist's Paradox. Pro and devoted cyclists have incredibly well-developed aerobic engines, but they are often unaccustomed to weight-bearing activities and their joints and bones are therefore poorly prepared for them. Worse than that, cycling—in the absence of other athletic activities—can breed significant muscle imbalances, creating great strength and power in muscles that drive the pedal stroke while leaving the hip and leg muscles responsible for sideways (lateral) movement weak and underdeveloped.

But, you say, you're a cyclist, and you've made the choice to focus on the sport you love. That's great, but more well-rounded fitness gives you more options for adventures and won't take away from your abilities on the bike. I live at the foot of Pikes Peak, and I know cyclists who have lived here for a decade yet have not experienced the sense of accomplishment and wonder that comes from hiking to the summit. It's not a particularly difficult climb; every year thousands of out-of-shape tourists conquer it. But it's a nearly impossible challenge for highly specialized cyclists because the 13-mile trail is too hard on their feet and hips, and they struggle under the weight of packs if they choose to turn the adventure into a 2-day camping trip. I'm all for maximizing sport-specific performance, but unless you're making a living as a cyclist, I also believe that the benefits of nonspecific fitness are worth pursuing.

To break free of the Cyclist's Paradox and stop being a prisoner to the bike yet still perform like a competitive racer when you're on the bike, I recommend strength training movements that enhance joint mobility and range of motion through the hips and back. Cyclists perform better when they have good flexibility in their hips and backs because greater flexibility gives them the opportunity to produce power through a larger range of motion (or greater power through the same range of motion). Exercises such as lateral lunges and step-ups, which are included in the strength training program in this chapter, are an important component of improving hip mobility and strength. And because a strong torso is crucial for strong cycling as well as for pain-free performance throughout life, the program in this chapter also incorporates a lot of core strengthening exercises.

As always, time is a central problem. Even pro athletes who have a lot of time to devote to training reach a point when they have to direct their full energy to their primary sport. The same thing happens to time-crunched athletes who have less time available for training; it just happens sooner. There is a limit to the amount of time and energy any athlete can devote to meaningful, productive training. There are only so many days and hours in a week, and the more you train, the more you need to recover. Pretty soon you reach a tipping point where adding more training will compromise your recovery and performance.

You're not a professional cyclist, and you're already limited in the amount of time you can devote to training. My contention is that athletes with limited training time benefit most from focusing on their primary sport. In other words, if you only have 6 hours a week to devote to training, you're better off spending that time on your bike. There is one major reason why this is true: Dividing your limited time between strength training and cycling training often results in workloads that are insufficient to lead to significant progress in either arena. Generally speaking, I reserve combined strength training and aerobic performance programs for athletes who can spend more than 14 hours a week on their training goals.

So, if I don't think it's wise for time-crunched athletes to combine strength training with their on-bike training, why have I included a strength training program in this book? Because as mentioned in Chapter 2, the Time-Crunched Periodization Plan calls for a relatively significant period of less-intense cycling training once you're done with the 11-week TCTP. I believe that it is during this recuperation/maintenance phase that strength training will enhance your overall health and performance in life.

Strength Training for Life

The strength training program described in this chapter is not designed to improve your cycling-specific performance. Instead, it promotes full-body strength so you can live an active and healthy life for years to come.

There is a lot of talk these days about metabolism (the energy your body burns on a daily basis through a combination of normal bodily functions, the thermal effect of digesting food, and your activity level and exercise), particularly the notion that metabolism inevitably declines as we get older. This idea has fueled countless late-night infomercials that blame middle-age weight gain on declining metabolism and tout pills and potions that claim to reverse the effects of aging by boosting said metabolism. The truth is, the primary reason metabolism declines as we age is that people tend to be less active as we grow older. When we were younger, we were more active, so we needed, and therefore carried, more lean muscle mass on our bodies. That muscle burned calories, not only to maintain itself but to power our activities, and as we grew less active we lost some of this calorie-burning muscle. At the same time, we either maintained or increased our caloric intake, and hence gained weight.

If you want to keep your metabolism elevated, you need to focus on building—or at least maintaining—lean muscle mass. Cycling may help you maintain or build leg muscle, but it doesn't do much for the rest of your body. In truth, the strength training program in this chapter probably won't build a significant amount of muscle on your upper body either (cyclists are generally averse to increased upper-body bulk, anyway, as it detracts from PWR), but it provides a balanced approach that will help you build a good base of strength and keep the lean muscle you have now.

For me the benefits of generalized strength training go beyond maintaining or boosting metabolism. I'm in my 50s and have three kids, Anna, Connor, and Vivian. For me, strength training is an essential part of being the kind of father I want to be for my kids. At least for right now, Anna is an avid equestrian, Connor is into BMX racing and snowboarding, and little Vivian doesn't stand still for more than a few seconds. I don't want to sit in a chair and watch them; I want to be a part of their activities, and that requires not only a lot of energy but the ability to jump, twist, lift, push, and pull. I'm a devoted cyclist because cycling is the sport I fell in love with as a kid, but I'm a well-rounded athlete because my overall fitness and strength give me the opportunity to be a fully engaged father and still keep up with the demands of my travel and business schedule.

Case Study: The Rise of John Fallon

Compared to Sterling Swaim and Taylor Carrington, John Fallon came to cycling late in life. He was in his early 30s before he started riding and initially had no interest in racing. Long rides in the mountains west of his home in Evergreen, Colorado, were his passion. He trained for and completed the Triple Bypass (a 120-mile epic that includes three major mountain passes as it travels from Evergreen to Avon, Colorado) several times, while raising two children with his wife, Ali, and working as a stockbroker in Denver.

By sheer coincidence, Taylor Carrington joined the firm John worked for, and the two quickly became friends. A few years later, Taylor noticed John was frustrated with his cycling fitness and losing interest in the long weekend rides he had previously enjoyed. Taylor recommended John call his CTS coach, Jim Rutberg, for some guidance and perhaps to consider getting coaching. Rutberg asked all the usual questions about John's goals, his history as an athlete, his interests and obligations outside of athletics, and his personal and professional schedule. During their 90-minute conversation Rutberg provided some very actionable guidance and offered his services as a coach, but John decided to continue training on his own.

A year passed before John contacted Rutberg again. By that point John's training had deteriorated to the extent that he was heavier than he'd been in 5 years. Although he'd just finished the Triple Bypass again, his finishing time was slower than ever before, and he did not enjoy the experience very much.

Rutberg, who was by this time a vocal proponent of the TCTP, readily suggested it to John. Initially, John was skeptical. He had recently gone for lactate threshold testing at a local performance center, and the sports scientist who analyzed his results had recommended long, steady, subthreshold, base building aerobic rides. Rutberg agreed that such training would be quite effective, as long as John didn't mind quitting his job and losing his house. John could only ride about 7 hours a week, which was about half the time that would have been required for the training plan recommended by the sports scientist. Rutberg made the case described in this book, that only through higher-intensity workouts would John achieve the workloads necessary to significantly improve his cycling performance. And then there was the skiing.

Years ago, before housing prices skyrocketed in Colorado ski towns, the Fallons had purchased a condo in Vail. And John wasn't just a man for the "groomers"; he liked to escape into the back bowls early in the morning and ski hard until the sun disappeared behind the peaks to the west.

Over the course of a recent summer, John made big improvements in his sustainable power on the bike by using the TCTP. As the months passed, he dropped about 10 pounds and took 1, then 4, then 9 minutes off his time up Lookout Mountain, his favorite serpentine climb outside Evergreen. As the leaves on the aspen trees turned bright yellow, Rutberg congratulated him on a fine season of work and suggested it was time to devote his energy to preparing for ski season. For the next several weeks, as the base deepened in the bowls behind Vail, Rutberg cut John's riding back to one or two rides on weekends and focused his weekday workouts on strength training.

The following winter was a blockbuster year for skiing in the Rocky Mountains. The snow was the deepest it had been in a decade (more than 47 feet fell on Wolf Creek Ski Area alone!), and storms kept blanketing the backcountry with thick layers of fresh powder. Between his weight loss, increased aerobic fitness, and continued strength training, John had the best ski season he could remember. He wasn't as winded at the end of long runs, was able to complete more runs per day, and gained the confidence to return to challenging slopes he hadn't attempted in years. He even booked a weeklong heli-skiing trip in Alaska and reported back to Rutberg that he had the endurance and power to enjoy the longest and steepest runs the guides found for the group.

The following spring, despite working in San Francisco and commuting back to Denver a couple of weekends each month, John refocused his training on cycling. The cycling scene in San Francisco was different than in Denver, and John soon became interested in local criteriums. Due to John's intense work and travel schedule, Rutberg put him back on the TCTP. And even though he had only been riding one or two times a week during ski season, his overall workload had been high enough that 4 weeks into the cycling program he was sustaining higher power outputs in SteadyState and Power-Interval workouts than he had at any point in the previous season. Though he was a relative novice in terms of racing tactics, John had the fitness to finish in the top half of masters Cat. IV to V races in California right from his first race. Within a few weeks he was consistently finishing in the top 10.

John Fallon is representative of a huge group of athletes out there. He's a cyclist, but he also has passions outside cycling. He wants to perform well on the bike, but not at the cost of being restricted to one sport or activity. In some ways he may represent the greater ideal we should all strive for: diversity through greater overall fitness. John's not going to win a masters national championship, but he's a guy in his mid-40s who can say "yes" to a wider variety of activities, sports, events, and adventures—at a moment's notice—than most athletes who have been devoted single-focus cyclists for 20 years.

Making Strength Training Work for You

I hate having to travel somewhere just so I can start training. As a cyclist I put on my clothes, grab my bike from the garage or the rack in the office, and am training as soon as I roll out the door. Runners are probably the only athletes who have it easier than cyclists, but only because they have less gear to contend with. Maybe that's why I've never been a big fan of gyms (or sports played on fields or courts).

There was a time during the early days of Carmichael Training Systems when I had pretty much given up on being a cyclist. One particular winter, I think it was 2001 to 2002, I barely touched my bike for about 4 months. During that time I decided I'd follow the "normal" path to fitness for a middle-aged guy: I joined a gym. I quickly realized that the most frustrating part of my entire day was the drive to and from the gym. The whole point of going to the gym was to work out, but between getting there and getting back, I was in the car nearly as long as I worked out. Clearly this was not a good use of limited time, so I got back on my bike and started doing my strength training at home. Now we have a workout space at CTS headquarters in Colorado Springs, so it's even easier.

To make strength training work for you, it has to address certain principles.

CONVENIENCE AND COST

First off, strength training has to fit into your personal and professional schedule. That's why I believe in at-home strength training as opposed to going to the gym. At the same time, it has to be cost effective. I don't expect you to spend thousands of dollars on a home gym setup and a menagerie of equipment just so you can work out effectively in your house. With a small investment in a limited amount of equipment (and some creativity), you can achieve all the benefits you're looking for. The two items I believe you should invest in are dumbbells and resistance cords. They don't take up much room, and they can be used for a wide range of exercises. The dumbbells are great for chest and shoulder presses; can be used for some pulling exercises like a bent-over row; and can even be used to add resistance to step-ups, lunges, and squats. The resistance bands can be used for many of the same exercises as dumbbells, but in addition can be anchored on door frames or other immovable objects so you can perform a seated row or a pull-down.

As cyclists, we tend to have access to a number of inner tubes. When you puncture a tube on a ride, keep it instead of throwing it out. It may no longer be good for holding air, but it can still be useful. To use a bicycle tube for a resistance band, I recommend cutting the valve off. This is purely for safety, to remove a relatively sharp piece of metal from the proximity of your body. However, don't cut the entire valve out of the tube (this weakens the tube itself), but rather use a hacksaw or clipper to cut the valve itself close to its base. You can also use a variety of methods to adjust the amount of resistance offered by bicycle tubes:

- **Lightest resistance:** Cut a road bike tube once so it becomes one long tube. Tie a loop in each end so you can anchor one end and use the other loop for a handle.
- **Light resistance:** Leave a road bike tube as an intact loop. Anchor one side and hold on to the other. This will create more resistance because you have to stretch two lengths of tube. If you need to increase the length of this tubing, tie two road bike tubes together.
- **Heavier resistance:** Use mountain bike tubes. A tube designed to fit a 26 × 2.0 tire will offer more resistance than a tube designed for a 700c × 25 tire. Again, you can cut one tube to make a long, single piece of tubing, or tie two intact tubes together to add length.
- **Even more resistance:** Add tubes. Adding a second or even a third tube increases the amount of resistance you will experience. You can even combine mountain bike and road tubes to make smaller, incremental increases in resistance.

NOTHING WRONG WITH THE BASICS

Some of the best strength training exercises are the simplest, and there's nothing wrong with continuing to perform some of the basic movements you learned in middle school. Push-ups and pull-ups, for instance, are solid exercises for upper-body strength. A body-weight squat and lunges are good exercises for lower-body strength. You can make these exercises more challenging by adding weight to a squat or lunge, or putting your feet up on a bench or chair for push-ups. Or you can simply add more repetitions or incorporate more speed into the movement to develop power as well as strength.

BALANCE MATTERS

The primary reason I include strength training in this book is to help you maintain a healthy and active lifestyle, and I believe a balance component is essential. When you perform movements that challenge your balance, you engage muscles throughout your body.

For instance, when you start doing lunges, you may notice you have a hard time keeping your upper body balanced over your legs. As you practice the movement, you will engage muscles in your core and hips and learn to better balance your body in this position. The same is true of overhead lifts. As you press a weight over your head, you will engage muscles from your feet to your fingers to control the weight in space. This whole-body integration is as important as the weight you're able to move, because when you train your body to act as one coordinated unit, you are better able to maintain your balance in increasingly unstable conditions.

Outside the realm of athletics, researchers have examined the impact of strength training on mobility and longevity in elderly populations. Engaging in resistance training consistently throughout our adult years can help us maintain greater bone density as we get older, as well as preserve more lean muscle mass. From a balance perspective, older people who exercise regularly are less likely to fall, are more able to catch themselves when they trip or slip, and suffer fewer or less severe injuries when they do fall down. Breaking a hip, a common injury among elderly men and women, reduces a person's lifespan. Not only does it involve a significant period of recovery, but people often lose confidence in their stability and further reduce their activity levels. You may be many years away from having to worry about slipping in the kitchen and breaking your hip, but the point is that the positive effects of training—and the negative ramifications of not training—have wide-ranging impacts on the quality of your life, now and in the future.

MOVEMENTS MATTER

When we get to the actual exercises in the strength training program, you'll notice that there are no isolated movements to target triceps, biceps, or hamstrings. Instead you'll find multijoint exercises that engage large muscle groups because these are the exercises that prepare you for real-world demands. An exercise like a push-up or overhead press, for example, engages your triceps but works muscles in your chest and shoulder at the same time. All of these muscles must work together to complete the movement, which is similar to the reality that you rarely use your triceps in isolation. Similarly, you'll be using exercises like squats and lunges to work your hamstrings, but these movements also engage muscles throughout your legs, hips, and torso.

You'll also notice that some of the exercises take you out of that standard "feet shoulder-width apart" stance that's so common in strength training movements. I'm not really concerned about what you're capable of lifting or doing while you have both feet planted firmly on the ground, shoulder-width apart. Think about the last time you needed strength or power in an unexpected moment (something or someone was falling and you needed to catch and hold the weight, perhaps). Were you perfectly balanced? Like many 7-year-olds, my son, Connor, is fearless, and he doesn't always realize the potential consequences of his "adventures." Last summer he was standing on the top of a stone retaining wall, about 4 feet above a concrete driveway. He called his dog, Hank, who came running as he always does, but the dog was going a little too fast to stop in time and knocked Connor right off the wall. I was standing in the driveway below and managed to catch Connor, which probably saved him from a bad headache if not a trip to the ER. The reason I bring this up is that it happened so fast that all I had time to do was reach out one arm and lunge with one leg to get there in time. I got him, I didn't hurt myself in the process, and true to form, Connor thought it was a ton of fun and wanted to do it again (we didn't).

The movements included in the strength training program in this chapter are among the most applicable to real-life situations. You're going to develop strength with flexibility, power when you're extended or reaching instead of just when your feet are firmly planted and your arms are close to your chest. As an added benefit for cyclists, the lower-body exercises in this program are great for improving range of motion and flexibility through the hips.

How to Use the Time-Crunched Strength Training Program

Three workouts make up the Time-Crunched Strength Training Program. The first is a simple core strength workout, and then there are two fullbodyroutines. The core strength workout is something you can and should do year-round, even while you're in the midst of your high-intensity cycling training. It should take fewer than 10 minutes to complete and is a good add-on immediately after you get off your bike.

Variety is an important component of an effective strength training program, because different exercises present specific challenges, even when they target very similar muscle groups. For instance, squats and step-ups are both good exercises for developing lower-body strength and power, but squats work both legs at the same time, and step-ups incorporate a balance component because you're lifting your body weight with one leg at a time. The same can be said for a curl and press compared with an alternating overhead press.

Because I want to keep the strength workouts short, and there's little reason to target the same area of the body more than once during each workout, I have created two routines so you can complete a wide variety of exercises each week. You should aim to complete two or three strength workouts a week, leaving a full day between them, and I recommend alternating the two full-body routines. That could mean doing Routine 1 on Tuesday, Routine 2 on Thursday, and if you want to add a third, doing Routine 1 again on Saturday. The following week would start with Routine 2.

Whichever strength routine you're doing, core strength is such a vital aspect of sports performance and an active lifestyle that you should always add the core routine as well. In total, the core routine and one of the strength routines should only take you about 30 minutes to complete.

In terms of how much resistance you should use, the final few repetitions of each exercise should be challenging, but maintaining good form is more important than working to failure. This is especially true when working with resistance bands, dumbbells, and dynamic movements, because reaching failure typically means losing control of the weight or compromising your balance. As you get stronger and need to increase your workload, I want you to do so by increasing the resistance (heavier band or dumbbell, or holding weights during some of the dynamic movements) rather than increasing the number of repetitions or sets you complete.

Just as there is debate about endurance training methods, there are different approaches to strength training. In terms of repetitions and sets, you can move more weight or move against more resistance if you reduce the number of repetitions in a set. In other words, I may be able to press 50-pound dumb-bells over my head 6 times, but I could complete the same movement 12 times if I use 30-pound dumbbells. As you manipulate these two variables (resistance and repetitions), you start to change the impact the exercise will have on your muscles.

If you're going for sheer strength gains, doing fewer reps (1 to 6) with very high resistance is generally the way to go. If you're going for muscular endurance and little to no increase in muscle mass, then 15 to 20 reps with relatively light resistance will do the trick. In the middle you get a significant increase in strength and a moderate increase in muscle mass, which is exactly what we're looking for. As a result, you'll be doing sets of 12 repetitions per exercise in the strength routines and 20 repetitions per exercise in the core routine (see Table 11.1).

TABLE 11.1 | **Time-Crunched Strength Training Program**

CORE STRENGTH ROUTINE	
Reverse Crunch	
Back Extension	
Bicycle Crunch	
Windshield Wipers	
For each core exercise, complete 20 repetitions. No rest between exercises, but rest 1 minute between the Core Routine and the beginning of either Strength Routine 1 or 2.	

STRENGTH ROUTINE 1	STRENGTH ROUTINE 2
Squat and Jump	Step-up
Push-up	Push-up
Standing Overhead Press	Reverse Wood Chop with Bands
Lateral Lunge	Lateral Lunge
Seated Row	One-Arm Row
For each exercise, complete 12 repetitions. Rest between exercises is 30 seconds. Repeat Core Strength + Routine 1 three times; rest 2 minutes between the cycles.	For each exercise, complete 12 repetitions. Rest between exercises is 30 seconds. Repeat Core Strength + Routine 2 three times; rest 2 minutes between the cycles.

Workout Descriptions

Back Extension

Lie flat on your stomach with your arms by your side and your legs completely straight (Figure 11.1). Push your legs into the ground and use your back to lift your shoulders and chest off the floor (Figure 11.2). Lift 1 to 3 inches off the floor, but don't strain too hard to lift very high. Slowly lower your chest back to the floor and repeat. For an added challenge, extend your arms out to the side (Figure 11.3) or out in front of you (Figure 11.4) and lift them off the ground as well (Figures 11.5 and 11.6). A more advanced version of this exercise would be to lift your right arm and left leg off the ground simultaneously (Figure 11.7), and then lower back to the ground before lifting your left arm and right leg off the ground simultaneously.

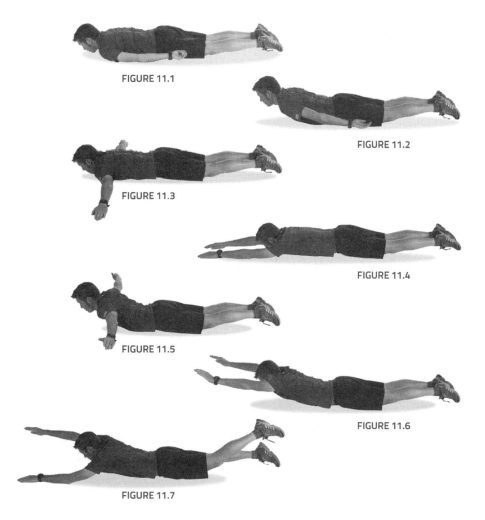

FIGURE 11.1

FIGURE 11.2

FIGURE 11.3

FIGURE 11.4

FIGURE 11.5

FIGURE 11.6

FIGURE 11.7

Bicycle Crunch

Studies have shown this exercise to be one of the best abdominal movements because it engages your upper and lower abdominals and incorporates a twist as well. Lie on your back on the floor. Your hands should be lightly touching the back of your ears. Raise your right foot off the ground 4 to 6 inches and keep that leg straight. At the same time, bring your left knee toward your chest (Figure 11.8). Using your abdominal muscles (don't pull your head forward with your arm), raise your right shoulder off the ground and twist to the left, with the goal of touching your right elbow to your left knee. If you can't make contact, that's fine. Lower your right shoulder back to the ground and extend your left leg until it is straight and your foot is 4 to 6 inches off the floor. Complete the same movement on the other side by bringing your right knee toward your chest and raising your left shoulder off the ground (Figure 11.9). One repetition of this exercise consists of completing the movement on both sides, and all repetitions of this exercise should be done at a moderate, continuous tempo with no pauses or rest between repetitions.

FIGURE 11.8

FIGURE 11.9

Lateral Lunge

This may be the most important exercise in the program, because most cyclists are in dire need of lateral stability and strength. Stand with your feet together and your arms extended out in front of you (Figure 11.10). Step to the right with your right foot, keeping your left leg straight and your left foot flat at its starting position (Figure 11.11). Keeping your right knee behind your right foot, and your chest high and back straight, drop your hips as you sit into a squat. Aim to go low enough that your right thigh is parallel to the ground. Pause for 1 to 2 seconds, then drive with your right leg to return to the starting position. As soon as you return to the starting position, step to the left with your left leg and repeat the same movement. One repetition of this exercise consists of lunging to both sides.

FIGURE 11.10

Beginners may want to step forward and to the side at about a 45-degree angle, as it can be easier to maintain your balance using this method (Figure 11.12). As you get stronger, gradually shift to stepping directly to the side.

FIGURE 11.11

For more of a challenge, hold a weight in front of your chest and do the exercise. If you hold the weight close to your chest, you're mainly adding resistance for your legs; if you hold it out in front of your body, you'll add work for your back and shoulders. When you add a weight, make sure you don't roll your shoulders forward or curve your back.

FIGURE 11.12

One-Arm Row

This exercise for your upper back and the rear portion of your shoulder is ideally done with a dumbbell but can be completed with a resistance band anchored close to the floor. If you have a bench, put your left knee on the bench while your right leg is straight and your right foot is on the floor. Bend forward at the waist, place your left hand directly under your shoulder on the bench, and keep your back straight. Hold a dumbbell in your right hand, straight below your right shoulder (Figure 11.13). Using the muscles in your upper back and shoulder (rather than just the muscles in your arm), lift the barbell up, pulling your elbow high but keeping it close to your side. Lift until you've drawn the weight close to your side (Figure 11.14). In a controlled manner, lower the weight to the starting position and repeat. Complete a set using your right arm before switching sides and using your left arm. Figures 11.15 and 11.16 show a variation of this exercise using an exercise band.

Additional tips: Don't drop your shoulder as you lower the weight, in an attempt to get a stretch or make the range of motion longer. Similarly, don't use your core muscles to twist your torso as you raise the weight. The majority of your upper body will be very still during this exercise. The movement should be confined to your arm and shoulder, utilizing the muscles in your upper back to make them move.

FIGURE 11.13

FIGURE 11.14

FIGURE 11.15

FIGURE 11.16

Push-up Variations (Easy, Intermediate, and Advanced)

Easy: Lie facedown on the floor with your hands placed even with your chest, just slightly wider than shoulder width apart (Figure 11.17). Keep your head, shoulders, and hips in a rigid line and push your chest away from the floor so your weight is supported on your knees and hands. Push yourself up until your arms are fully extended (Figure 11.18), but be careful not to lock your elbows. Slowly lower yourself until your chest barely touches the floor, and then immediately push yourself back up. Repeat for the prescribed number of repetitions.

Intermediate: Same exercise as Easy, but make the contact points with the ground your hands and your toes, not your hands and your knees (Figure 11.19). Make sure to keep your body in a straight line from your shoulders all the way to your feet. Your hands should be slightly wider than shoulder width apart (Figure 11.20).

Advanced: When a regular push-up is no longer challenging, put your feet up on a box bench or chair (Figures 11.21 and 11.22) and then complete your push-ups.

FIGURE 11.17

FIGURE 11.18

FIGURE 11.19

FIGURE 11.20

FIGURE 11.21

FIGURE 11.22

Reverse Crunch

I like reverse crunches because there is no temptation to pull your head and neck forward as many people do during traditional crunches. Lie on your back with your knees bent, feet together. Hold your arms straight at a 45-degree angle out from your torso, palms facing down (Figure 11.23). Bring your knees to your chest by tightening your abdominal muscles and curling your hips off the floor (Figure 11.24). Be careful to engage your abdominal muscles to produce the movement instead of relying on the muscles in the front of your hips and legs. When your knees have reached your chest, or as close as you can get, curl back down and return to the start position.

FIGURE 11.23

FIGURE 11.24

Reverse Wood Chop with Band

This is a twisting lift that starts by your ankle and finishes at shoulder height or higher. Start by anchoring a resistance band at about ankle height to something sturdy such as a heavy desk or bed frame. Some resistance bands come with an adapter so you can anchor them between a door and a doorjamb. If you can't anchor the band, stand on it. Stand with a wide stance, your knees bent, and your right foot toward the anchored end of the band. Bend down and grasp the handle(s) in both hands at about knee height (Figure 11.25). You want there to be light to moderate tension on the band in this starting position. Keeping your back straight, your core engaged, and your eyes up, pull the band up and across your torso as you twist with your core and shoulders (Figure 11.26). You can finish the movement with your hands at shoulder height, or continue up (Figure 11.27) until your hands are overhead (this will be harder on the shoulders; if you have shoulder trouble, stop at shoulder height). In a controlled manner, return to the starting position and repeat. When you're done on one side, turn around so your left foot is toward the anchored end of the band and repeat the exercise.

FIGURE 11.25

FIGURE 11.26

FIGURE 11.27

Seated Row

Sit on the floor with a resistance band anchored to something sturdy, such as a heavy desk or bed frame. Some resistance bands come with an adapter so you can anchor them between a door and a doorjamb. The band should be anchored about chest height when you're sitting, but it's OK if it is a bit lower than that. If you don't have anything to anchor the band to, loop it around your feet. Sit with your back perpendicular to the floor and extend your arms straight forward as you hold on to the ends of the bands. In this starting position, with your palms facing each other, there should be light to moderate tension on the band. With your chest high and your back straight, pull your hands straight back, keeping your elbows close to your sides, until your hands reach the sides of your chest (Figure 11.28). In a controlled manner, bring your hands back to the starting position and repeat. Do not lean back as you perform this movement; keep your back perpendicular to the ground. To make this exercise more challenging, you can perform it one arm at a time (Figures 11.29 and 11.30).

FIGURE 11.28

FIGURE 11.29

FIGURE 11.30

Squat and Jump

This exercise adds a speed-and-power component to a body weight squat. Stand with your feet slightly wider than shoulder width apart (Figure 11.31). With your arms at your sides, squat until your hips reach knee level (Figure 11.32), then explode straight up and jump as high as you can (Figure 11.33). As you begin to drive upward, swing your arms up to generate momentum and more height. Bend your knees to absorb the impact as you land. Return to a standing position and repeat. It's important that you aim to propel yourself as high as you can with each jump.

FIGURE 11.31

FIGURE 11.32

FIGURE 11.33

Standing Overhead Press

Not only is this a great exercise for your shoulders, triceps, and the upper portions of both your chest and back, but it also engages muscles from your toes all the way to your fingers. Stand with your feet shoulder width apart and knees slightly bent (Figure 11.34). You can use dumbbells or a resistance band for this exercise. Curl the weight (dumbbells or resistance band) so your hands are shoulder height and your palms are facing forward or slightly toward the midline of your body. Keep your chest high and your abdominal muscles engaged as you press both hands straight

FIGURE 11.34   FIGURE 11.35   FIGURE 11.36

up over your head (Figure 11.35). As you extend your arms to the top of the movement, keep your palms facing forward. Bring your arms back down to the starting position and repeat.

If you're using a resistance band, stand on the band with one or both feet and follow the same instructions as above (Figures 11.36 and 11.37).

To make this movement a greater challenge for your abdominal muscles, alternate one arm at a time (Figures 11.38 and 11.39).

FIGURE 11.37   **FIGURE 11.38**   **FIGURE 11.39**

Step-up

I particularly like the single-leg nature of this exercise, because it forces you to balance on one leg and use hip and torso muscles to maintain stability. In addition, the movement develops strength and power that's not only useful in life but also applicable to your on-bike performance. Start by standing facing a bench that's about knee height (Figure 11.40). Place your right foot on the bench and, keeping your back straight and chest high, use your hip extensors and leg to step up onto the bench (Figures 11.41 and 11.42). Bring your left foot even with your right foot, then step down in a controlled manner, leading with your left foot. Bring your right foot down to the floor and then alternate sides, stepping up with your left foot.

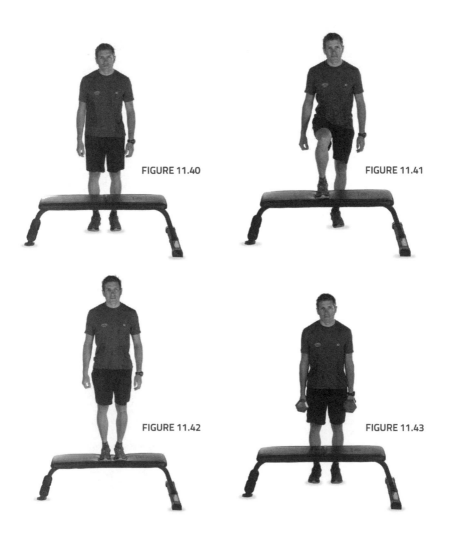

FIGURE 11.40

FIGURE 11.41

FIGURE 11.42

FIGURE 11.43

You can make this exercise more challenging by holding weight in your hands at your sides (Figures 11.43, 11.44, and 11.45). To add a greater balance component to the exercise, and for more of a challenge, you can hold a weight in front of you (Figures 11.46 and 11.47). But it's essential that the weight not be so heavy that it causes your shoulders to roll forward or pitch your upper body forward.

If you don't have a bench, this exercise can be done on a staircase (step up onto the second step). The only issue with using a staircase is that you have to step a bit forward as you step up. This is a minor issue, but just make sure you're able to keep your chest high and back straight throughout the exercise. If you have to lean your upper body forward significantly to step up onto the second stair, your staircase may not be well suited to this exercise.

FIGURE 11.44

FIGURE 11.45

FIGURE 11.46

FIGURE 11.47

Windshield Wipers

This is a great exercise for developing the core muscles responsible for twisting; on the bike, these muscles also resist twisting so your pedal stroke can be more powerful. Lie on your back with legs together and extended straight and arms extended perpendicular to your body. Lift your legs so your toes are pointed straight up and hold them perpendicular to the floor (Figure 11.48). Keeping your arms and shoulders flat against the floor and your legs straight, lower your legs to the left (Figure 11.49). Raise your legs back over center and then lower them to the right (Figure 11.50). Lowering to both sides once completes one repetition.

FIGURE 11.48   FIGURE 11.49

FIGURE 11.50

References

Barnett, C., M. Carey, J. Proietto, E. Cerin, M. Febbraio, and D. Jenkins. 2004. Muscle metabolism during sprint exercise in man: Influence of sprint training. *Journal of Science and Medicine in Sport* 7 (3) (September): 314–322.

Billat, V. 2001. Interval training for performance: A scientific and empirical practice. *Sports Medicine* 31 (2): 75–90.

Brooks, G. A., and J. Mercier. 1994. Balance of carbohydrate and lipid utilization during exercise: The "crossover" concept. *Journal of Applied Physiology* 76: 2253–2261.

Burgomaster, K., K. Howarth, S. Phillips, M. Rakobowchuk, et al. 2008. Similar metabolic adaptations during exercise after low-volume sprint interval and traditional endurance training in humans. *Journal of Physiology* 586 (1): 151–160.

Burgomaster, K., S. Hughes, G. Heigenhauser, S. Bradwell, and M. Gibala. 2005. Six sessions of sprint interval training increases muscle oxidative potential and cycle endurance capacity in humans. *Journal of Applied Physiology* 98 (6) (June): 1985–1990.

Coyle, E. F. 2005. Very intense exercise-training is extremely potent and time efficient: A reminder. *Journal of Applied Physiology* 98: 1983–1984.

Daniels, J., and N. Scardina. 1984. Interval training and performance. *Sports Medicine* 1 (4) (July): 327–334.

Dempsey, J. A. 1986. Is the lung built for exercise? *Medicine and Science in Sports and Exercise* 18: 143–155.

Dudley, G., W. Abraham, and R. Terjung. 1982. Influence of exercise intensity and duration on biochemical adaptations in skeletal muscle. *Journal of Applied Physiology* 53 (4) (October): 844–850.

Esfarjani, F., and P. B. Laursen. 2007. Manipulating high-intensity interval training: Effects on VO_2max, the lactate threshold, and 3000 m running performance in moderately trained males. *Journal of Science and Medicine in Sport* 10 (1) (February): 27–35. (E-publication, July 28, 2006).

Faria, E. W., D. K. Parker, and I. E. Faria. 2005. The science of cycling: Factors affecting performance—part 2. *Sports Medicine* 35: 313–337.

Faude, O., T. Meyer, J. Scharhag, F. Weins, A. Urhausen, and W. Kindermann. 2008. Volume vs. intensity in the training of competitive swimmers. *International Journal of Sports Medicine* 29 (11) (November): 906–912.

Fox, E. L., R. L. Bartels, and C. E. Billing. 1975. Frequency and duration of interval training programs and changes in aerobic power. *Journal of Applied Physiology* 38: 481–484.

Franch, J., K. Madsen, M. S. Djurhuus, et al. 1998. Improved running economy following intensified training correlates with reduced ventilatory demands. *Medicine and Science in Sports and Exercise* 30: 1250–1256.

Gastin, P. 2001. Energy system interaction and relative contribution during maximal exercise. *Sports Medicine* 31 (10): 725–741.

Gibala, M., J. Little, M. van Essen, G. Wilkin, K. Burgomaster, A. Safdar, S. Raha, and M. Tarnopolsky. 2006. Short-term sprint interval versus traditional endurance training: Similar initial adaptations in human skeletal muscle and exercise performance. *Journal of Physiology* 575 (3): 901–911.

Gorostiaga, E. M., C. B. Walter, C. Foster, et al. 1991. Uniqueness of interval and continuous training at the same maintained exercise intensity. *European Journal of Applied Physiology* 63: 101–107.

Hardman, A., C. Williams, and S. Wootton. 1986. The influence of short-term endurance training on maximum oxygen uptake, submaximum endurance, and the ability to perform brief, maximal exercise. *Journal of Sports Sciences* [online] 4 (2) (Autumn): 109–116.

Harmer, A. R., M. J. McKenna, J. R. Sutto, R. J. Snow, P. A. Ruell, J. Booth, M. W. Thompson, N. A. Mackay, C. G. Stathis, R. M. Crameri, M. F. Carey, and D. M. Enger. 2000. Skeletal muscle metabolic and ionic adaptation during intense exercise following sprint training in humans. *Journal of Applied Physiology* 89: 1793–1803.

Hawley, J. A., K. H. Myburgh, T. D. Noakes, et al. 1997. Training techniques to improve fatigue resistance and enhance endurance performance. *Journal of Sports Science* 15: 325–333.

Jacobs, I., M. Esbjoernsson, C. Sylven, I. Holm, and E. Jansson. 1987. Sprint training effects on muscle myoglobin, enzymes, fiber types, and blood lactate. *Medicine and Science in Sports and Exercise* 19 (4) (August): 368–374.

Jones, A., and H. Carter. 2000. The effect of endurance training on parameters of aerobic fitness. *Sports Medicine* 6: 373–386.

Karp, Jason R. 2008. Chasing Pheidippides: The science of endurance. *IDEA Fitness Journal* 5 (9) (October): 28.

Krustrup, P., Y. Hellsten, and J. Bangsbo. 2004. Intense interval training enhances human skeletal muscle oxygen uptake in the initial phase of dynamic exercise at high but not at low intensities. *Journal of Physiology* 559 (1): 335–345.

Laursen, P., M. Blanchard, and D. Jenkins. 2002. Acute high-intensity interval training improves Tvent and peak power output in highly trained males. *Canadian Journal of Applied Physiology* 27 (4) (August): 336–348.

Laursen, P. B., and D. G. Jenkins. 2002. The scientific basis for high-intensity interval training: Optimising training programmes and maximising performance in highly trained endurance athletes. *Sports Medicine* 32 (1): 53–73.

Laursen, P. B., C. M. Shing, J. M. Peake, J.S. Coombes, and D. G. Jenkins. 2002. Interval training program optimization in highly trained endurance cyclists. *Medicine and Science in Sports and Exercise* 34 (11) (November): 1801–1807.

Laursen, P. B., C. M. Shing, J. M. Peake, J. S. Coombes, and D. G. Jenkins. 2005. Influence of high-intensity interval training on adaptations in well-trained cyclists. *Journal of Strength and Conditioning Research* 19 (3) (August): 527–533.

Linossier, M. T., C. Dennis, D. Dormois, et al. 1993. Ergometric and metabolic adaptation to a 5-s sprint training programmer. *European Journal of Applied Physiology* 67: 408–414.

Little, J., A. Safdar, G. Wilkin, M. Tarnopolsky, and M. Gibala. 2010. A practical model of low-volume high-intensity interval training induces mitochondrial biogenesis in human skeletal muscle. *Journal of Physiology* 588 (6): 1011–1022.

Londeree, B. 1997. Effect of training on lactate/ventilatory thresholds: A meta-analysis. *Medicine and Science in Sports and Exercise* 29 (6) (June): 837–843.

MacDougall, D., A. Hicks, J. MacDonald, R. McKelvie, H. Green, and K. Smith. 1998. Muscle performance and enzymatic adaptations to sprint interval training. *Journal of Applied Physiology* 84: 2138–2142.

Marles, A., R. Legrand, N. Blondel, P. Mucci, D. Bebeder, and F. Prieur. 2007. Effect of high-intensity interval training and detraining on extra vo_2 and on the vo_2 slow component. *European Journal of Applied Physiology* 99: 633–640.

Midgley, A. W., L. R. McNaughton, and A. M. Jones. 2007. Training to enhance the physiological determinants of long-distance running performance. *Sports Medicine* 37 (10): 857–880.

Neufer, P. D. 1989. The effect of detraining and reduced training on the physiological adaptations to aerobic exercise training. *Sports Medicine* 8 (5) (November): 302–320.

Parra, J., J. A. Cadefau, G. Rodas, N. Amigó, and R. Cussó. 2000. The distribution of rest periods affects performance and adaptations of energy metabolism induced by high-intensity training in human muscle. *Acta Physiologica Scandinavica* 169 (2) (June): 157–165.

Rakobowchuk, M., S. Tanguay, K. Burgomaster, K. Howarth, M. Gibala, and M. MacDonald. 2008. Sprint interval and traditional endurance training induce similar improvements in peripheral arterial stiffness and flow-mediated dilation in healthy humans. *American Journal of Physiology—Regulatory, Integrative, and Comparative Physiology* 295 (1) (July): R236–R242.

Robinson, M., J. Plasschaert, and N. Kisaalita. 2011. Effects of high-intensity training by heart rate or power in recreational cyclists. *Journal of Sports Science and Medicine* 10: 498–501. Rodas, G., J. Ventura, J. Cadefau, R. Cusso, and J. Parra. 2000. A short training programme for the rapid improvement of both aerobic and anaerbic metabolism. *European Journal of Applied Physiology* 82: 480–486.

Simoneau, J. A., G. Lortie, M. R. Boulay, et al. 1986. Inheritance of human skeletal muscle and anaerobic capacity adaptation to high-intensity intermittent training: Human skeletal muscle fiber type alteration with high-intensity intermittent training. *International Journal of Sports Medicine* 7: 167–171.

Talanian, J., S. Galloway, G. Heigenhauser, A. Bonen, and L. Spriet. 2007. Two weeks of high-intensity aerobic interval training increases the capacity for fat oxidation during exercise in women. *Journal of Applied Physiology* 102: 1439–1447.

Tanaka, H., and D. R. Seals. 2008. Endurance exercise performance in Masters athletes: Age-associated changes and underlying physiological mechanisms. *Journal of Physiology* 586 (1) (January 1): 55–63.

Westgarth-Taylor, C., J. Hawley, S. Rickard, K. Myburgh, T. Noakes, and S. Dennis. 1997. Metabolic and performance adaptations to interval training in endurance-trained cyclists. *European Journal of Applied Physiology* 75 (4) (April): 298–304.

Weston, A. R., K. H. Myburgh, F. H. Lindsay, S. C. Dennis, T. D. Noakes, and J. A. Hawley. 1997. Skeletal muscle buffering capacity and endurance performance after high-intensity training by well-trained cyclists. *European Journal of Applied Physiology* 75: 7–13.

Willett, K. 2006. Mitochondria: The aerobic engines. www.biketechreview.com/performance/mitochondira.htm.

Index

Absorption, 170, 172, 178
Acceleration, 2, 63, 85, 95, 194, 198, 200,
    202, 205
  cornering and, 204
  energy for, 165
  responding to, 195, 197, 203
Adaptations, 7, 8, 31, 40, 60, 98, 129, 138,
    140, 180
  biological, 51
  cardiovascular, 41
  metabolic, 51
  muscular, 41
  physiological, 10, 24, 44
  training, 12 14, 88, 99
Adenosine triphosphate (ATP), 19, 21, 25
Advanced Commuter training plan, 133,
    136–137 (table), 138
Aerobic base, 46, 81, 164
  building, 2, 26, 51, 94, 193, 226
Aerobic engine, 19, 22, 24, 25, 27, 46, 58,
    68, 69, 129, 162, 165, 219
  building, 45
  described, 20–21
  fat burning by, 201
Aerodynamics, 59, 64
Alexander, Craig, 81
Allen, Hunter, 9, 11, 61, 79, 107
Altitude training, benefits of, 7
American College of Sports Medicine, 172
American Heart Association, 168
Anaerobic system, 19, 21, 27, 51
ANT+ signals, 132
Aquaphor, 155, 210
Armstrong, Lance, 8, 10–12, 30
ATP/CP system, described, 19–20
Attacks, 165, 193, 195, 201

  cornering and, 204
  launching, 202–205
  pace and, 203
  pitch and, 203–204

Back extension, 231 (fig.)
  described, 231
Balance, 228
  strength training and, 227
Bascomb, Neal, 6
Base building, 2, 9, 26, 51, 54, 94, 193,
    222, 226
Bicycle crunch, 232 (fig.)
  described, 232
Biochemical reactions, 25, 162
Body weight, 81, 174
Bolt, Usain, 6
Bompa, Tudor, 7
Bonking, 147, 177, 178
Borg Scale, 83, 84
Braking, 146, 195, 200
Breakaways, 194, 199, 200, 203, 204, 205
Broker, Jeff, 8
Browning, Ray, 11
Burke, Edmund, 8, 11, 61
Burney, Simon, 142
Burton, Justin, 142

Cadence, 37, 82, 86, 92, 200
  described, 40–41
  high, 41, 95, 124
  increase in, 85, 197
  pedal, 93, 94, 97
Caffeine, 62, 169, 173, 177
Caloric expenditure, 182 (table), 185–186
  calculating, 182, 183

perspective on, 182–183
Caloric overcompensation, 185–187
Calories
    burning, 39, 124, 155, 162, 163, 174,
        197, 222
    consuming, 162, 166, 171–174, 176,
        179–187, 201–202, 222
    exercise, 181–182
    RMR and, 181–182
Carbohydrates, 45, 173, 195
    aerobic metabolism and, 69
    burning, 20, 23, 25, 26, 45, 165, 201
    consuming, 165, 166, 167, 170, 171, 172,
        174, 175, 176, 178, 179, 201, 202, 212
    endurance and, 174, 185
    energy from, 162, 163
    glycolysis and, 163
    lactate and, 21
    low-glycemic, 166, 170
    nutrition and, 166, 167
    performance and, 165
    pre-workout, 167–168, 168 (table)
    processing, 162, 163, 202
    sports drinks and, 174–175
    storing, 184, 193, 201, 202
Cardiac drift, 71, 72, 73, 73 (fig.)
Carmichael, Anna, 222
Carmichael, Chris, 129, 161, 165
Carmichael, Connor, 222, 228
Carmichael, Vivian, 222
Carmichael Training Systems (CTS), viii,
        3, 4, 13, 15, 42, 47, 56, 58, 82
    classes at, 86
    launching of, 12
Carrington, Megan, 48
Carrington, Sally, 48
Carrington, Taylor, 52, 53, 54, 56, 100,
        139, 222, 223
    resurgence of, 47–50
Carrington, Tyler, 3
Century program, 99, 101, 102–103,
        106–107 (table), 108–109 (table),
        115, 118–119, 150
Century riders, tips for, 200–201
Chafing, treating, 155
Cholesterol, reducing, 168
Climbing, 8, 13, 31, 40, 53, 58, 63, 64, 65,
        85, 94, 96, 97, 118, 120

dirt-road, 157
    energy for, 165
    rides/described, 154
    slow-cadence, 37
ClimbingRepeats (CR), 93, 96, 98, 111,
        157
    described, 94
Coach Rides, 199
Coaching, 10, 12, 13, 14, 15, 69, 180
    strength training and, 219
Coggan, Andrew, 9, 11, 61, 79, 107
Commuter bikes, described, 130–131
Commuting, 16, 123
    accommodation for, 127–128
    arguments against, 125
    commitment to, 128, 129
    fitness and, 126
    hydration/nutrition and, 131–133
    intensity and, 133
    lifestyle, 127–129
    performance and, 126, 132
    plans for, 124, 127, 133, 136–137
        (table), 138
    racing and, 125–126
    training and, 125, 129, 131, 132
    workload of, 123, 124, 128
Competition, 54, 55, 139, 141, 147
    preparing for, 99
    structures, 53
Competitor program, 99, 115, 133, 139,
        150
    Cyclocross plan and, 140
    structure of, 103
Conditions, 41–47, 100
    course, 82, 156
    weather, 82, 85, 156
Consumption, 178, 179
    body weight and, 174
Cool-down, 51, 87, 114
Cornering, 204
Coyle, Ed, 29, 171
CR. See ClimbingRepeats
Cramping, 177, 178
Creatine phosphate (CP), 19
Criteriums, 9, 16, 118, 150
Crotch, protecting, 210
CTS. See Carmichael Training
        Systems

CTS Field Tests, 13, 47, 71, 73–80, 84, 88, 89, 91, 146
    data from, 79
    instructions for, 82–83, 85–87
    other performance tests versus, 78–80
    repeating, 117–118
    workload from, 111
Cycling tours, 213, 216
Cyclist's Paradox, 219–220
Cyclist's Training Bible, The (Friel), 11
Cyclocross, 8, 9, 16, 139
    skill instruction for, 142
    TCTP and, 49
    training for, 141, 142–143, 147
Cyclocross bikes, 130
Cyclocross Training and Technique (Burney), 142
Cyclocross training plan, 140–142, 143, 144–145 (table)
    Competitor plan and, 140

Data, 62, 79, 132
    gathering, 60–61, 80, 87
Davis, Grant, 158, 191, 192, 197
Decelerating, coasting and, 197
Dehydration, 62, 155, 162, 173
Detraining, 57, 58
Diet, 166, 182, 187
Digestion, 170, 221
Doping, 7
Drafting, 195, 197
Duration, 16, 68, 157, 185

Eating, 155, 177, 186
    focusing on, 183–184
    pre-workout, 167–168, 173
    race-day, 147, 212
Effectiveness, 8, 13, 22, 41, 70, 124
Electrolyte drinks, 131, 132, 202
Electrolytes, 132, 171, 172, 173
    carbohydrates and, 176
    consuming, 174, 175, 177
    cramping and, 177
EM. See EnduranceMiles
Endurance, 2, 20, 21, 26–28, 30, 40, 47, 60, 69, 93, 165, 183, 199, 203, 206, 209, 230
    aerobic, 57
    building, 1, 35, 213

carbohydrates and, 174, 185
    focus on, 8, 9
    intensity of, 25, 72, 113
    power and, 194, 224
    training and, vii, 3, 4, 9, 13, 14–15, 46, 50
Endurance MTB program, 150–151, 152–153 (table), 154–155, 178
    for multiday events, 158–159
Endurance rides, 124
    moderate-intensity, 207, 216
Endurance string theory, described, 23–24
Endurance Training Blocks, 93, 116, 207, 217
    nutrition for, 211–213
    one-week, 213, 214 (table)
    two-week, 208–209, 213
    working cyclist's, 214–216
    workload/fatigue and, 210
Endurance training models, 34
    classic, 4, 9–12, 15, 30, 31, 38, 41, 42, 45
EnduranceMiles (EM), 114, 120, 121, 138, 154, 209, 215
    described, 92
Energy, 65, 116, 132, 163, 164–165, 170, 221, 222
    from aerobic metabolism, 162
    conserving, 194, 195–199
    demand for, 20, 21
    intensity and, 23
    pedaling, 195
    performance and, 202
    required, 180
    training and, 68, 185
Energy bars, 174, 175, 212
Energy expenditure, 124, 163, 185, 202
    power output and, 68
Energy systems, 31, 61, 87, 112, 146
    immediate, 19–20
    overloading, 32
Epic rides, 118, 189, 199, 209, 217
Ergometer, 73
Experienced Century program, 108–109 (table)
    described, 102–103
Experienced Competitor program, 99, 104–105 (table)
    described, 100–101

Fallon, Ali, 223
Fallon, John, 3, 222–224
Fartlek running, 6, 157
FastPedal (FP), 112
    described, 91–92
Fatigue, 13, 45, 46, 54, 84, 85, 95, 106, 109,
        113, 115, 116, 138, 208, 210
    focusing on, 62, 65–66
    generating, 123
    importance of, 69–70
    intervals and, 69, 111, 112
    performance and, 165
    power outputs and, 200
    responding to, 60, 151
    training and, 67, 69, 70
Fats
    burning, 20, 23, 25, 45, 69, 162, 163,
        165, 201
    carbohydrates and, 163
    consuming, 166, 169, 187
    energy from, 162, 164–165
    pre-workout, 167, 168
Fibers, fast-twitch/slow-twitch, 27
Field tests, 74, 77, 78, 96, 117
    bad, 77 (fig.)
    good, 75 (fig.)
Fitness, 13, 35, 53, 54, 63, 84, 116, 117,
        129, 143, 158, 192, 207, 223
    aerobic, 4, 36, 45, 46, 47, 99, 150, 163,
        217
    building, viii, 4, 32, 41, 46, 55, 68, 99,
        101, 125, 140, 183, 189, 205, 225
    commuting and, 126
    decline in, 15, 118
    endurance, 2
    general, 185, 220, 222, 224
    intensity and, 163
    maintaining, vii, 55
    nutrition and, 161–162
    performance and, 52, 56, 57, 117, 150
    strength training and, 225
    TCTP and, 44–47
    workouts and, 67
5 Essentials for a Winning Life, 161–162
Flexibility, 220, 228
Fluids, consuming, 72, 171, 173, 174, 175,
        185

Focus, 8–9, 62, 65–66, 121, 176, 183–184,
        208, 216, 221, 222, 224
Food for Fitness (Carmichael), 161, 165
Foods
    carbohydrate-rich, 201
    choosing, 168
    consuming, 171, 172, 176, 201
    emergency, 177
    lower-glycemic-index, 170
    post-workout, 186
    pre-workout, 80, 167–168, 167–168
        (table)
Foundation/preparation period, 55, 56
    described, 57–58
FP. See FastPedal
Frederick, Scott, 54
Frequency, 37, 38–39, 125
Friel, Joel, 11
Fuel, 20, 163, 172, 183–184, 185
    high-quality, 187

Gears, 92, 94, 95, 97, 197
    finding, 85–86
Gels, 154, 173, 174, 177, 178, 184
    carbohydrate-rich, 169, 170
    consuming, 171, 172, 175, 176, 202
Gerschler, Woldemar, 6
Global positioning system (GPS) units,
        2, 132
Glucose, 21, 164, 166
Glycogen, 26, 27, 165, 171, 176, 184, 201
    burning, 172
    caffeine and, 169
    replenishing, 179
Glycolysis, 21, 23, 45, 162, 163, 164
Glycolytic system, 19, 20, 23, 24, 26, 31,
        69, 200
    burning by, 45, 57, 195
    described, 21–22
Goals, 17, 37, 50, 99, 154, 207, 221, 223
    racing/touring, 53, 118–119
    TCTP and, 118–119
Golich, Dean, 8, 61
GPS. See Global positioning system
        units
Grazing, 212–213
GU Electrolyte Brew, 174

GU Energy, 155, 202
Heart disease, 168
Heart rate, 39, 60, 62, 67, 69, 74, 83, 91, 92, 94
  average, 82, 88
  drop in, 197
  EM, 120
  increase in, 71, 72, 138
  intensity of, 13
  at lactate threshold, 78
  power outputs and, 77, 78, 84
  ranges of, 8, 61, 72, 73
  training with, 8, 38, 70–73
Heart rate monitors, 2, 8, 38, 71, 74
High Performance Cycling (Jeukendrup), 11
Hincapie, George, 5
Hip mobility, improving, 220
Hips, breaking, 227
Hitz, Mick, 216–217
Hoy, Chris, 6
Hydration, 7, 72, 73, 175, 176, 211
  commuters and, 131–133
  strategy for, 150, 154, 173

Improvement, 35, 56, 74–75, 151
  defining, 25–27
Individuality principle, 31
  described, 33–34
Insulin, increase in, 166
Intensity, 6, 14, 25, 27, 36, 51, 55, 56, 72, 98, 106, 113, 115, 138, 147, 151, 156, 161, 172, 185, 207, 208, 216
  aerobic, 155
  calculating, 87–89
  commuting and, 133
  decrease in, 120
  described, 37–38
  energy and, 23
  fitness and, 163
  heart rate, 13
  high, 12, 28–30, 81, 96, 114, 186
  increase in, 16, 21, 23, 57, 95, 97, 174, 179
  interval, 10, 15, 43, 45, 73, 92, 114
  lactate threshold and, 30, 52, 93, 140, 155
  low, 186
  moderate, 24, 38
  performance and, 16

physiological adaptations and, 24
power and, 71, 140
recording, 89 (table)
specific training at, 20–21
SteadyState, 89
sustaining, 29, 66
TCTP and, 28
temperature and, 171
training, 8, 9, 11, 33, 47, 62, 71, 73–80, 82–83, 85–87, 87–89, 87 (table), 91, 92, 94, 111, 112, 115, 132, 145
variations in, 9, 35
VO$_2$max and, 29, 30
workloads and, 15
Intensity ranges, 88 (table), 97
  effective, 73–80, 82–83, 85–87
Intermediate Commuter training plan, 133, 134–135 (table), 138
Intervals, 6, 29, 46, 52, 82, 93–97, 105, 120
  energy for, 163
  fatigue and, 69, 111, 112
  high-intensity, viii, 25, 26, 27, 28–29 (table), 32, 33, 35, 36, 40, 42, 45, 46, 47, 68, 115, 116, 118, 176
  high-quality, 112, 121
  intensity of, 9, 10, 11, 15, 43, 45, 73, 114
  lactate threshold, 51, 71, 100
  moderate-intensity, 56
  number/type of, 33, 36
  priority for, 114
  recovery periods and, 97, 110
  skipping, 111–113
  SteadyState, 92
  stopping, 106–111
    training, 87–88
    two-day, 113–114
    understanding, 7–8
  VO$_2$max, 82, 84, 108
Izzard, Colin, 216

Jagassar, Simon, 55
Jeukendrup, Asker, 11
Joint mobility, 129, 220
Jorgensen, Jeff, 116
Journal of Applied Physiology, 29, 51
Journal of Strength and Conditioning Research, 75

Kearney, Jay T., 8
Kilocalories, 66, 162
Kilojoules, 60, 62, 123–124, 163, 174, 180,
    181, 182, 183, 197
  producing, 66–69
Klem, Jeff, 158
Krebs Cycle, 62

Lactate, 10, 73, 76, 93, 96, 98
  generating, 21, 24, 26, 27, 30, 45, 95,
    146, 202
  glucose and, 21
  processing, 22, 23, 99, 146, 151
  tolerance for, 199
Lactate threshold, 10–11, 13, 23, 31, 47,
    54, 69, 73, 92, 193
  heart rate at, 78
  increase in, 37
  intensity and, 30, 52, 93, 140, 155
  intervals at, 51, 100
  power outputs at, 16, 20–21, 22, 30, 35,
    39, 40, 45, 53, 57, 58, 66, 74, 78, 79,
    81, 94, 118, 167
  tests for, 8, 82, 83
  training at, 9, 28, 120
  work at, 55, 84
  workouts and, 100, 185
Lactate Threshold/VO$_2$max Test, 73
Lance Armstrong Performance Program,
    The, 11, 101
Lateral lunges, 220, 233 (fig.)
  described, 233
Leadville 100: 150, 155, 158, 178, 189, 190,
    191
Leipheimer, Levi, 65
Lifestyles, 15, 127–129, 181 (table), 182
  healthy/active, 227, 229
  RMR and, 181
Lunges, 220, 226, 227, 228, 233

Macronutrients, 162
Magliozzi, Ray and Tom, 163
Maintenance programs, 47, 58, 120–121
    (table), 150
Mann, Brent, 202
Merckx, Eddy, 11
Metabolism
  aerobic, 19, 20, 21, 22, 25, 27, 68, 69,
    162, 165
  anaerobic, 19, 21, 27, 51
  boosting, 221, 222
  fatty acid, 26
  weight gain and, 221
Mifflin-St. Jeor equation, 180–181, 182
Minerals, 162
Mitochondria, 23, 25, 26, 35, 45, 68
Motivation, 15, 47, 112, 113, 169, 192,
    204
MOTOACTV, 132
Motorola, 132
Mountain bike racing, 9, 16, 118, 150,
    151, 194
  road biking and, 156–158
Multijoint exercises, 227
Muscle mass, 11, 222, 230

New Century program, 106–107 (table)
  described, 101
New Competitor program, 99, 101, 102–
    103 (table), 158
  described, 100
Nutrition, 7, 175, 177, 186
  carbohydrates and, 166, 167
  commuters and, 131–133
  for Endurance Training Blocks, 211–213
  fitness and, 161–162
  key concepts in, 161–163
  performance and, 161, 164, 165
  periodization, 161, 165
  plans for, 154, 166, 183, 184
  post-workout, 176, 178–179, 185, 212
  pre-workout, 80, 167–170, 211
  race-day, 147, 150, 155
  recovery and, 212
  training and, 61, 155, 161, 163–165, 167,
    169, 171–176, 187
  See also Sports nutrition

One-arm row, 234 (fig.)
  described, 234
Overeating, 184, 186
Overhead presses, 227
Overheating, 138, 155, 179
Overload, 6, 69, 151
  reaching, 110 (fig.)
  recovery and, 31–33

Overload and recovery principle, described, 31–33
OverUnder (OU) intervals, 94, 97 (fig.), 99, 111, 114, 118, 119, 141, 151
  described, 96–98
Owens, Jesse, 5, 6
Oxidizing, 25, 26, 27, 68
Oxygen, 20, 86, 151
  energy and, 21
  maximum amount of, 140

Pace, 8, 68, 99, 193, 194, 198, 199, 200, 217
  aerobic, 51
  attacks and, 203
  changes in, 23, 197
  endurance, 69
  finding, 85–87
  pushing, 165
  steady, 196
Park-and-Ride, using, 127
Peak-and-Fade PowerIntervals (PFPI), 94, 96 (fig.), 143
  described, 95
Peaksware, 60
Pedaling, 84, 85, 86, 93, 143, 157, 197, 198, 203, 220
  drafting and, 195
  energy for, 195
  mechanics, 111
  performance and, 195
  power and, 41
  speed, 91, 92
Pelotons, 98, 199, 203, 204, 205
  positioning in, 195, 200
Perceived exertion, 8, 69, 70, 111, 185, 200
Perfect Mile, The (Bascomb), 6
Performance, 50, 57, 69, 73, 79, 81, 85, 118, 227
  aerobic, 221
  best, 42, 44, 115
  caffeine and, 169
  carbohydrates and, 165
  commuting and, 126, 132
  cramping and, 178
  data, 60
  decline in, 15, 42, 46, 56, 117
  improving, viii, 7, 13, 24, 25–27, 39, 43, 47, 56, 77, 91, 125, 165, 166, 179, 194,
    200, 202, 221, 223
  nutrition and, 161, 164, 165, 211
  optimizing, 22, 202
  pedaling and, 195
  problems with, 49, 111, 221
  strength training and, 219, 220
  tests, 13, 73, 74, 79
  tips for, 193–205
  training and, 12, 22, 67, 96, 109, 112, 124
Periodization, 5, 6, 50, 54–56, 161
PFPI. See Peak-and-Fade PowerIntervals
Physiology, 10, 24, 44, 62, 129, 176, 217
PI. See PowerIntervals
Power, 9, 28, 54, 60, 78, 82, 91, 197, 206
  aerobic, 41, 93
  developing, 36, 37, 41, 45, 65, 66, 71, 79, 98, 130, 143, 213, 226
  endurance and, 194, 224
  heart rate and, 84
  intensity and, 140
  at lactate threshold, 20, 21, 22, 30, 35, 39, 40, 45, 53, 57, 66, 71, 74, 94, 118, 195
  measuring, 13
  pedaling and, 41
  ranges, 92
  readings, 141
  sustainable, 11, 23, 40, 66, 93, 116, 118, 142
  training with, 38, 55, 61, 62, 65–70
  using, 63, 195, 199–205
  at VO$_2$max, 41, 45
Power files, 9, 61, 65, 94, 195
Power meters, 2, 66, 67, 71, 74, 116, 130, 132, 141, 163, 157, 181, 182, 183
  advances in, 26
  fatigue and, 70
  using, 38, 46, 60, 62, 69, 73, 200
Power outputs, 13, 38, 40, 70, 72, 74, 76, 85, 88, 95, 109, 111, 113, 157
  aerodynamics and, 64
  drop in, 39, 59, 64, 65, 107, 171
  energy expenditure and, 68
  exercise duration and, 68
  fatigue and, 200
  field testing, 53–54, 117
  heart rate and, 77, 78
  high, 102, 108, 165
  improving, 34, 66, 190–191

at lactate threshold, 16, 20–21, 22, 30,
    35, 39, 40, 45, 53, 57, 58, 66, 74, 78,
    79, 81, 167
maintaining, 106, 201
submaximal efforts at, 11
sustainable, 57, 63, 78, 79, 103, 199
Power-to-Weight Ratio (PWR), 63–65,
    204, 222
PowerIntervals (PI), 31, 41, 52, 53, 82, 98,
    100, 103, 108–114, 116, 118, 119,
    142, 157
commuting and, 131
concentration on, 140
cyclocross and, 143
described, 94–95
intensities for, 94, 143
maximum-intensity, 34, 56, 99
riding, 38, 39
with run-ups, 143
steady effort, 143
training and, 140
Preparation period, 55, 86
described, 56–57
Progression principle, 31, 35, 36
Protein, 20, 164, 165, 212
consuming, 166, 187, 211
energy from, 162
pre-workout, 167, 168
Pull-ups, 226
Pulls, 165
skipping, 198–199
taking, 196, 197, 199
Push-ups, 226, 227, 235 (fig.)
described, 235
PWR. See Power-to-Weight Ratio

Race-and-recover periods, 9
Racing, 11, 138, 142, 155, 157
commuting and, 125–126
high-intensity, 9
physical/psychological demands of, 12
successful, 194
training and, 8, 9, 12, 100, 141, 217
Randall, Tim, 213
Range of motion, 220, 228
Rating of Perceived Exertion (RPE), 70, 91
described, 83–84
Recovery, 9, 26, 44, 69, 70, 76, 95, 125,
    129, 147, 176, 190, 193, 227
active, 56, 138
between-ride, 212, 217
compromising on, 221
guidelines for, 32, 32 (table)
importance of, 6, 104–113
nutrition and, 212
optimal, 124
overload and, 31–33
post-ride, 212
rapid, 133, 155
spinning, 2, 30, 74, 76, 85, 86, 98, 108,
    109, 111, 209, 213
stress and, 7
TCTP and, 30
time for, 30, 39, 55, 85, 86, 93, 94, 110,
    111
training and, 115, 129, 187
Recovery drinks, 131, 169
carbohydrate-rich, 176, 212
post-workout, 176, 185
using, 147, 184, 212
Recovery periods, 36, 39, 115, 117, 119,
    120, 133, 150, 216
extended, 46
intervals and, 97
10-minute, 76
Recovery rides, 114, 124
Recuperation/maintenance phase, 56, 221
Repetitions, 37, 230
described, 38–39
Resistance, 37, 93, 219, 227
bands, 225, 226, 229
heavy, 226
increasing, 226, 229
light, 226, 230
Rest, 8, 14, 31, 33, 95, 104–113, 209, 216
scheduling, 54
skipping, 154
Resting metabolic rate (RMR), 180–182
Reverse crunch, 235 (fig.)
described, 235
Reverse wood chop with band, 237 (fig.)
described, 237
Riding
aggressive, 201, 206
high-volume, 207
pack, 195

smarter, 194, 206
Risk, Dan, 101
RMR. See Resting metabolic rate
Road biking, mountain bike racing and,
    156–158
RPE. See Rating of Perceived Exertion
Rutberg, Elliot, 189, 190
Rutberg, Jim, 15, 47, 54, 158, 189, 190, 191,
    192, 197, 223
    Carrington and, 48, 49, 50
    Fallon and, 100
    TCTP and, 4, 5, 52–53, 224
Ruth, Babe, 6

Saddle position, improper, 210
Schedules, 7, 54, 58, 111–112, 116, 117, 126,
    128
    perfectly structured, 104
    rearranging, 113–114, 119
Science, 6, 7, 9, 15, 24
Seated row, 238 (fig.)
    described, 238
SEPI. See Steady Effort PowerIntervals
Serious Cycling (Burke), 11
Serious Training for Endurance Athletes
    (Sleamaker and Browning), 11
Skills, 34, 49, 141, 142
    cyclocross, 143–145
Skin
    cooling by, 171
    protecting, 210
Sleamaker, Rob, 11
Snacks, 213
    pre-workout, 80, 167, 168–170, 171, 173,
    184
Sodium, 177, 178
    consuming, 172, 179, 185
Software programs, 9, 60, 87, 89
Specialization period, 54, 55–56
Specificity principle, 31, 34–35
Speed, 101, 116, 132
    average, 201
    increase in, 36, 119, 197
    maintaining, 201
    maximizing, 65
    pedal, 91, 92
Spinning, 110, 197
    easy, 114, 116

recovery, 2, 30, 74, 76, 85, 86, 98, 108, 109,
    111, 209, 213
    warm-up, 173
Sports drinks, 154, 172, 173, 178, 184
    carbohydrate-rich, 169, 175, 176, 177,
    201, 202
    carbohydrates and, 170, 174–175
    consuming, 171, 176, 201, 202, 211–212
    pre-workout, 211–212
Sports nutrition, 161, 162, 164, 170, 175,
    177, 183, 187, 212
    guidelines for, 184
    performance and, 211
    sodium-free, 178–179
    See also Nutrition
Sprinting, 8, 31, 36, 51, 193, 194, 195, 199
Squat and jump, 239 (fig.)
    described, 239
Squats, 226, 228, 229
SRM power meters, 8, 132, 157
SS. See SteadyState
Stage races, mountain bike, 150
Standing overhead press, 240 (fig.), 241
    (fig.)
    described, 240–241
Steady Effort PowerIntervals (SEPI), 95
    (fig.), 143
    described, 94
SteadyState (SS), 89, 92, 96, 98, 99, 111, 112,
    113, 114, 118, 138, 151, 157
    described, 93
Step-up, 220, 242 (fig.), 243 (fig.)
    described, 242–243
Stimulants, 62, 169
Strength, 196, 199, 201, 222
    developing, 220, 226, 228, 230
    lower-body/upper-body, 226
Strength training, 224
    balance and, 227
    benefits of, 221–222
    fitness and, 225
    movement and, 227–228
    performance and, 219, 220
    program for, 228–230, 230 (table)
    using, 219, 220, 225–228
Stress, 7, 140, 210
Sunscreen, using, 210
Swaim, Ben, 3

Swaim, Sterling, 15, 16, 48, 50, 56, 100, 192, 216, 222
  case of, 3–4, 5
Sweating, 71, 72, 171, 173, 175, 178

T. See Tempo
Taylor, Major, 5, 6
TCTP. See Time-Crunched Training Program
Technology, vii, 7, 9, 10, 58, 59, 84
Temperature, 131, 171
Tempo (T), 92, 100, 114, 163, 173, 208
  described, 93
  training intensity for, 93
Terms, described, 41–47
Terrain, 37, 156, 204
  described, 39–40
Thorpe, Jim, 6
3-hour limit, using, 42–44
ThresholdLadder (TL) intervals, 141, 151, 157
  described, 98
  training intensity for, 98
Time, 15, 35, 110, 156, 201
Time-Crunched Training Program (TCTP), 29, 33, 34, 35, 37, 42, 43, 44, 46, 47, 52, 53, 57, 58, 60, 62, 68, 71, 80, 82, 93, 94, 95, 100, 108
  cyclocross and, 49
  demands of, 31
  described, 16, 17
  manipulating, 36
  periods of, 55–56
  questions about, 115–121
  success with, 38, 167
  using, viii, 2–3, 4, 5, 63
  workouts, 41, 49
Time trials, 11, 74, 75–76, 118, 205
TL. See ThresholdLadder intervals
Tour de France, 11, 12, 64, 103, 192, 211
Training, 10, 16, 36, 37, 38, 70, 101, 119, 124, 140, 157, 158, 161, 174
  adaptations to, 7, 12–14, 60, 113–114
  aerobic, 41, 51, 55
  antiquated, 5, 44
  back-to-back, 151, 154

breakdown of, 15
designing, 2, 23
effective, 8, 13, 22, 41, 50, 62, 69, 104, 123
focusing on, 208, 216, 224
high-intensity, 24, 26, 27, 28, 30, 33, 44, 45, 46, 47, 53, 57, 115, 118, 176, 184, 207, 229
high-volume, 9, 36, 42, 44, 46, 51, 55, 57, 179, 183, 190, 193, 194, 209
history of, 5–9
individual, 33, 217
indoor, 49, 74, 79, 86, 118, 206
less-structured, 54
levels of, 15
low-volume, 24, 44, 47, 49, 55, 57, 176, 186, 207
methods, 10, 12, 17
moderate-intensity, 9, 35–36, 45, 176
morning, 131
positive effects of, 31
precision with, 8
principles of, 30–31, 37–41
pro-level, 12–14
quality, 39, 62, 167, 168, 171
resistance, 37, 219, 227
specific-event, 56
structured, 53, 54, 99, 121
successful, 31, 36
target-specific, 8–9
theories in, 2
time for, 99–103, 118, 120, 207, 220, 221
Training and Racing with a Power Meter (Allen and Coggan), 11, 61, 79, 107
Training blocks, 138, 154, 213, 214, 217
  consultations about, 215–216
Training logs, 61, 87, 89
Training ranges, 75, 77–78, 88
Training rides, 2, 67, 141
  nutrition for, 155
Training stimulus, 9, 15, 35, 114, 125, 151, 215
Training time, 14–15, 34
  limited, vii, viii, 17, 36, 114
Trainingpeaks software, 9
Transition periods, 56, 57
Trebon, Ryan, 50
24 Hours of Elephant Rock, 189, 190, 191

Two-Week Endurance Training Block, 209
(table), 213
described, 208–209

Ultimate Ride, The (Carmichael), 11, 30, 31,
41, 101, 202
Ultraendurance races, 16, 150
Union Cycliste International (UCI), 48, 49,
50
United States Cycling Federation (USCF),
3, 193
U.S. Olympic Committee, 8, 61
USA Cycling, 8, 12, 61
Upset stomachs, 78, 170, 173, 173, 176

Vacation time, using, 214, 216
Vitamins, 162
VO$_2$max (maximum aerobic capacity), 3,
8, 22–23, 24, 28, 43, 47, 71, 84
endurance performance and, 27
genetics and, 81
improving, 26, 35
intensity and, 27, 29, 30, 45
interval sessions, 69
measuring, 25–26
power at, 23, 41, 45, 57, 66
testing, 81, 82
Volume, 37
blood, 72
decrease in, 57
intensity and, 33, 38
low, 38
training, 9, 16, 24, 35, 36, 42, 44, 46, 51,
55, 57, 59, 120, 179, 183, 190, 193, 194,
205, 207, 208, 209

Warm-ups, 77, 78, 80, 114, 146
Water, 170, 213
consuming, 176, 179, 212
gels and, 175
Watts, 60, 65, 132, 197
Weather, 82, 85, 156
Week 10, demands of, 154–156
Weekend rides, 16, 151,154
commuting and, 129
Weight gain, metabolism and, 221
Weight loss, 180, 212
Weight-management, 124, 183

Weight training, 220
balance and, 227
White, Nick, 81
Windshield wipers, 244 (fig.)
described, 244
WKO+, using, 60, 61
Work-to-recovery ratio, 95, 108
Working Cyclist's Endurance Training
Block, 215 (table)
using, 214–216
Workloads, 13, 39, 45, 55, 105, 111, 163,
185, 210, 221
commuting and, 123, 124, 128
cumulative, 39, 115, 117, 151
high, 99, 114
increase in, 20, 33, 57, 99, 125, 138,
229
initial, 100
kilojoules and, 67
measure of, 84
mountain bike/road, 157
overload and, 33
time/intensity and, 15
training, 31, 35, 47, 67, 128
Workouts, 6, 8, 10, 13, 33, 55, 80, 103, 106,
110, 114, 151, 158, 167, 180, 184
afternoon, 105
calories for, 182 (table), 185, 186
climbing-specific, 63
components of, 31, 37–41
core, 220, 228–229
described, 91–98, 231–244
development of, 60, 115
difficult, 53, 138, 167, 186, 189
early-morning, 172–173
endurance-building, 209
high-intensity, 51, 54, 106, 107, 129, 138,
163, 167, 171, 186, 223
intensity of, 15, 51, 87–89, 106, 172
interval, 116–117, 119, 156, 167, 173,
176, 183, 186, 208, 216
moderate-intensity, 80, 171
quality of, 166, 180
skipping, 111–113, 114, 117, 154
time for, 116–117, 134
types of, 145
weekday, 16, 151, 224
World Anti-Doping Agency, 169

About the Authors

CHRIS CARMICHAEL was an Olympian and a professional cyclist before beginning his career as a coach, best-selling author, and entrepreneur. He was recognized as the U.S. Olympic Committee Coach of the Year and was inducted into the U.S. Bicycling Hall of Fame in 2003. He served as the men's road coach for the U.S. Olympic Cycling Team during the 1992 Olympic Games, was the head coach for the U.S. Cycling Team for the 1996 Olympic Games, and coached 7-time Tour de France Champion Lance Armstrong for more than 20 years. Chris founded Carmichael Training Systems, Inc. (CTS) in 2000 to make world-class coaching expertise available to everyone.

Through Chris's leadership and an unsurpassed education program that develops the highest-trained coaches in the industry, CTS immediately established itself as the premier destination for personal fitness, nutrition, and performance coaching and camps. CTS's proven track record for producing champions continues to attract top amateur and professional athletes. Athletes who work or have worked with CTS include Ironman world champions Craig Alexander, Tim DeBoom, and Normann Stadler; Olympic triathlon gold and silver medalist Simon Whitfield; NASCAR drivers Carl Edwards, Bobby Labonte, and Max Papis; and U.S. national cyclocross champions Katie Compton and Ryan Trebon. In addition, Chris has created more than 20 training DVDs and authored 10 books, including *The Ultimate Ride* (2003), the New York Times bestseller *Chris Carmichael's Food for Fitness* (2004), *5 Essentials for a Winning Life* (2006), and *The Time-Crunched Triathlete* (2010).

A native of Miami, Chris and his wife, Paige, live in Colorado Springs with their three children, Anna, Connor, and Vivian.

JIM RUTBERG is the editorial director and a coach for Carmichael Training Systems, and co-author, with Chris Carmichael, of *The Ultimate Ride, Chris Carmichael's Food for Fitness, Chris Carmichael's Fitness Cookbook, The Carmichael Training Systems Cyclist's Training Diary, 5 Essentials for a Winning Life, The Time-Crunched Triathlete,* and innumerable web and magazine articles. His work has appeared in *Bicycling, Outside, Men's Health, Men's Journal, VeloNews, Inside Triathlon, Triathlete,* and more. A graduate of Wake Forest University and former elite-level cyclist, Rutberg lives in Colorado Springs with his wife, Leslie, and their two sons, Oliver and Elliot.